Ancient Trackways
of
Wessex

Ancient Trackways
of
Wessex

H.W. Timperley & Edith Brill

First published 1965

Copyright © in this edition in 2005 by
Nonsuch Publishing Ltd, an imprint of The History Press

Reprinted in 2013 by
The History Press
The Mill, Brimscombe Port,
Stroud, Gloucestershire, GL5 2QG
www.thehistorypress.co.uk

British Library Cataloguing in Publication Data.
A catalogue record for this book is available from the British Library.

ISBN 978-1-84588-006-4

Printed and bound in England.

CONTENTS

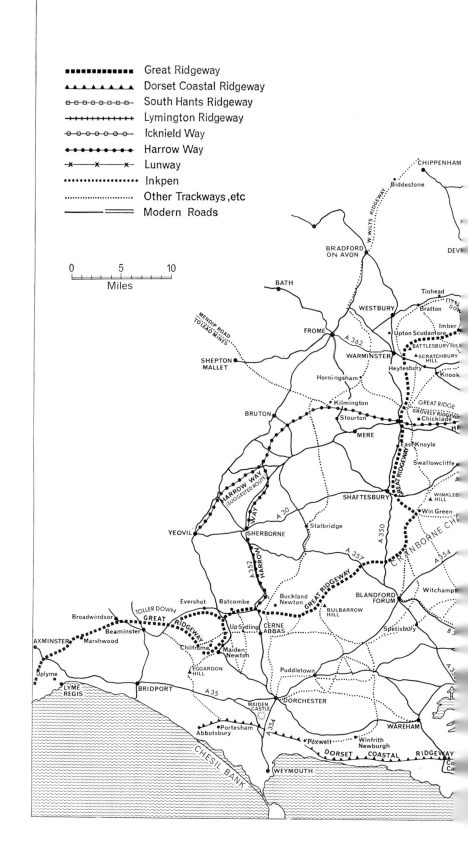

Great Ridgeway

▲▲▲▲▲▲▲ Dorset Coastal Ridgeway

South Hants Ridgeway

+++++++++ Lymington Ridgeway

Icknield Way

Harrow Way

x — x — x — Lunway

Inkpen

Other Trackways ,etc

Modern Roads

0   5   10
Miles

CHIPPENHAM
Biddestone
BRADFORD ON AVON
DEV
BATH
Tinhead
WESTBURY
Bratton
MENDIP ROAD TO LEAD MINES
FROME
A 362
Imber
Upton Scudamore
WARMINSTER
BATTLESBURY HILL
SHEPTON MALLET
Horningsham
SCRATCHBURY HILL
Heytesbury
Knook
Kilmington
GREAT RIDGE
BRUTON
Stourton
GROVELY RIDGEWAY
Chicklade
H
MERE
East Knoyle
Swallowcliffe
HARROW WAY (SUGGESTED ROUTE)
SHAFTESBURY
WINKLEBY HILL
Win Green
A 30
YEOVIL
SHERBORNE
Stalbridge
A 350
A 357
BLANDFORD FORUM
Witchamp
Evershot
Batcombe
Buckland Newton
Evershot
Up Sydling
BULBARROW HILL
Spetisbury
B 3
TOLLER DOWN
GREAT RIDGEWAY
Broadwindsor
Beaminster
A 352
HARROW
GREAT RIDGEWAY
AXMINSTER
Marshwood
Chilfrome
Maiden Newton
Uplyme
EGGARDON HILL
Puddletown
LYME REGIS
BRIDPORT
A 35
MAIDEN CASTLE
DORCHESTER
WAREHAM
Portesham
A 354
Poxwell
Winfrith Newburgh
Abbotsbury
CHESIL BANK
DORSET COASTAL RIDGEWAY
WEYMOUTH
Co
Ca
CRANBORNE CH
A 354

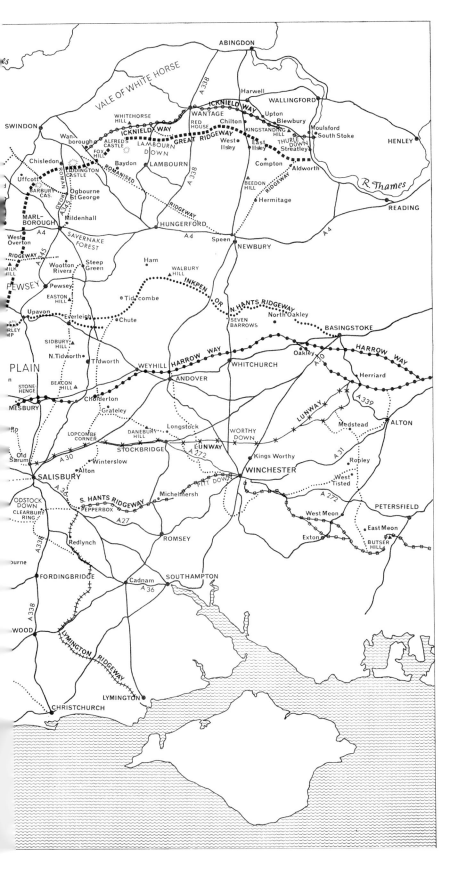

INTRODUCTION TO THE
MODERN EDITION

The ancient kingdom of Wessex, where Alfred the Great once ruled the West Saxons, covers a large swathe of countryside in the south-west of England, including Hampshire, Berkshire, southern Oxfordshire, Wiltshire, Somerset, Dorset and eastern Devon. As well as having been one of the greatest English kingdoms before the Norman Conquest of 1066, Wessex is famous as the setting for Thomas Hardy's great nineteenth-century novels and, to many, it is synonymous with *Tess of the d'Urbervilles*, *The Mayor of Casterbridge* and *Far From the Madding Crowd*. Meticulously and comprehensively researched, *Ancient Trackways of Wessex* is a delightful exploration of this enchanting corner of England.

Wessex itself is mostly a chalk plateau. With Salisbury Plain at its centre, the chalk hills and downs of southern England radiate out in all directions, and the ridgeways provided natural routes from one place to another, along which the early inhabitants of Britain travelled. Northwards from the Plain the Marlborough Downs run into the White Horse Hills (so called because of the vast, ancient picture of a horse which was carved out of the hillside) and then on to the Chiltern Hills, while to the west the downs carry on through Wiltshire and Dorset to the Isle of Purbeck. To the east lie the Hampshire Downs, the North and South Downs and, eventually, the White Cliffs of Dover and Beachy Head. Along the coastline, from Portland Bill to Selsey Bill, are numerous natural harbours, which made the extremely habitable chalk uplands an attractive place to settle thousands of years ago.

The ridges connecting the chalk plateaus formed natural routes between them, which were being used for trade by the Bronze Age. There is evidence of Iron Age settlements along these routes and during the early Middle Ages they were used as boundaries; in general, they survived the enclosures of the eighteenth century and it was only really when the railways began to to provide a superior network of communication that the decline set in. Nevertheless, although they are no longer as well-used as they were for centuries, the trackways along the chalk ridgeways of Wessex are still there, and, as this book demonstrates, have much to offer those who take the trouble to explore them.

The Great Ridgeway cuts across Wessex from Axmouth in the south west through Cranborne Chase, Salisbury Plain, the Vale of Pewsey, the Vale of the White Horse and on, eventually, to the Wash in East Anglia. Icknield Way, which may originally have stretched from East Anglia to the far west, can now only be traced for a fraction of its length near Wantage. The Great Ridgeway is bisected by the Harrow Way, which runs more-or-less east to west through Wessex on its way from Cornwall to Kent. During the later Middle Ages this was one of the routes used by pilgrims travelling to the shrine of St. Thomas à Becket at Canterbury. From these ancient 'trunk roads' lesser trackways branch off, connecting them with places not directly in their way; many were formerly of much greater importance, such as Winchester, on the South Hampshire Ridgeway and close to the Lunway (or London Way), which was the capital of England during the tenth and early eleventh centuries. They provide a look into England's past, clues as to the shape of the country before the railways and tarmac roads changed it forever.

Ancient Trackways of Wessex is both an historical and a practical guide to these ridgeway routes. Through examination of sources ancient and modern as well as walking along them for themselves, the authors have managed to reconstruct the routes even where little or no evidence of where they went exists on the ground. Nor are their descriptions limited to mere directions to follow: they explain why the trackways follow particular routes, combining history and geology with topography. The geology of the area is particularly important, because it is the chalk uplands and the ridges between them which provided habitable areas with natural lines of communication. It is geology, therefore, which has shaped Wessex, both literally and historically, because without its ridge-roads and natural harbours, both providing easy access from outside, the pattern of settlement would have been very different.

For thousands of years the ancient trackways of Wessex connected centres of habitation with each other and the area itself with the outside world. For much of that time there were no other means of communication. Everything travelled along them, people, animals and goods, and they helped to define Wessex. Sadly, modern, mechanised farming methods, road-building and the ever-increasing need for more housing threatens to and somethimes does destroy these trackways. Before too many years have passed they may have disappeared entirely. Although the onslaught shows no signs of abating, in this book the routes and histories of Wessex's ancient trackways are set down for posterity. Well-researched and written with an evident passion for the subject, *Ancient Trackways of Wessex* is a very important account of the system of communciation which served a large part of south-west England for hundreds or even thousands of years.

Harold William Timperley was educated at the University of Manchester and was by profession a teacher. He wrote several books about the English countryside and its natural history, including *A Cotswold Book*, *The Cotswold Scene*, *English Scenes and Birds*, *The Vale of Pewsey*, *Ridge Way Country* and *Shropshire Hills*. His wife, Edith Brill, a graduate of the University of London, was a prolific author, who wrote numerous books about the Cotswolds, including *The Cotswolds*, *Cotswold Crafts*, *Cotswold Ways* and *Life and Tradition on the Cotswolds*, as well as *The Golden Bird*, *London Ladies*, *The Mink Coat* and *Three Maids of Islington*.

ACKNOWLEDGEMENTS

EVEN if I knew their names it would be impossible to mention individually all the people who helped us in the field when we were in pursuit of the old trackways, but I feel that the kindness of the many country people who delved into their memories and often went out of their way to direct us should be gratefully recorded.

To R. E. Sandell, honorary librarian of the Wiltshire Archaeological and Natural History Society, we are deeply indebted. He was always willing to help us with his intimate knowledge of the books and papers in his care, and he also came to our aid in every possible way. The Society kindly gave their permission for the reproduction of the two drawings from Sir Richard Colt Hoare's *Ancient History of Wiltshire*.

Mrs. M. Nurse, Mr. Denis Grant King, Mrs. and Mr. Grose also encouraged us with transport, hospitality and advice. The criticisms of the late Dr. O.G.S. Crawford on the first draft of the manuscript must also be gratefully acknowledged. In the later stages Professor Ronald Good kindly advised me on several problems connected with Dorset.

I owe special thanks to Monica Hutchings, who is always ready to explore, photograph and enjoy the roughest track or byway, and to Roderick Standing, who made particular journeys to take his pictures.

My husband, H.W. Timperley, died before the book was finally prepared for publication. I have endeavoured to carry out his original wishes concerning it as faithfully as possible. The book now comes as an offering to his memory.

EDITH BRILL

INTRODUCTION

ALTHOUGH Wessex, the old kingdom of the West Saxons, has a clear historic content, it has no distinct boundaries, at least not as we determine the boundaries of a province today. King Alfred's Wessex covered approximately the central south region lying between Sussex and Cornwall and reaching down from the upper Thames to the Channel coast, but for the purposes of this book Wessex is roughly the counties of Berkshire, Hampshire, Wiltshire, Dorset and Somerset, with short extensions into Oxfordshire, the Cotswolds and Devon, and we are dealing with it as the Wessex of the prehistorian rather than of the historian.

At its centre is the chalk plateau of Salisbury Plain, from which ranges of chalk hills radiate in most directions. To the north are the Marlborough Downs and their extension eastward from Wiltshire into Berkshire as the White Horse Hills, these becoming on the other side of the Thames gap the Chilterns, which die away into the East Anglian chalk ridge leading to the Wash. To the south-west run the downs which lead from Wiltshire into Dorset and on towards the coast between Weymouth and Bridport, and send off below Dorchester a narrow coastal extension running eastward along the Isle of Purbeck and ending at Swanage Bay. With their inward-facing escarpment overlooking the Vale of Blackmoor, the Dorset heights link up westward with the hills of Devon. Away to the east Salisbury Plain passes into the Hampshire Downs, which divide into the separate arms of the North and South Downs terminating in the chalk cliffs of Dover and Beachy Head respectively. Instead of a southward extension of chalk hills from the Plain to the Channel coast there is the Hampshire basin holding the heathy gravels of the New Forest between Cranborne Chase and Southampton Water.

A few miles to the north-west of the central plateau of chalkland the range of Cotswold oolite leads away from Bath and out of Wessex through Gloucestershire, Oxfordshire and Northamptonshire to Lincolnshire and Yorkshire. Salisbury Plain and the Marlborough Downs are separated from these limestone hills by the upper valley of the Bristol Avon, whilst the Uffington White Horse escarpment, with a more easterly trend, is separated from them by the upper Thames valley or Vale of the White Horse, the watershed dividing the river heads being a low ridge linking the limestone wolds and the chalk downs a little west of Swindon.

In the main, much of Wessex was an open region in prehistoric times, an area of undulating and river-intersected uplands never overtopping a thousand feet. Little if any of the downland was originally quite free from some kind of woodland and scrub; it was grazing animals and primitive cultivation which kept it open. Air photographs show how intensively the downs were cultivated in the Early Iron Age. There is no lack of evidence to show that before then—in the Bronze Age and Neolithic times—the chalk and limestone uplands were the inhabited regions.

Upland Wessex was hemmed in by an almost continuous belt of clay forest and waste land impossible for prehistoric man to clear and cultivate with the implements at his command. The cross-dykes, which often end where ancient woodland began, give an indication of the impenetrability of woodland on heavier soils. Wild animals and epizootic disease would also help to keep men from the wet forest lands.

On the north were the waterlogged plains of the Vale of the White Horse, and along the west side the clay forests reaching down lowland Wiltshire to Dorset from Braydon Forest in the north to Selwood and Gillingham in the south, there joining those of the Vale of Blackmoor in Dorset. To the north-east lay the forest and marsh land under the Chilterns, to the east the broken and wooded region of east Berkshire, and to the south of this, beyond the eastern margins of Hampshire, were the impassable clay forests of the Weald. The chalk uplands of north Hampshire were—and still are—not very open terrain: as well as holding many steep-sided valleys they are capped with clay that supports plenty of woodland cover, which thins out towards the open downland of Salisbury Plain.

There were four main natural lines of land passage through the marginal forests of Wessex to the rest of Britain: the Test-Loddon divide at Basingstoke leading into Surrey and along the North and South Downs; the Chiltern continuation of the Berkshire Downs leading towards East Anglia from the Thames gap in the chalk at Goring; the Thames-Avon divide at Wootton Bassett in north Wiltshire leading into the Cotswolds; and the ridge of downs leading from Winchester through Droxford to Butser Hill and going on with the South Downs into Sussex. It will be seen later how these forest passes, and others within Wessex, determined the lines of the landways.

O.G.S. Crawford in *Man and His Past* says that 'taking the coastline of Wessex from Portland Bill to Selsey Bill, including the Isle of Wight, most of the prehistoric ports are found within these limits'. It was to these natural harbours and estuaries that many important trackways led. They were the termini of inland trade routes as well as the gateways by which many of the waves of migrants and invaders entered Britain. Sir Cyril Fox in his *Personality of Britain* brings this vividly to life in a single sentence. Discussing the vulnerability of south and south-east England to invasion from the Continent he says: 'It is the tragedy of British prehistory and history, and the key thereto, that the most habitable and most easily conquerable areas are adjacent to the shores whence invaders are most likely to come.'

It is impossible to have concrete evidence of the trackways in Neolithic times; we know only the approximate lines along which it would have been possible to travel. Yet there must have been tracks beaten out by animals and men in their pastoral wanderings, tracks to settlements and watering-places, and tracks along which were brought the polished stone axes found in Wessex and made from the igneous rocks of the west of Britain—Cornwall, Wales and the Lake District.

Where such tracks existed it is difficult to believe that whenever possible they were not used in later times. It is natural to follow a path where one exists, and the advantage of any track, however ill-defined, in uncharted open country is obvious. Doubtless there were guides who carried the pattern of a landscape, its smaller differences, in their minds, and in those days the bump of locality and sense of direction would be much stronger than they are today. Some countrymen still possess those instincts, difficult to define and something more than a good memory, phenomenal eyesight and a sub-conscious reaction to natural conditions.

It was in the Bronze Age, broadly speaking, that landways and waterways began to take shape as a network of prehistoric communications. One way of discovering trade routes is by tracing raw materials back to their sources. There are, for example, the bronze axes found all over Britain and now known to be of Irish origin. As the Bronze Age passes into its middle and late periods trade must have been an important part of life, for in burial mounds in Wessex many objects of gold, amber and bronze have been found, and from bronze hoards found near river crossings and other places it can be assumed that by this time there were traders and pedlars who used the ridgeways and upland trackways for their professional occasions. Many of these objects have been found in regions devoid of natural sources of these metals and stones and thus could only have been brought from outside. The tracks the traders followed would be those connecting one settlement with the next, and in time trunk roads would evolve.

The nearest harbours for traders working the Salisbury Plain and Cranborne Chase areas were those between the Isle of Portland and Southampton Water, such as Weymouth Bay and Christchurch. From the density of finds, as illustrated by Sir Cyril Fox on the maps in his *Personality of Britain,* the Thames, also, was a natural approach, 'in the Bronze Age if not earlier', up which came goods traded from overseas.

It is when we come to the Early Iron Age that we can feel more certain that the remnants of the tracks strung out along the escarpments and ridges, connecting hilltop camp to hilltop camp, are survivals of the roads used by people of that period. Not only can they be traced in the field, but there is written evidence in the Anglo-Saxon land charters and medieval copies of these charters showing that the Saxons used existing ridgeways as boundary lines.

Crossing and reaching outward from Salisbury Plain the trackways led along the hills to the ports and estuaries of the North Sea and Channel coasts, to the Severn estuary, to the Cotswolds and the Midlands beyond. These tracks were literally highways because they were watershed ways that only descended to cross even a small valley when there was no practicable line round the valley head to the hilltops on the other side. We do not find many remains of the pre-Roman inhabitants of Britain away from the hills and their green roads. One of the striking things about the main trackways is that they link together country-wide successions of the great prehistoric earthworks as well as other habitation sites and the fading outlines of what were their cultivated fields.

The names we have used for many of the roads in this book are, of course, post-Roman. Some can be found in medieval and later documents, others down the centuries have named themselves, as familiar places and things will. Association has given them a patina which adds to their attraction. The earliest names which have come down to us can be found in the Anglo-Saxon charters—a few local names for short stretches which happened to coincide with land boundaries, and these are descriptive or are the names of families who had settled there. In the charters the general name Ridgeway appears either as *Hrycweg* or one of the variant spellings. *Weala-Weg* also occurs, meaning Welsh Way, the name 'Welsh' being used by the Saxons to describe the British people they had conquered.

Herepath, or *Harepath*, was also a Saxon name for through roads, but not every herepath was a ridgeway. It was applied to roads of Saxon origin as well as to parts of older roads useful to the Saxons. Herepaths are sometimes known as 'war' roads, from *here* (army).

During the normal wear and tear of ancient times these green ways would, by their nature, renew themselves. To them frost is a friend, breaking down the ridges and footprints made by wheels and animals in wet weather, whereas frost is an enemy to a waterlogged made road, lifting the stones out of their beds. On the porous chalk and limestone hills heavy rain soon drains away; but under the made Roman roads, which fell into disrepair when the Romans left Britain, there were culverts to become blocked, with the result that these parts became flooded and deteriorated all the time.

During the enclosing of farms and the making of great estates in the eighteenth century many of the green roads were defined by low banks and hedges to mark their course and keep travellers and beasts from encroaching upon private land, for even then they still remained important highways. The courses of some of the old roads were changed to go round instead of through a new estate, which explains many a deviation from an original line. Although this often considerably reduced their width it still left them continuous. They lasted as useful workaday roads until well into the nineteenth century, enabling travellers to escape from the mire of the valley roads.

The turnpike roads took away most of their usefulness for ordinary travellers though some of the 'flying coaches' still preferred the upland ways. And they were still used by shepherds and drovers taking their flocks and herds to markets in the towns or to the hilltop fairs. The width of their turf-covered surface provided food as well as a natural tread for slow-travelling unshod animals. The turnpike fees were evaded by using them and there was no danger from faster-moving vehicles.

With the coming first of the railways and then of motor transport it became possible to carry cattle and sheep by road and rail, and the real decline of the ridgeways set in. Stretches of old roads still bear the name Ox Drove, a name given to them because of their use as cattle ways. Wiltshire has many such stretches and until recently there were still old men to be found in the villages who had used them for this purpose. The name, however, must go back further than the eighteenth century, for it has been said that the first roads of all were those trodden out by cattle—beasts that would look strange to us today but whose bones have been found in prehistoric settlements and burial mounds beside many an ancient Ox Drove.

The maps we have mainly used in tracing the old roads have been the 1-inch Ordnance Survey editions, and we have found that where their courses have not been followed by present-day roads these maps often give more or less definite indications of the other parts, though sometimes, as is to be expected, not continuously. Too many reaches of the trackways have been lost for complete continuity to be represented. Here and there a length of parish boundary suggests a possible line by spanning a gap. In the field it was often discovered that a track which is a blank on the map is not so on the ground: an obviously long-standing row of trees, or an old hedge that is broadening itself into a thicket, or a field-dividing bank standing between the last faint traces of a way are clues to a possible line. Sometimes a definite hollow grooved across a field gives a clue, though in these days of ploughing old pasture for temporary leys these hollows soon become obliterated. When, to piece in the gaps or else to find confirmation of a line, we have used maps other than those mentioned, we have named them in the text. Most of the maps we used have been superseded by the Seventh Series of the 1-inch Ordnance Survey editions, and not all the landmarks and tracks mentioned in the text are to be found on the latest maps.

A road is a living thing and gathers about itself a personality as long as it is being used. Now only a thin ghost of their one-time importance lingers about the old trackways. The line of some of them has been kept by modern roads, and more are being taken into the road system. Some serve hill farms and have been given a width of metalled surface while keeping their broad green margins, margins rutted and sunken lower than the new centre and telling of their past use as cattle ways along the hills. Stretches of the old green roads left to us have become places of recreation, and come alive at week-ends and holidays. Encroachment on the few remains is going on all the time. In one place an open section is enclosed, in another an airfield, housing estate or factory swallows up a length.

Once every line scored on the chalk and limestone uplands left a scar for the conjectures and theories of future archaeologists, but modern farm machinery and bulldozers have the power to wipe out these signs of the past, which was why we wanted to record the vanishing trackways before they are entirely obliterated.

H. W. T.

E. B.

September 1962

1

THE GREAT RIDGEWAY

Approximately 23 miles

THOUGH evidence of the presence of a great highway in prehistoric times across Britain from East Anglia to Devon must be eked out with theory, conjecture and imagination, there seems little doubt that one existed, with branches going off along other main ridges or linked to them by minor tracks, and forming a complicated system of communication over the whole of the higher country. Many prehistoric burial mounds, or the remains of them, still stand alongside or within sight of the Great Ridgeway, and in them have been found not only the bones or ashes of the dead but a variety of implements and ornaments made of materials not local in origin. Some came from distant parts of the British Isles, others from the mainland of Europe and a few from as far off as Egypt. Among these materials were amber from the east coast and from the shores of the Baltic, jet from Yorkshire, tin, in bronze objects, from Cornwall, copper from Ireland, gold from Ireland and Wales and blue faience beads from Egypt. There was also flint from mines such as those discovered in Sussex and East Anglia.

This main highway, traversing ridge after ridge from East Anglia to Devon, has come to typify all ridge roads, and has taken upon itself since Saxon times, as the Saxon charters show, the generic name of Ridgeway. For the purpose of this book we are calling this through way the Great Ridgeway. It is, perhaps, the best loved and best known of all the ancient trackways.

The Great Ridgeway enters Wessex from the Chiltern heights through the gap cut by the Thames at Goring (Map 30). Here the river is wide and shallow, its gravelly banks shelve gently, and it was obviously a good crossing-place before the channel was more closely confined in modern times. There were probably other places of crossing, for pack trails can be seen on Apple Pie Hill linking up with the track on Roden Downs, but it is generally accepted that to continue its journey westward over the Berkshire Downs the Great Ridgeway crossed the river at or near Streatley. Another ancient road, a parallel way, coming from Thetford in the north-east, also crossed the river at Streatley. This is the Icknield Way—perhaps a summer way of the Great Ridgeway—which continues west from Streatley on lower slopes but going in the same direction until the two come very close together at Wanborough in Wiltshire, where the lie of the land makes its continuance as a summer way difficult to work out, if indeed it went on from there independently.

Most main ridgeways in Berkshire, Hampshire and Wiltshire had their summer ways, in part if not for the whole of their length. These were routes on the lower slopes made possible in dry weather by the tendency of the upper courses of chalk streams to dry up in summer. Many of these summer ways are represented today by modern roads.

As well as the intermingling of folk memory, the activities of topographers and early map-makers have confused the line of the Great Ridgeway with the Icknield Way in Berkshire and Wiltshire, but if one remembers that the Ridgeway must always have been the higher road, and considers the physical relief of these hills, then the two trackways sort themselves out. The Saxon charters and the Tithe Awards of Berkshire refer to them again and again and to minor ridgeways branching from them in all directions. There are also many records that they were still used as droves for cattle in the eighteenth and nineteenth centuries. To mention one, Defoe in his *Tour through England and Wales* says that because the clay roads of the valleys were practically impassable for cattle in winter, the graziers of the Midlands used to bring their stock near London in the autumn and keep them there to sell in the capital in the winter.

From Streatley there are two ways by which the Great Ridgeway could get on to the high downland west of the Thames valley and reach and follow the crest of the scarp through Berkshire into Wiltshire. The main and most direct way is by the ridge, leading approximately west from the river, which carries the minor road climbing steeply through woods to Westridge Green and on to Hungerford Green. From Hungerford Green a wide lane branches north-west from this road and runs past Starveall to a meeting-place of tracks about half a mile south of Lowbury Hill.

Alternatively there is the way which follows the main road to Wantage, the A417, for its first half-mile as it climbs out of the valley. At Lough Down a metalled byway branches west from the main road and begins the rise to higher ground, soon becoming a deeply sunken way between high chalk banks. In a little more than a mile it becomes a rough track. It passes between Streatley Warren and the south-west corner of Ham Wood and for the next twenty-three miles to Fox Hill, about two miles within Wiltshire, it is a green road practically all the way, never passing through a village and for a good deal of its length unhedged if not unfenced, although from Roden Downs to Gore Hill the track we walk today is not on the actual line of the Ridgeway, as will be seen later in the chapter.

When the track reaches the head of the coomb which holds Streatley Warren the road is nearly 600 feet up, with cultivated downs rising and falling on each side.

About 500 yards past the second Warren Farm—the more westerly one—the track descends a little to a meeting-place of tracks south of Lowbury Hill, where it joins the branch of the Ridgeway coming from Hungerford Green. From it a track called White Hollow Way in an Anglo-Saxon charter rises between Lowbury Hill and Deans Bottom before crossing the Fair Mile track from Kingstanding Hill and following the ridge of Langdon Hill, after which it makes a gradual descent to Aston Upthorpe, a village at the foot of Blewburton Hill on which there is a spectacular stepping of cultivation terraces, or lynchets, below the banks of the summit camp.

From the cross-ways south of Lowbury a half-mile of rough sunken lane brings the Great Ridgeway to Roden Downs and another meeting-place of trackways. From here to where it crosses the Abingdon-Newbury road some five miles westward its line today has become involved and it is difficult to decide which is the main route, the summer way or modern deviations. As we see it today the Ridgeway goes past Lowbury Hill and over Roden Downs for a mile and a half, then turns a little south of west for a mile, but instead of keeping that line and going to East Ilsley it makes a right-angled turn north-west on East Ilsley Down to cross Several Down and the main road from Abingdon in coming to Bury Down.

The 1-inch O.S. map gives—as a dotted line and not a definite track—a former and more direct course for the Great Ridgeway, past the railway halt on Blewbury Down and going a little south of Fox Barrow and Grim's Ditch, on Compton Downs and Several Down, in coming to Abingdon Lane Down and a tumulus where it crosses the Abingdon–Newbury main road at Gore Hill. The 1830 edition of the 1-inch O.S. map issued before the railway across Blewbury Plain was made shows a more direct line between Lowbury Hill and Gore Hill which more or less coincides with the dotted line on the latest map.

Once the Abingdon–Newbury road is crossed the Great Ridgeway flows on uninterrupted as a wide green drove (Map 29). In about three miles it reaches Scutchamer Knob, a Saxon mound, whose plume of beeches was once a landmark for miles around. Now the old trees have been cut down and it has lost its flamboyance, revealing a crescent-shaped mound on which young trees of beech, chestnut and conifers have been planted giving promise that in years to come it will once again be a landmark for the surrounding countryside. The old maps name it Scutchamfly Barrow—a teasing name—but the local people called it Scotchman's Hob for a long time. Edward Thomas, in *The Icknield Way*, says an old carter justified the name to himself by the fact that a nearby old road called Hungerford Lane comes from the north and so presumably from Scotland.

The green road winds over Ridgeway Down, with its slender white monument on a high point nearby erected in memory of Robert Loyd-Lindsay, Baron Wantage, and bearing that text most moving to all hill-lovers: 'I will lift up mine eyes to the hills from whence cometh my help.'

Keeping well south of Lockinge Park the Great Ridgeway descends as a narrower hedged lane to White House, where it makes a sharp northward turn and then another as abruptly in regaining its westward line, the small crook in its course being probably due to the making of a later track crossing it. Still hedged, narrow and rather sunken now, it comes out at the Wantage–Hungerford road at a point called Red House. Red House has disappeared, but the pillar box near some red-brick cottages by the crossroads has 'Red House' lettered on it. For fifty yards or so before it comes to the crossroads the centre has been metalled to make a road to a farmhouse, and at the entrance from the main road there is a signpost saying TO THE FARM ONLY. No lover of old roads, however, would be taken in by this, for the sunken grassy margins on each side are far wider than the metalled strip and show unmistakable signs of age.

Along its eleven miles from Segsbury Camp to Fox Hill the old road is named Ridge Way on the O.S. map (Map 28). It is also signposted as a green road. Today these eleven miles form its best known and perhaps best loved reaches. Yet it is not the Ridgeway as the ancients saw it, for in those days no low banks outlined its width, though we like to think it was marked by old thorns and other trees, including the Wayfaring Tree, and that the happily named plant traveller's-joy climbed about them as it does today.

Its generous width, the long curving reaches one can see ahead following the contours, have become a part not only of the benign amplitude of the downs but of our conception of downland landscape. This stretch, also, holds sudden revelations of coombs great and small curving into the scarp. Although these coombs are a feature of all downland the northern downs excel in them. There is the Devil's Punchbowl, passed before one comes to White Horse Hill, and the Bishopstone coombs soon after the Wiltshire border is crossed, and many another. Prehistoric earthworks lie close to the track and the tumuli include Wayland's Smithy in its oval of tall beeches. The strange attenuated White Horse cut in the turf just below the crest of White Horse Hill lies out of sight of the Ridgeway. Below it is another great coomb called the Manger.

The trackway does not keep to the very edge of the chalk but lies a little behind it (Map 27). Often the view into the Vale of the White Horse is cut out by a short and gentle lift of field to the crest, and then the widest view is in the opposite direction over the downs rolling away to the Kennet valley and Inkpen beyond it, where another ridgeway goes into Hampshire and beyond.

Where, above Ashbury and Bishopstone, the old road runs from Uffington Camp westward to Charlbury Hill, a sweep of higher ridges within the downs curves away from and back to the Ridgeway and makes the southern skyline. These crests hold their own branch ridgeways, not easy to follow now that most of the downs are arable and cattle pastures.

Many local tales used to be told about this sweep of higher downs. Idlebush Barrow just off the Ridgeway has many variations of the idle shepherd boy story woven about its low tump, a tump which seems surprisingly insignificant when one stands near it yet is visible for miles around as a mound on the smooth ridge leading towards Lambourn. Two ragged groups of bushes about half a mile apart on the southern skyline are known as One o'clock Bush and Two o'clock Bush because it is said that shepherds once used them for telling the time. On all these downs one can pick up sherds of Romano-British and earlier pottery. There are sunken ways and linear earthworks, some now being lost under the plough. A pavement and other remains of a Roman villa lie under the earth in the angle of a field about halfway between the Ridgeway and the top of the down on which the bushes stand.

Ordnance Survey Maps

Oxford and Newbury. Sheet 158. 1 inch to 1 mile. 1940
Oxford and Henley-on-Thames. Sheet 105. 1 inch to 1 mile. Popular Edition, 1919
Sheet 3, West Berkshire. Published 1830 at Ordnance Map Office in the Tower

Fox Hill to St. Joan à Gores

Approximately 29 miles

Where the Great Ridgeway comes to the end of the ridge that has carried it westward above White Horse Vale it drops down from 750 feet to 650 feet to join the metalled road slanting up the scarp from Little Hinton and goes with it for a furlong to cross the Roman road to Baydon at Fox Hill (Map 27). Just before it comes to the minor road there are traces of hollowed trails in the pasture along its south margin which look very much like indications of the Ridgeway's earlier width here. Often when an ancient road descends a spur of downland we find these abandoned hollow ways fanning out from the brow of the slope.

From its crossing of the Roman road at Fox Hill the Ridgeway's next two and a half miles have been modernized into the main road leading over Wanborough Plain and along the north foot of Liddington Hill to a second Roman road going south to Ogbourne St. George. In between, at the east end of Liddington Hill, it crosses the main road going south-east from Swindon to Aldbourne, and though today the crossing is a simple inter-section of two roads, it was very different in 1773 when the Andrews' and Dury's map of Wiltshire was first published. On this map it is a star-like criss-crossing of half a dozen ways.

From one Roman road to the other the Ridgeway is shown keeping the line it follows today, passing the now vanished Ridgeway Bush landmark—known to Colt Hoare—before reaching the cross-ways we have mentioned and then continuing under the north-facing slopes of Liddington Hill. Here, shelved between the hillside steeps and the fields gently tilting down from it to the damp brookland below Badbury village, the modernized way now has a sign naming it *The Ridgeway*. The late Mr J. B. Jones, an adventurous discoverer in local geology and a great fighter for the preservation of local antiquities, was instrumental in having it erected just before he died, and to the many people who respect J. B. Jones and his work this sign must renew their memory of him every time they see it.

Because of the course of the next few miles of the Great Ridgeway (Map 26), this is the place to point out that west of Liddington Hill the North Wiltshire Downs have a main, or outer, escarpment of the lower chalk and an inner one of the upper chalk. The outer scarp makes a south-westerly sweep from Wroughton to Cherhill Down west of Avebury and is separated from the foot of the inner scarp by a shelf of downland that gradually widens southward from about two miles to four. At Liddington Hill the inner scarp does not run direct to Barbury but turns south to Ogbourne St. George, where it is gapped by the River Og flowing to join the Kennet at Marlborough. On the west side of the Og the scarp turns back north-west and, as Smeathe's Ridge, leads to Barbury Castle, where it bends south again as Hackpen Hill, which continues the ridge of downs on the Marlborough side of Avebury. To get from Liddington Hill to Barbury, the Ridgeway threads the four miles of lower ground which lies between them. After skirting Liddington Hill and crossing the Swindon–Marlborough main road (the Roman road to Ogbourne St. George) it continues south-west to pass a little beyond the intermittent sources of the Og at Draycot Foliat, first as a lesser metalled road and then as a green lane and trackway to the foot of Barbury slopes. These four miles of its course thus form the base of a triangle of lower ground which has its apex at Ogbourne St. George and contains the often dry head-reaches of the Og.

But before going on with the Great Ridgeway south from Barbury Castle we should return to the east end of Liddington Hill, to the former criss-cross of tracks shown on Andrews' and Dury's map. For one of those tracks branches from the Ridgeway and follows a much higher though much longer course to Barbury and, as lane and track, can still be walked for most of the way. Today we pick it up where it leaves the Swindon–Aldbourne road a little south of the Great Ridgeway crossing, and opposite the end of the hill.

It goes up this to the summit plateau, there bends south along the ridge that brings it to Round Hill Downs above Ogbourne St. George, descends to cross the Og at Southend, rises again on the other side of the stream to reach Barbury by way of Coombe Down and Smeathe's Ridge, and passes through the Barbury earthworks to rejoin the Ridgeway on Uffcott Down. On today's map there is only a parish boundary leading past the tumuli on Coombe Down, but in Andrews' and Dury's map a trackway follows the same line to Smeathe's Ridge. We have often wondered if this longer route may not have been the earliest course of the Great Ridgeway between the earthworks of Liddington Castle and Barbury Castle, with the lower, shorter route past Draycot Foliat coming into use as a summer way which, in the end, superseded the longer way round. Perhaps it is a question that will never be answered.

The next six miles of the Great Ridgeway begin with a southward swing towards the Kennet valley (Map 25). After passing under Barbury it takes a rise to Uffcott Down like a prelude to the greater height and spaciousness of the Hackpen ridge that carried it above the Hackpen White Horse and on past the derelict barn and the old pond at Glory Ann. On Hackpen the only part of the Ridgeway that is off its natural course is at Glory Ann where, for about a furlong, it should follow the parish boundary across dry, open ground above the pond but has been turned aside into the damp, rushy depression in which the pond lies. Here it passes between the pond and the ruins of the barn before making a right-angled turn back to its natural course.

All the way along the two and a half miles of Hackpen Hill the Ridgeway is very near to an altitude of 900 feet, a broad ribbon of track lined in several places with wind-toughened, lichen-encrusted thorns on one side or the other. Close on the right the hill's west flank falls away steeply to the shelf of lower downland that is edged on the other side by the fall of the outer scarp to the clay lowlands of northern Wiltshire. The east flank of the hill drops much less steeply to Dean Bottom and Rockley Hollow, the downs on this side of the ridge being patched with the woods at Old Totterdown and Rockley. Always seen ahead are the downs rising southward from the Kennet to the high skyline ridge which overlooks the Vale of Pewsey immediately beyond it.

As a wide green track it goes on across Overton and Avebury Downs with Windmill Hill and Avebury on lower ground a mile or so to the west, and Fyfield and Clatford Downs with their sarsen stone 'grey wethers' to the east. This is upland country, less tamed and benign than the downs the Great Ridgeway traversed through Berkshire and the Wiltshire-Berkshire borderland between Uffington Camp and Fox Hill.

On Overton Hill the trackway passes the site of the stone circle known as the Sanctuary, and still keeping its southward course crosses the Roman road and the River Kennet to skirt West Kennett village and continue up the south side of the river valley. For about a furlong from East Kennett village it has been metalled, but the metalled road bends south-east while the Ridgeway goes on first as a lane past the East Kennett long barrow in its shroud of trees, and then, rising with the downs again, takes the slope as a much diminished way, overgrown by thorns and brambles until, reaching the open heights, it comes into the saddle between Walker's Hill and Knap Hill overlooking the Vale of Pewsey (Map 24).

From Barbury to this point the way has been clear, but now the Great Ridgeway has to cross the five miles of the Vale of Pewsey and its greensand to reach the northern escarpment of Salisbury Plain.

Today it is not possible to trace with certainty the Ridgeway's course across the valley from the two Alton villages—Barnes and Priors—lying side by side at the foot of Walker's Hill. Yet unless we question the general belief that it aimed to regain the chalk at or close to Broadbury Banks on the edge of Salisbury Plain, no part of it could have been far from the line of the present cross-valley road which, after rising from Lockeridge in the Kennet valley to the saddle between Walker's Hill and Knap Hill, descends under Walker's Hill to lead along the west side of Alton Barnes and on through Honey Street and Broad Street—significant names both—to Wilsford on the Vale's west branch of the Avon close to the scarp foot of the Plain. The earlier 1-inch O.S. maps, together with Saxon boundary references in the charters of Beechingstoke and North Newnton, help us to see where the Ridgeway's course may have varied from this. Earlier O.S. maps show a track through Alton Priors towards the Kennet and Avon canal, and vestiges of this track could be traced a few years ago in the fields south of the village until they died out short of the canal, which suggests that the cutting of the canal finally put it out of use. If the line be continued over the canal it meets the present road after a bend a little south of Honey Street farm, and from this point the metalled road probably represents the Ridgeway as far as Broad Street.

But here the Beechingstoke and North Newnton charters indicate that it probably diverged on the west along the parish boundary and footpath which leads towards 'Wivelesford', so named in the Beechingstoke charter, a ford in the Vale's west branch of the Avon where it passes Puck Shipton and Wilsford, the latter place taking its name from the ford. The present footpath crosses the infant river on a brick bridge and then leads through the fields to a short lane at the west end of Wilsford. That the now almost disused footpath is a much diminished trackway is easily seen in the field, especially where it is following the parish boundary from Broad Street to the ford. In the Beechingstoke charter it is called the 'Way to Wivelesford', and in the North Newnton charter the 'Highway through the Brushwood'. Dr Grundy, whose translations of the charters we are quoting, states that it was 'probably part of a great highway of pre-Saxon times'.

South of Wilsford (Map 23) the trackway mounts to the Plain, passing Broadbury Banks and going on as an open track to a tumulus on Wilsford Hill, where it enters War Department country. For its first mile westward it has a centre of short close turf, a darker green than the rough grasses covering the parallel grooves showing its once generous width, but soon after passing a beech grove the turf is replaced by a military hard road for a mile or so over Chirton Down to the top of Redhorn Hill. From here the view opens out to reveal the length of Pewsey Vale, a view the eye welcomes, for along the last two miles behind the scarp there has been only the rolling Plain stretching away southward, where a flock of sheep, a herd of cattle, a clump of trees seemed reduced to pygmy size in the wide prairie-like desolation.

About a mile and a half farther west the scarp turns south-west, and the trackway follows it above Lavington villages (Map 22) to St. Joan à Gores Cross on the Devizes-Amesbury road as a wide track, open all the way, with cornfields on the inner side reaching towards the forbidden regions of the Plain. On the outer or scarp side there are many furrows of cart tracks, and as it descends to St. Joan à Gores these are multiplied: in places there are as many as sixteen parallel ruts under a shaggy growth of weeds and grasses.

Ordnance Survey Maps

Swindon. Sheet 157. 1 inch to 1 mile. 1940
Swindon and Cirencester. Sheet 104. 1 inch to 1 mile. Popular Edition, 1919
Salisbury. Sheet 167. 1 inch to 1 mile. 1940
Andrews and Dury. Map of Wiltshire. Published 1773

St. Joan à Gores to Win Green

Approximately 29 miles

Across the Devizes–Amesbury main road (A 360) the Great Ridgeway becomes a narrow surfaced road which soon begins an easy rise and in little more than a mile and a half comes to a tumulus on West Lavington Down. It continues as such through and beyond the deserted village of Imber. The first half-mile or so from the main road gives access to several downland farms sheltered in small hollows on the right, but with the farms left behind we come again to forbidden War Department country.

At the tumulus there is a meeting-place of at least four ways, including the Ridgeway. They come to it over the Plain from north-west, north-east, south-west and south-east, and which of the two westward tracks is the main Ridgeway is open to doubt. On the high, waterless Plain it would not be necessary for tracks to keep to the scarp ridge, and tracks would develop as need arose. Some must have been altered and adapted down the ages to suit the many generations of farmers who have occupied the Plain from earliest times, and the Army has added others to confuse us.

The most direct route the Great Ridgeway could take from West Lavington Down is the one which goes on to the east end of Imber (Map 21). As a metalled road it leads through the village and westwards along a hollow to pass tumuli and Ladywell Barn, and then swings south-west in coming to the edge of the Plain, first passing a long barrow on Boreham Down before descending Sack Hill and past Battlesbury Camp to the Wylye valley.

An alternative loop leaves the east end of Imber and has the look of being the most likely course. It follows higher ground, and passes the long barrow called Bowls Barrow, where it turns approximately north-west and joins the metalled road from Imber halfway between Ladywell Barn and the long barrow on Boreham Down. An ancient ditch lies parallel to it along the south side for one and a half miles to this junction. Here there is a meeting-place of several tracks, one of which comes south from Bratton Castle, crosses the Great Ridgeway, coincides with it nearly to Bowls Barrow, and then goes south-east across the Plain to Yarnbury Castle, which is another great meeting-place of trackways (see pages 60-61). Bowls Barrow is remarkable because in it was discovered a block of stone similar to the bluestones transported from South Wales to become a circle of foreign stones incorporated into Stonehenge. The way these bluestones were brought to Stonehenge has been the subject of much interesting argument, and the discovery of this stone makes one wonder how far Bowls Barrow lies from the route along which they were transported.

The next major passing-place of the Great Ridgeway is the hill-fort of Battlesbury on the edge of the Plain above Warminster near the head of the Wylye valley (Map 20). Here it turns south to follow the chalk on the other side of the Wylye river from Wiltshire into Dorset by way of East Knoyle and Shaftesbury, but before letting the Ridgeway take us out of Wiltshire let us go back to West Lavington Down for a look at a track which branches off north-west and which may have been an alternative, though less direct, loop-way along the scarp to Warminster.

For about two and a half miles a very gradual rise from the West Lavington tumulus takes a trackway past New Zealand Farm and Brouncker's Farm (Map 21) to come to the scarp where Stoke Hill carries it along to Coulston Hill. Except for a short stretch of metalled surface on Stoke Hill it is a broad green way grooved with multiple wheel-ruts, and no doubt this full width survival is associated with the fact that in later times it formed the last downland reach of the coach road from Salisbury to Bath which passed by Yarnbury in going north-west over the Plain. Several milestones can be discovered in the herbage beside the trackway—one stands at Yarnbury, another lies on its side in the hedge-bottom on Coulston Hill, and its lettering tells us we are XIX miles from Sarum, and XVII from Bath, with the date 1753 below.

During its coach-road phase this track forked at the west end of Coulston Hill soon after it reached 'XIX miles from Sarum', descending the scarp at the narrow bottom of a steep-sided, ravine-like notch in the chalk to reach Tinhead village and the valley it had to cross in heading for Bath. The Ridgeway branch, true to character, turns south-west to pass near the beech-shaded Tinhead long barrow on the west side of Tottenham Wood, then south over Patcombe Hill, and finally west above Longcombe Bottom in rounding a jumble of coombs between Tinhead long barrow and the earthworks of Bratton Camp (Map 20), visible two miles in front on the level summit of Westbury Hill. Cultivation has made the track little more than traceable along a hedge as far as the Tinhead barrow, but it, or today's version of it, is plain enough for the rest of the distance to the camp.

From Bratton Camp the ridge of Westbury Hill takes the trackway along to pass Beggar's Knoll and then across cornland to the gate by which it enters Upton Cow Down, a broad, smoothly rounded shoulder of ancient pasture leading down from the Plain to the Frome valley and bringing the track with it, to become one with the scarp-foot main road from Westbury to Warminster. It joins this road above Biss Bottom near Upton Scudamore and so, passing under Arn Hill, reaches Warminster and the Wylye valley, thus completing the loop it began by leaving the Great Ridgeway on West Lavington Down.

As usual when crossing a river valley the line of the Great Ridgeway becomes obscure, and there is no clear evidence in the field as to where it crossed the Wylye. The young river flows almost north from Monkton Deverill and through the other Deverill villages towards Warminster, but about half a mile short of the town turns east under the edge of the Plain. Two crossing-places suggest themselves—one near Longbridge Deverill, the other at Boreham soon after the river has turned east. On the edge of the Plain overlooking Boreham the earthworks of Battlesbury and Scratchbury Camps dominate the landscape, and the scarp here has a number of deeply scored parallel tracks leading down to the valley.

If we take the line to have been that of the surfaced road from Imber to the east end of Warminster, it then looks as if its continuation beyond Warminster should be that of the Shaftesbury road (A 350), which keeps west of the river until it crosses at Longbridge Deverill (Map 19) and goes up Lord's Hill to the cluster of tumuli on Parsonage Down. Here it bends south and runs over Pertwood Down to Upper Pertwood Bushes. But if, instead of the last mile and a half of the surfaced road, we take the line of the Ridgeway to have been that of the track which branches from it on Sack Hill and touches the west side of Battlesbury Camp, it will bring us over the railway and Chalk Hill to Boreham on the Warminster–Salisbury main road and, immediately south of the road, to the second river crossing.

Thence the line is approximately represented by the metalled road through Bishopstrow to Sutton Veny, and south from Sutton Veny (Map 19) by the broad track leading over Whiten Hill and on past a tumulus on Littlecombe Hill before suddenly dipping and rising again in crossing the upper-most part of Long Bottom and at once becoming for about a quarter of a mile a narrow hidden way through a small wood.

After the wood it is a wide green lane, its width lessened by thickets of thorn within the hedges. In about half a mile and just after crossing the line of the Roman road from Great Ridge it comes to a meeting-place of five tracks about five furlongs north-east of Pertwood. This is also the meeting-place of parish boundaries. In earlier times it must have been an important meeting-place of ways.

The Great Ridgeway would seem to be the track going south-west and passing a little north of Pertwood to join the main Warminster—Shaftesbury road (A 350) at the west end of Upper Pertwood Bushes, which is also, it should be remembered, the point we reached on the Shaftesbury road after crossing the Wylye at Longbridge Deverill.

South of Pertwood Bushes there is the choice of lines to East Knoyle. Perhaps the main road is on the line, or maybe the original line is the track which branches south-west three furlongs on and passes tumuli and a long barrow in coming to and crossing the main road and the Harrow Way between Mere and Chicklade (A 303). As a track it leads south for about 300 yards across the angle formed by the metalled road to Hindon, and continues as a minor road past Chapel Field Barn to Chapel Farm and so to Windmill Hill, where it bends eastward to join the Shaftesbury road passing through East Knoyle village.

From East Knoyle to Shaftesbury the main road must be pretty well on the line (Map 18). The Dorset boundary is crossed on Little Down about half a mile from Shaftesbury. To keep above the coombs between Shaftesbury and Melbury Abbas the Great Ridgeway would have turned away south-east from the town at Ivy Cross, and the line may be represented by the road running across the outskirts of the town from Ivy Cross to Butt's Knap. To get from Butt's Knap to the west end of Charlton Down the course could not have been far from that followed by today's road to Cann Common and up the western flank of Breeze Hill.

The Ox Drove (*see* page 175) joins the Great Ridgeway at the east end of Charlton Down and at the junction there are tumuli and ancient entrenchments. The Ridgeway then swings through half a circle to follow the ridge of Ashmore Down more or less south-westward to Fontmell Down, where it joins the Upper Blandford road from Shaftesbury.

Ordnance Survey Maps

Salisbury. Sheet 167. 1 inch to 1 mile. 1940
Frome. Sheet 166. 1 inch to 1 mile. 1946
Dorchester. Sheet 178. 1 inch to 1 mile. 1945

Win Green to Bulbarrow Hill

Approximately 15 miles

The lie of the land just west of Win Green, where the scarp of the Dorset chalk begins, suggests no alternative course for the Great Ridgeway on its journey through Dorset; the line flows on as easily and naturally as the contours of the hills. Curving away from Win Green it first follows the by-road over Ashmore Down and after a couple of south-westerly miles turns south into the Upper Blandford road to Shaftesbury, with Fontmell Wood on its east side and on the west the steep slopes and cross-dykes of Fontmell Down. It keeps to this road for about four and a half miles, and at intervals along each side of it are tumuli and minor earthworks (Map 17).

Near Everley Hill Farm, about three miles from Blandford, an inconspicuous green lane branches off to the west, and this may have been the line the track took on its way into the valley to cross the Stour, where, with Hambledon Hill and Hod Hill, those massive outliers of the chalk, over-looking the nearer bank, the river enters the gap it cut through the chalk uplands in flowing south-east to Blandford and Wimborne. This lane is now called Smugglers' Lane.

After an entrance made unobtrusive by shrubs and bramble clumps it becomes a wide grassy track, with fields and woodland on each side. In about a third of a mile it comes to a derelict lodge lost in the ragged shrubs of a long-neglected garden. Here there is a lost meeting-place of ways. Three now lead out to the fields and coppice, but Smugglers' Lane carries on narrowed almost to a path, and after a hardly perceptible descent of a mile or so there comes an abrupt fall to the valley as a stony path. This path ends at the lower or main Blandford to Shaftesbury road (A 350) by the lodge, beyond which the line is lost in the meadows of the Iwerne stream, a small south-flowing tributary reaching the Stour through a gap between the scarp and Hod Hill.

It is significant that opposite the end of Smugglers' Lane the main road makes a sharp turn by which is continued the lane's course towards the stream and almost immediately bridges it where the current looks as if it could be easily forded. Shortly afterwards, round the north-east corner of Hod Hill, the main road sends off a branch that leads behind the hill to Hanford and then on between the Stour and Hambledon Hill to Child Okeford, whilst the main road bends away to recross the stream and return to the foot of the scarp. It seems likely that the modern road over the Iwerne bridge and its branch behind Hod Hill are not far from the line the trackway took from the end of Smugglers' Lane to Hanford.

This still leaves the Stour to be crossed. It is impossible to tell now which of the two possible crossings was originally used by the Great Ridgeway in regaining its upland world on Shillingstone Hill. Perhaps it used both. There may once have been a ford—though it is difficult to think so today—somewhere at the head of the deep bend the meandering river makes in flowing across rather than along its valley bottom from the railway to the north-west corner of Hod Hill and then, almost parallel, back again right across the valley, the first half of the return being along the very foot of the precipitous and heavily wooded west side of Hod Hill. What looks like a narrow sunken track, long disused, goes down through the hill-foot trees and undergrowth from the road behind Hod Hill to this bend in the river, but it leads to no shelving banks such as might indicate an abandoned ford.

Yet if we were to cross the river here and go on for about a quarter of a mile into the marsh and rushy meadows between the two arms of the bend we should come to the blind end of a green drove which, as Ronald Good points out in his *Old Roads of Dorset*, is known as Hodway Lane, a name which suggests that the missing part may have led back through a ford to Hod Hill. Following the lane it takes us to the main road below Shillingstone Hill and there makes the cross-ways called Gains Cross by continuing as a track up the side of Shillingstone Hill to its summit.

A more likely looking crossing of the river today is opposite the grounds of Hanford House at Hanford immediately west of Hod Hill. The ford can still be found, but even if all traces of it had vanished the name 'Hanford' would prove that it once existed. The way through it leads, like Hodway Lane, to Shillingstone Hill, to a shoulder the hill pushes out towards the river a little farther up the valley. From the road that runs between Hod and Hambledon to Child Okeford it looks as if the approach would have been along the line now represented by a footpath going through the grounds of Hanford House to the river where, in rounding Alders Coppice, it is flowing towards Shillingstone Hill. The ford is opposite the south-east corner of the coppice just before the river bends away from it. Here flowing over a bed of large slabs of stone the water shallows between an embayed beach on the east side of the river with the river bank worn back behind it, and a similarly eroded bank on the west side. There is a tumbling of broken water over the downstream edge of the stony bed below which the river widens out like a reedy pool.

As there are no riverside fences or hedges it seems odd to discover on the west bank opposite the ford an old wooden bridle-gate, complete with side posts, erect in isolation as if to substantiate the way to the crossing.

Leading away from this gate a shallowing depression marks the line of a path towards the south-east corner of Alders Coppice and the end of a lane that keeps at first to the south end of the coppice and then goes on to pass under the railway in reaching the valley-side main road. Above this it becomes a track to the summit plateau of Shillingstone Hill where it is joined by a track that is a continuation of Hodway Lane from Gains Cross.

From the water meadows Hod and Hambledon Hills are in close view. Turning one's back on the river one can see the track going on over Shillingstone Hill like an invitation to the traveller. The passing of the centuries has obliterated clear evidence of where the Great Ridgeway actually crossed the Stour in ancient times. Only when the track ascends the hills again on the other side can one feel sure that one's feet are on the right road. Shillingstone Hill and its associated ridge have the remains of many ancient settlements and earthworks: the crossing must have been a busy one in those times. But all one can say today is that the Stour had to be crossed at its easiest point, and even today the twin hills, Hambledon and Hod, still seem to be guarding the gap the river made below them in the chalk hills.

Beyond the high commons of Shillingstone and Okeford Hills, now newly afforested, the chalk escarpment can be said really to begin again (Map 16). At the top of Okeford Hill many small tracks between the gorse go off in all directions. One, wider than the others, goes on inevitably in the direction of Bell Hill and Ibberton Hill to Bulbarrow. Along the south side of its generous width are deeply sunken furrows under a tangle of thorny shrubs and trees. The two miles or so from Okeford Hill across the summit of Bell Hill to where it becomes the made road from Okeford Fitzpaine is one of the widest and most open stretches of the Great Ridgeway in Dorset, recalling its passage through the Berkshire and North Wiltshire Downs. One becomes aware of the kinship though the turf is made up of the hair-like grasses of heathland, and instead of daisies starring the track there are the small yellow flowers of tormentil. Below the crest the pale green slopes of Bell Hill hold the dark double line of another ancient but narrower green road slanting in the direction of the hamlet of Belchalwell Street, and suggesting a Roman byway.

Bell Hill has lifted the Great Ridgeway to an altitude of nearly 850 feet before the ridge begins to fall away as it comes nearer to Bulbarrow. The fall is gradual but it reveals the view ahead and in it the Ridgeway recovering height on Ibberton Hill, while the valley opens out from the foot of the scarp to distances backed by the hills of Somerset. The way narrows in bending round a small spur of the ridge, goes through an almost perfect example of a cross-dyke and descends to 690 feet to join and become the metalled road slanting up the scarp from Belchalwell Street. The ascent to Bulbarrow's 900 feet is accomplished in the mile and a half in which, on Ibberton Hill and Woodland Hill in succession, the scarp-crest carries the road above the great wooded coomb hollowed in the side of Bulbarrow Hill to the summit.

Bulbarrow is one of those hills which seem to have a magnetic pull. As well as drawing the imagination it gathers to itself all the roads of the surrounding district; they come in from Wiltshire, Somerset and Hampshire, from the four corners of Dorset and from the sea. These roads do not meet in one crossing but branch off from the three acute corners of the summit triangle, which is a modern arrangement made when the summit was occupied by a small R.A.F. station. Each branch splits into two almost immediately to wind down the ridges of the hills and the side of the great coombs, and these branches in many instances divide again to link farms, small hamlets and villages in the sheltered valleys.

Bulbarrow takes its name from Bul Barrow, a tumulus on the summit, but this tumulus has lost all resemblance to a smooth mound and is now a jumble of hillocks covered with nettles and briars and much too uncomfortable for a look-out post. At a point near the debased tumulus where there is a gap in the hedge there is a sweep of view which is one of the most stimulating along the whole section of the Great Ridgeway in Dorset. On the coastal horizon a little east of south is the long ridge of the Purbecks, and at the opposite extreme, but much farther off, are the dim shapes of Somerset hills more coastal than inland and thus basing an arch of sky spanning almost the full width of Wessex between the bounds of its two channels.

South-west of Bulbarrow Hill, beginning at the middle distance, Nordon Hill curves up from the Ansty valley in leading away to the wilder more ragged heights of Nettlecombe Tout headland. There lies the westward continuation of the Great Ridgeway. Crowning a bluff thrust out from Bulbarrow itself and joined to it by a neck left between two coombs hollowed in the north and south sides of the hill, are the moulded green banks and ditches of Rawlsbury Camp. This camp overlooks the south part of Blackmoor Vale known as the Vale of the White Hart, a secluded corner watered by streams which must have made it almost impenetrable marsh when the newly-made banks and ditches of Rawlsbury were gleaming white. At Rawlsbury the chalk lies just under the turf and the heath is banished. The whole of this last five-mile stretch from where the Great Ridgeway ascends to the hills after the Stour crossing must have been a well-populated area in prehistoric times. There are the sites of at least two settlements, one on Shillingstone Hill and another at Ringmoor about a mile from Okeford Hill. There are tumuli on the uplands behind the edge of the escarpment and no doubt many more have been obliterated by the plough.

Ordnance Survey Maps

Salisbury. Sheet 167. 1 inch to 1 mile. 1940
Dorchester. Sheet 178. 1 inch to 1 mile. 1945

BULBARROW HILL TO THE SEA

Approximately 45 miles

Immediately after Bulbarrow Hill there is a definite but narrow gap in the scarp (Map 16). How this gap was crossed in ancient times there are now only the barest visible indications. The Great Ridgeway is aiming at Dorsetshire Gap and Nettlecombe Tout about two and a half miles away on the other side of a little valley which tapers back into the hills. At this distance from Bulbarrow Hill, Dorsetshire Gap looks such an unimpressive nick in a hill-crest that at first sight it must often disappoint the expectations stimulated by its name, but Nettlecombe Tout looms up beyond the Gap, though its shaggy wooded side and jutting spur give no hint of a trackway on it.

A low swell across the valley between Bulbarrow Hill and the Dorsetshire Gap forms a watershed dividing the Devil's Brook, flowing south through the hills to Dewlish, from several tributaries of the Lydden flowing north into Blackmoor Vale. Ronald Good suggests that the Ridgeway's direct course to Nettlecombe Tout would first be along the spur leading south from Bulbarrow, then across the Devil's Brook in the neighbourhood of Lower Ansty—though it seems to us that this part of the valley bottom can at times be very wet—and then along the ridge of Nordon Hill above Melcombe Horsey.

An alternative route we discovered in the field lies across the valley from Moots Copse to Breach Wood on the line of the low watershed we have mentioned. Opposite the south corner of Moots Copse a bridle-path—much of it now lost but still shown complete on the 1-inch O.S. map—led down a slope of what are today's cultivated fields and on to cross the road from Ansty Cross to Mappowder, coming out at a bridle-gate half hidden in the roadside hedge by a cottage (Map 15). Across this road the field on the other side shows no obvious traces of a path following the line towards Breach Wood, but in the wood itself there are traces of an old track, and from the south-west corner of the wood a wide, drove-like lane ascends gradually to a farm at the foot of Nordon Hill. This old lane has a deeply sunken part on its left side overgrown by ancient oak and thorn trees and a tangle of scrub. The centre of the open way is roughly metalled but on each side of the metalling there are old cart ruts and furrows thickly overgrown with coarse herbage. Tall dense hedges hung with bramble and rose briars enclose the whole width of the track which, after coming to the farm, slants up the side of the hill along a shelf of rough pasture dotted with bushes to reach the top of the ridge. The track comes out into the open near a broken tumulus standing in a cornfield and continues westward along the ridge for about a furlong to Dorsetshire Gap. Where the end of the ridge falls steeply into the Gap there are deep hollow trails which divide and come round each side of the shoulder.

How Dorsetshire Gap got its name we have not been able to discover; nor do we know whether the gap is the result of rushing water or wind, or perhaps both, funnelling through an original notch in the scarp-crest, or whether it was artificially deepened to form a barrier or a boundary in ancient times. Its striking character is not revealed until one comes almost upon it to find the ridge of Nordon Hill coming to an abrupt and almost vertical end with the shoulder of the opposite ridge less than a stone's throw beyond, rising with the same steepness, and a narrow track or gully winding between the two shoulders.

The small downland plants on the almost vertical sides of the slopes have a precarious roothold in the chalk which must be often torn away when heavy rain cascades from the summits. Deep hollows filled with woodland cut off the view on the right and help to shut in this narrow pass at the edge of the hills. On the left the tunnel-like track goes away from the Cap to descend gently to Melcombe Horsey secluded in the broad valley-amphitheatre below. If the scarp here were denuded of its woods the Gap would stand out with more dramatic emphasis, particularly when seen from Blackmoor Vale. The first O.S. maps indicate that this was not such a lonely region of Dorset in the early nineteenth century as it is today, for they show that the Gap drew to itself several roads that were obviously used by more than local farm traffic, which must have helped to score the pass deeper.

On the west side of the Gap a number of broken hollow ways worn deeply into the chalk, with later trails going roughly parallel to the sunken gulleys, rise to the top of the ridge. Here the hollow ways fade out and the track goes through an arable field and is not deeply marked. Where the shoulder of the ridge begins to fall to the saddle between Nettlecombe Tout and Ball Hill the track becomes another hollow way which is a tunnel of rank and thorny growth so overgrown that only a stoat or slinking fox could weave a path along it. Nettles stand waist-high in its damp bottom, luxuriating in the black mould of dead and decaying vegetation, and the struggle of all the living plants has produced a tangle of elongated weedy growth of blanched intertwined stems. The traveller today must keep to the fields beyond until the trackway fans out into several broken hollow ways, lined with trees and shrubs, as it comes to the end of its fall and then unites into a green rutted drove to pass some cottages and come to the crossroads at Folly Inn near Plush just off the metalled road from Mappowder to Piddletrenthide. The Folly Inn, which has only recently been closed, must have been one of the loneliest inns in Dorset, and one regrets its closing. Its presence in this remote region suggests that there were more long-distance travellers coming over the hills in the last century than there are today.

There can be little doubt of the line of the Ridgeway at this point. The green road past the inn narrows and deepens as it continues up Ball Hill and along Church Hill, passing tumuli and an ancient field system to come to the B 3143 road from Buckland Newton to Piddletrenthide. From the end of the Church Hill ridge to the road the last 200 yards or so are not clear, but a parish boundary continues the line to the road almost opposite a hedged lane. This wide lane follows a ridge westward between Henley and Alton Pancras to the south-east end of Little Minterne Hill, where it is crossed by the Old Sherborne road above Minterne Parva.

This lane is the nearest we can get to the line of the Great Ridgeway today. From it a footpath goes north-west along Little Minterne Hill to a tumulus and then on as a track to Dogbury Camp and Dogbury Gate on the present main road from Sherborne to Cerne Abbas (A 352), which here leaves Blackmoor Vale behind in going through the pass between Dogbury and High Stoy on the west side of the road. The Ridgeway takes us along behind High Stoy, where vestiges of tracks in the turf on the hillside just above the half-mile of road from Dogbury Gate to Telegraph Hill suggest the line; after which there can be no other line for it but that of the next two miles or so of the present highway going west from Telegraph Hill to where it bends round the head of the deep coomb in the scarp slope of Batcombe Hill (Map 14).

It passes the Cross and Hand, an odd short pillar of grey stone holding no cross today or sign that it ever held one. Who placed this stone on the side of the road and why it was placed there has been explained in many ways, the likeliest being that it is a parish boundary stone. Perhaps because of its position on the crest of this lonely escarpment in the heart of some of the most magical of Dorset scenery, the legend grew up that it was the place where a miracle was worked. Another story is that a murder was committed at this spot, and yet another that the almost obliterated carving at its top represents a bowl held in a hand and was put there to receive alms for poor wayfarers. This last story appeals to us most.

The amplitude of the great curve of highway along Batcombe Hill, the exhilarating depth and sweep of the coomb under the hill, the magnificent spread of view across Blackmoor Vale to the hills about Sherborne, with the Mendip ridges in the distance beyond them, and the untamed nature of the wide margins of the open road, where great oaks stand with full horizontal spread of boughs and the heath is dotted with gorse, patches of heather in summer and floods of bluebells in spring, make this stretch of the Great Ridgeway unforgettable. There is also the satisfying assurance that there can be no doubt at all that this was the very same ground the Ridgeway traversed, for it could have taken no other course along this reach of the escarpment. Here it is truly a ridge road, the ground falling away on each side, northward in sheer steeps, southward in more gentle slopes.

As it comes to the head of the Batcombe hollow the modern road, which for about two miles has so definitely perpetuated the Great Ridgeway, turns north-west to descend the shoulder of the hill on its way to Holywell, but a track and a lane continue the south-west line to the main road from Yeovil to Dorchester (A 37). This part of the road to Dorchester has a long history, for it was once a Roman road, and before that a trackway.

At Batcombe Hill the question arises of how the Great Ridgeway crossed the Frome and the wide gap in the chalk the river has made as far south as Maiden Newton. Did it continue to Holywell and along the lesser ridge by way of Evershot, Horsey Knap and Benville Lane to Toller Down Gate, or did it turn south to follow the main escarpment, cross the Frome near Maiden Newton, and make its way to Toller Down Gate from there? It had to get on to the Toller ridge to continue its course south-westward. The chalk escarpment turns south at Batcombe Hill for about three miles and then at Maiden Newton, where it is cut by the Frome, swings back north-east to Toller Down Gate, while the lesser ridge from Holywell is off the chalk and crosses several streams, though it looks the more direct and simple route on modern maps.

Maybe this line was a branch used as a summer way, but it seems likely that the earlier and all-season way kept to the chalk ridge by branching at Batcombe Hill to the Roman road, known locally as Long Ash Lane, and followed this line south to Stagg's Folly or, maybe, three furlongs beyond to Folly Hill, there descending to cross the Frome somewhere between Cattistock Camp and Maiden Newton. From Stagg's Folly a metalled by-road leads to and around the north side of Castle Hill to Cattistock village, but soon after this byway has left the main road a footpath branches from it and becomes a track running under the south side of Castle Hill to the village, beyond which the line is continued by today's metalled road across the river and then by a short track to Chilfrome. From Chilfrome a lane called Upper Drove runs across a ridge between the Frome and the River Hooke to the main road going up Whitesheet Hill from Maiden Newton to Toller Down Gate. We remembered the chalk quarries on the Wiltshire White Sheet Hill where the Salisbury Way ends when we saw the white scar of chalk quarrying on this Dorset Whitesheet Hill.

An alternative line takes us to where, on Folly Hill, the minor road branches south-west and leads along the ridge of Nordon Hill and down to Maiden Newton to join the main Dorchester–Crewkerne road (A 356) which, after crossing the Frome at Maiden Newton, rises to Whitesheet Hill and follows the ridge to Toller Down Gate. The track keeps a little north of today's Toller Down Gate crossroads.

At Toller Down the Great Ridgeway is coming to the end of the chalk that has borne it thus far through Dorset, but the road must still go on across the county and into Devon to reach the sea at the mouth of the Axe (Map 13). The ridge westward along Beaminster Down, though formed of different deposits, provides the high ground on which it continues, and one quickly begins to notice the effect the difference in geological make-up has upon the road. The long, smooth and fairly level stretches are left behind, and instead there are more frequent dips between and curvings round separate hills, so that the road is more undulatory as well as more winding, although it keeps its general direction as purposefully as ever.

Three furlongs east of Toller Down Gate the Ridgeway leaves the A 356 road and forks west as today's lesser road over Beaminster Down. Thomas Hardy knew it as Crimmercrock Lane—obviously a rendering more easy on the tongue than Cromlech Crock Lane, an earlier local name for it—and made it the setting of one of his less tragic poems, the verses beginning: 'I pitched my day's leasings in Crimmercrock Lane.' We could not help wondering if, walking along it, he had experienced the same kind of joyousness as we had felt one autumn afternoon when we lingered there looking down at the little town of Beaminster, its golden-brown church tower, its clustering russet roofs and yellowish stone walls cupped in green hill-slopes that rise to encircle the place with ridges, rounded summits and shoulders from which the folds of other uplands reach away to spacious horizons in every direction.

At the road-fork after Toller Down Gate lie the Hore Stones, one on each side of the way. These are very massive irregular slabs of reddish-grey stone, seven feet or more across, embedded in the ground as well as in the shaggy grasses of the roadside margins. They show no signs of having been shaped or tooled, and Dr Grundy suggests they were Saxon boundary stones. They are not marked on the 1-inch O.S. map. On their broad flattish tops the pitted weather-worn hollows filled with moss and tiny plants, together with the patterning of lichen encrustment, give them the appearance of great age.

After rising to Beaminster Down the Great Ridgeway is joined by the Harrow Way, or Hard Way (*see* page 91), coming south-west from Corscombe and Yeovil. They meet in an area of rough pasture and common land dotted with gorse and brambles. About a quarter of a mile west of this junction a trackway to Eggardon (*see* page 69) branches south across the gorsy rough. From the opposite side of the Ridgeway this Eggardon track is continued north-east past Axnoller Farms to Richard's Ford, an ancient crossing of the very young Axe nearly a mile and a half on from the Ridgeway. At the ford the track turns north towards the Perrott villages, but this is lowland country intersected by many tributary brooks of the Axe and Parrott, which makes its further course and ultimate destination hard to determine.

Leaving Beaminster Down, with its glimpses of the Mendips on the northern skyline and layers of hill country stretching to the coast on the south, the Great Ridgeway dips gradually along Mintern's Hill and Buckham Down as a metalled road with broad margins which show definite signs that it was in use long before the middle strip was surfaced for motor transport. It continues over Horn Hill, where it crosses the tunnel cut through the hill for the main road north from Beaminster. The next place to the west of Horn Hill is Broadwindsor, about two miles on, and until the Beaminster tunnel was made in the middle of the nineteenth century the through road from Toller Down to Broadwindsor followed the line of the Great Ridgeway over Horn Hill. Today it bends from this line to join the main road at the north end of the tunnel and reaches Broadwindsor only after curving through Whetley Cross, whilst the Ridgeway, sunk between high ferny banks under tall beech trees, is the wide lane that keeps the direct course over the tunnelled hill and has the remains of a middle strip of asphalt still visible among stones and grass. Its original breadth is not so apparent now because of the encroachment of thicket-like hedges and narrow coppices, but even so there are grassy margins to keep it spacious.

In descending the shoulder of Horn Hill it narrows a little, its banks become deeper and above them willows, holly, oak and ash trees spread their boughs over the track and make it a shadowy woodland way. Primroses and wood sorrel grow between the mossy tree roots exposed on the sloping banks and drifts of bluebells make pools of colour under the trees. The only view is from field gates on the seaward side, where the bracken-covered ground falls away steeply at first towards broken country in which Gerrard's Hill with its plume of trees and Waddon Hill stand up boldly about a mile to the south.

As the track descends it leaves the woodland behind and its margins take on a lush waterlogged appearance. Soon reeds and sedges and a luxuriant growth of other water-plants along its margins indicate the beginnings of wet ground about the head of a small stream which flows north to feed the Axe. Broadwindsor is now about half a mile straight ahead along the remainder of the Horn Hill way, whilst the next great scarp-landmark for the Ridgeway, the densely timbered bulk of Lewesdon Hill rising almost to 900 feet, is about the same distance south of the village, which lies in a gap between Lewesdon and the end of a lesser ridge leading away from the scarp to the valley of the Axe. A small tributary of the Axe flows along the foot of each flank, and the one on this side of the village, Common Water, passes under the road and is the source of the waterlogging we have noticed. Before this stream was channelled in its deep narrow trench and the road made up, this must also have been a muddy part of the way until it breasted the rise up Hollis Hill to the village. In the village it enters today's road from Whetley Cross and on the western outskirts falls and rises again in bridging the other stream and going on to Cockpit Hill between Lewesdon and the massive spur that is Pilsdon Pen. A youth we spoke to at the door of a cottage near Common Water called the way up Hollis Hill the 'Roman road'. As country people often use the word 'Roman' for any ancient earthwork, building or trackway, and as this was the route Brian Vesey-Fitzgerald took when he was walking the Hard Way, or Harrow Way, it suggests that it may be the line of the Great Ridgeway as well, for the Horn Hill way coincides with the Harrow Way from Beaminster Down to Pilsdon Pen, and again from near Marshwood to the mouth of the Axe in Seaton Bay.

Yet the way through Broadwindsor was perhaps not the main course of the Ridgeway here, but a summer way loop which at some time or other superseded the original scarp-way above the streams; for there is a sequence of green lane and trail which leads by way of Clanden Hill, Waddon Hill, Stoke Knap and the north side of Lewesdon Hill to the Broadwindsor road at Cockpit Hill, thus by-passing the village on the south.

This branch begins two or three hundred yards before Common Water is crossed. A lane forks south along the side of Clanden Hill and in a quarter of a mile comes to the main road from Beaminster to Broadwindsor. Locally the lane is called Owls' or Owlers' Lane, which is only another way of calling it Smugglers' Lane, not an unusual name in Dorset and other parts of Wessex, especially near the coast; but though smugglers made use of these lanes because they traversed lonely and sparsely populated regions of the countryside, they were in existence long before the great period of smuggling in the eighteenth century, when they were given the name. Today this lane, shut in and narrowed by hedges spreading into thickets, is deeply rutted by field traffic, and when we walked it in the very wet summer of 1956 it was a miry way indeed. With ruts holding liquid mud, and with hedge-thickets and their tangles of undergrowth to check evaporation, it looked as if it would seldom give dry going now whether or not it did in the past. But it is not on chalk, and it is also more of a hill-foot than a hillside way.

On the other side of the Beaminster road the lane is continued south between very thick hedges by a more deeply hollowed way, obviously an ancient trail, rising across the end of Waddon Hill to Stoke Knap on the road from Broadwindsor to Bridport. The hill-slopes fall rather steeply and in folds that do not give room for a broad way to slant across them. From the main road at Stoke Knap the continuation is westward. A narrow lane leads under the woods on the north-facing front of Lewesdon Hill and enters the road from Broadwindsor above Swilletts Farm, the two branches of the loop thus uniting before going on to Pilsdon Pen.

On the right-hand side of the road as it curves under Pilsdon Pen the hill-slopes rise sharply to the camp on its summit; on the left the ground falls less steeply to Marshwood Vale with the hamlet of Pilsdon in the foreground and beyond the valley fields the coastal ridge, with a triangle of sea coming into view at the Bridport Gap and showing as a pale sparkling line on the horizon. On a clear day the view from this shelf-like reach of road is breath-taking. The long-distance traveller of old, knowing the end of his journey was now near, must often have rested at this spot, his traveller's fears banished for the moment by the beauty of the scene before him, though Marshwood Vale would not be the rich green cultivated valley of today but an area more deserving of its name. The modern traveller also pulls up, sensing that here is another of those magical places where he must stop and look his fill. Far too many, alas, when they do this, leave behind a litter of paper bags, cigarette packets and ice-cream cartons, for modern man, it seems, cannot refresh the spirit without refreshing the body also. I wonder what litter prehistoric man left behind when he stopped to look at the view. Perhaps he found it best to leave no traces that would tell an enemy he had passed by.

From Pilsdon Pen the line of the Great Ridgeway must be more or less the modern winding road which falls and rises to come to Birdsmoor Gate, a place called on earlier maps Furzemoorgate but which, at first sight, does not present such a charming picture as its two names suggest. At Birdsmoor Gate corner the line is taken up by the road B 3165, which keeps along the ridge to avoid the hollows and streams on either side of it (Map 12). It goes through the scattered village of Marshwood, which once possessed a Norman castle and a vineyard, and soon rises again to run under the beech woods of the north slope of Lambert's Castle, where the southward view to the sea is cut off by the hill.

The view north, however, is a rewarding one, particularly in autumn. Bracken-covered slopes fall away from the road and with the many coppices and patches of old woodland give the rich pastoral landscape spread between the ridge and Chard a hint of underlying wildness. It is a serene landscape, but not too placid, intricate in its flow and many-toned within its own green world, while the hills of Somerset lift up in the far distance to make an enclosing skyline. It is a prospect over which to muse and dream, less spectacular than the one from the earthworks at the top of the hill where, in a magnificent pattern of land and water, can be seen the pale bulk of Portland, the sea breaking on Chesil Beach, the Fleet and a long stretch of the Devon coastline.

Following the ridge west-south-west and then south-west the road comes to Monkton Wyld Cross where, with the Berkshire and Wiltshire reaches left many miles behind, the Great Ridgeway finally passes from Dorset into Devon. Here a delta of branches sprays forward, all leading to the Axminster–Charmouth main road, and one of them continues straight ahead to the Hunter's Lodge crossing and thence to Lyme Regis, curving south-east away from the line of the Ridgeway to get there. This upland top between Monkton Wyld Cross and Hunter's Lodge must originally have been one of those places where diverging trackways could duplicate themselves without restriction, and what we are left with now is a residue of the branches perpetuated by modern usage. Whether the present-day branch of the B 3165 road to Hunter's Lodge is on the line of the Great Ridgeway, or whether the line ran something north of it, the direction is towards the end of Trinity Hill, for it is along this hill that the old road at last begins to approach its end on the Devon coast.

It leaves the main highway near Hunter's Lodge as the minor road going south-west along Trinity Hill (Map 11) and then south over Shapwick Hill, close to the tumuli there, and on across the Lyme Regis road to reach Charton behind the tumbled cliffs of Charton Bay. Here it turns west, and with only a few hundred yards of down-like cliff-top between it and the expanses of the English Channel becomes a narrow upland lane within banks and hedges leading to Rousdon, Dowlands, Bindon and finally the Axe estuary. A quarter of a mile past Bindon it forks into two, one branch leading to the mouth of the Axe and the other to Axmouth village half a mile up the little estuary. The left-hand branch, keeping parallel to the coast, soon changes to a green track over a golf-course and then to a way down a deepening gully under the hill called Haven Hill, a tree-hidden way from which the river is not seen until one is almost in the main road alongside it. The right-hand branch reaches Axmouth by veering from the cliff-tops to enter the head of another wooded but broader hollow which it descends to the village. Seen from the upper part of the descent the tree-covered slopes of the open end make a wide notch in the angle of which the village is revealed as the foreground to green levels of marshy pastures threaded by the meandering river. Jutting up on the right of the notch is the summit of Hawkesdown Hill with the earthworks of its camp showing among the scrub there. So the Great Ridgeway ends—or begins—overlooked by a camp-crowned hill.

From medieval times onward there are records of great landslips on the east side of the mouth of the Axe, which not only set back the cliff-line but caused the river mouth to silt up by letting the run of the sea pile up a bank of pebbles across it, through which the river only just manages to force and keep its present narrow outlet under Haven Cliff. It is probable that similar landslips occurred before any were recorded. The changes here have been such that it is now impossible to say where the Great Ridgeway formerly came down to the river and the sea.

Ordnance Survey Maps

Dorchester. Sheet 178. 1 inch to 1 mile. 1945
Taunton and Lyme Regis. Sheet 177. 1 inch to 1 mile. 1946

2

SOME BERKSHIRE BRANCHES
OF THE GREAT RIDGEWAY

Fair Mile

Approximately 2 miles

WHERE the Great Ridgeway goes off over Roden Downs from a meeting-place of tracks and parish boundaries a quarter-mile west of Lowbury Hill, a track curves north-east to become the Fair Mile (*see* Map 30). This is the name given to the eastern end of a track leading from East Ilsley over East Ilsley Down, and which, after rounding the north-west side of Lowbury Hill, crosses a track called White Hollow Way in an Anglo-Saxon charter, coming south from Aston Upthorpe along Langdon Hill.

On this area of chalk downs there is a complicated series of trackways thrown off by the Great Ridgeway or connected to it by minor tracks, some of which have lost their original lines. This has been corn-growing country for centuries, and there have been alterations and, in some cases, a re-alignment of tracks in recent years, as can be seen by comparing the 1919 Popular Edition of the 1-inch O.S. map with later ones.

As soon as it has crossed the Aston Upthorpe track the Fair Mile receives its name on the map, and is indeed a fair mile to those who love walking an old road. As a broad green way it runs to Cholsey Downs, open on the north to rolling cultivated fields and on the south overlooking, first Deans Bottom, whose slopes are patterned with scrub and grey-green strips of old turf, and then the narrow trough of Unhill Bottom. Behind these hollows the broken line of Unhill Wood hides the Great Ridgeway or a branch of it going west from Streatley. In about a mile and a half—for this Fair Mile is as generous in its length as in its breadth—the track becomes a metalled way with narrow woodland on each side, and begins its descent of Kingstanding Hill to reach the Reading–Wantage road and join up with the Icknield Way.

East Hendred Down to Wittenham Clump

Approximately 8 miles

Where the Great Ridgeway comes to a meeting-place of tracks and parish boundaries on East Hendred Down (*see* Map 29), about half a mile east of Scutchamer Knob, a track leads down the scarp and past Upper Farm on Chilton Field to come to the inn on the Abingdon–Newbury main road (A 34). Dr Grundy named it the Wallingford Ridgeway. The continuation of this way is now a metalled road to West Hagbourne, but instead of following it the line of the Wallingford Ridgeway turns north and continues with the main road to just beyond the point where it crosses the Icknield Way at the Atomic Research Station on Harwell Field. Here a track continues the line west of Bag's Tree to Broadway, where the Wantage road forks for Wallingford and Reading.

The seven or eight miles of the main road east to Wallingford is a water-shed way between the Hagbourne and the streams flowing north to the Thames. At Brightwell a footpath and vestiges of tracks lead northward from it to Brightwell Barrow and the hill-fort beside Wittenham Clumps on the Sinodun Hills, so that the ridge provides a route linking them with the Icknield Way on Harwell Field and the Great Ridgeway on East Hendred Down. It seems likely that it was along this ridge from Wallingford that, in A.D. 1006, the Danish Army marched to Scutchamer Knob on its way to the battle of Cynete.

Hungerford Way, south to Great Shefford

Approximately 2 miles

North to the Icknield Way

Approximately 8½ miles

At the same meeting-place of tracks and parish boundaries east of Scutchamer Knob on East Hendred Down (*see* Map 29) a track came to the Great Ridgeway from the north which was once part of a through route from Oxford to Hungerford, and is mentioned as such in John Ogilby's *Book of Roads*, 1675. The part of it which goes north from the Great Ridgeway over Horn Hill a quarter-mile east of Aldfield Farm is called Hungerford Way in a Tithe Award of that district, and is still called Hungerford Lane by local people.

South from the Great Ridgeway it goes south-west over the downs as track, footpath and track to come to Lands End, where there is another meeting place of tracks and minor roads. From Lands End it continues its south-west line as a surfaced road to Farnborough, where it meets the Reading Way coming from the Great Ridgeway over Lattin Down (*see* page 50). A number of roads and tracks spray out from Farnborough, some of them leading to the various fords over the river in the Lambourn valley. The line of the Hungerford Way, however, is first a short length of footpath bending south of the village to join a minor road curving west to cross the Newbury–Wantage road (B 4494) at a copse. It continues approximately south-west past Woolley Home Farm and along the east side of Woolley House park to descend gradually from the downs to join the main Hungerford–Wantage road, about three-quarters of a mile west of Chaddleworth, and goes with it to Great Shefford (*see* Map 9). There is a footpath and then a track along the ridge on the left above the main road which goes down to the Lambourn at East Shefford. It leads from the minor road from Boxford just before this road begins its steep descent to the Hungerford road a mile south-west of Chaddleworth, and may be all that now remains of an earlier ridgeway. Its further course northward along the ridge is lost, though a short length of track which, if continued, would pass the west end of Spray Wood suggests the line. From Great Shefford the Hungerford Way follows the main road, a fairly high road all the way, passing between Long Ditch and a tumulus in its first mile.

North of the Great Ridgeway the Hungerford Way, called, as already mentioned, Hungerford Lane, went down the scarp of East Hendred Down, passing east of Aldfield Farm and crossing the Icknield Way in about two miles. On the most recent 1-inch O.S. map its first mile is a blank, though on earlier editions it is continuous. North of the Icknield Way it continues over Horn Down to Milton Hill and joins the main Newbury–Abingdon road. It must have continued along the line of this main road through Steventon and Drayton to Abingdon, for this seems the only possible way to avoid the headwaters of many north-flowing tributary streams of the Thames. From Abingdon the main road through South Hinksey to Oxford is a watershed way for its first two or three miles; after that it crosses the heads of many streams, though the road is comparatively high. The earlier travellers, before the Hungerford Way came into being as a coach road, would probably have taken a wide north-westerly detour south of Bagley Wood and over Boar's Hill to reach the ancient crossing of the Thames at North Hinksey.

Reading Way

Approximately 28 miles

A line of minor ridgeways which is practically continuous can be traced on the O.S. map of 1830 for nearly twenty-eight miles from the Great Ridgeway on Lattin Down to the Tilehurst ridge overlooking Reading; owing to modern road improvements this continuity is not now so apparent. Dr. Grundy calls this route the Reading Way and says it was along this line that the Danes came up from Reading to meet the Saxons at the Battle of Englefield in A.D. 871. Some of it became incorporated into Saxon and later roads: it may even consist in part of Saxon roads, as some lengths of it, particularly about Farnborough, Catmore, Chieveley, Beedon and Stanmore, are called Herepaths in the Anglo-Saxon charters of those districts (*see* Map 9).

For about six miles the Reading Way coincides with an old track named Old Street on the latest O.S. map, though the course of this today does not show the straight lengths we associate with the Roman roads the Saxons called Streets in their charters, meaning made roads. It may be worth mentioning that at its northern terminus, north-east of Farnborough, the Old Street track comes to a crossroads called Lands End, and not far from its southern terminus today, a little below Beedon Hill, there is a place called World's End. Though this has probably nothing to do with the actual beginning or end of Old Street, it does suggest that in the area it traverses Old Street may have superseded the ancient trackway in Roman times. Following the Roman occupation, this area of Berkshire south of the Great Ridgeway was colonized by some of the earliest Saxon settlers, as they spread out from the Thames valley; and if one remembers that, except for the commons which in their turn have now mostly been absorbed into farm land, much of it has been under cultivation for 1,500 years or more, the possibility of finding the original lines of the prehistoric trackways is very dim. The Saxon and medieval lanes and byways, now modernized into metalled roads, which wind from village to village and farmstead to farmstead, have taken their place, and some of these have been diverted to keep outside parkland enclosed in the eighteenth century and before. We can only suggest on the scantiest of evidence the route the trackway may have taken.

The beginning of the Reading Way, however, has the authentic feeling of antiquity. A track (*see* Map 29) which is also a parish boundary for half a mile or so branches from the Great Ridgeway at a tumulus about half a mile south-east of Pewit Farm and goes south-east over Lattin Down and through a coppice on Lockinge Down, keeping just east of South Ridgeway Farm and passing Moonlight Barn in reaching the west end of Farnborough (*see* Map 9). It would be pleasant to think that Moonlight Barn received its name because it was once used by 'moonlighters', or smugglers, for their secret trade, thus linking it by name with the stretches of ridgeways in other parts of Wessex that are known as smugglers' lanes, but we have been unable to find any evidence of this.

The line is continued through Farnborough as a metalled road and then goes east for nearly a mile of track until it joins Old Street at a copse near Kiln Barn. On an early O.S. map there are four kilns shown on this part of the track from the Great Ridgeway to Kiln Barn. The track turns south-east with Old Street and coincides with it for the next three miles or so, keeping east of Catmore and later passing a tumulus on the left and then Hailey Copse on the right before reaching Common Farm half a mile west of World's End. The approximate course of Old Street past Park Copse is indicated on the map by a dotted line only. From Common Farm the course is still south-east with a short farm-way leading to the minor road from Peasemore, and follows this road for nearly half a mile to Crossroads Farm on the East Ilsley–Newbury main road.

At Crossroads Farm it crosses the main road and continues as a well-defined track to the wooded Oareborough Hill, known locally as Oarebury Hill. Here the track forks. Old Street being the westerly fork, and it soon becomes the metalled road which, about a quarter-mile west of Hermitage station, is the B 4009 road to Newbury. It is interesting that it passes through a village called Long Lane, whose position suggests that it was so called because it is on the length of about three miles of road—a former lane—which goes direct to the north side of Newbury.

The continuation north-east of the B 4009 road is to Streatley through Hermitage, Hampstead Norris and Aldworth, and is part of an old road once called West Ridgeway. According to Edward Thomas in *The Icknield Way* this name was given to it by John Bennet, Bishop of Cloyne, in the late eighteenth century. John Bennet considered it a branch of the Icknield Way which, to quote his own words, 'went by Hampstead and Hermitage, under the name West Ridge, to Newbury, and thence it may be to Old Sarum'. Edward Thomas seemed to think that John Bennet gave this name to the road because it goes through the village of Westridge Green, and the road through the village was probably called Westridge Way in his time, as a road is often given the name of a village it passes through. Earlier O.S. maps call this road West Ridgeway where it comes to Aldworth, from where it presumably continued to Streatley past Hungerford Green and Westridge Green; on the latest map this last few miles to Streatley has become the Great Ridgeway itself. Be this as it may, the B 4009 road has many of the characteristics of a ridgeway for most of its course from Streatley to Newbury and may have been a branch of the Great Ridgeway at Hungerford Green going to join the ridgeways south of Newbury and the Kennet.

To return to the Reading Way. From Oareborough Hill, where the track forks, it is difficult to say what happens to it until we pick it up on the wooded ridge leading to Cold Ash village. Dr. Grundy takes it to Oare, and then by footpath to the railway halt. After a blank of half a mile or so a footpath leading from Little Hungerford through the woods of Hermitage, past Grimsbury Camp and then by a metalled road through Fence Wood to Cold Ash village suggests the line. There are several tracks about the camp and leading south through Fence Wood, but the modern road takes it through Cold Ash and then through woods past Turner's Green south of Upper Common. From Turner's Green it goes across Bucklebury Common to Upper Woolhampton, where the road turns south-east whilst the line of track is continued by a footpath for the three-quarters of a mile to Beenham. From Hermitage it has been on the watershed between the Pang and the Kennet.

From Beenham the ridge is then the watershed between the Bourne and the Kennet. Still following a winding metalled road it keeps north of the grounds of Beenham House and then goes along May Ridge—which used to be known as Mare Ridge—as a lane south of and above the Bourne. It passes through wooded country until it comes to the boundary of Englefield Park. Its course today can only be that of the minor road which keeps south of Englefield Park and goes past Parker's Corner to Theale, where the watershed narrows considerably; but the original line was probably lost in the park.

The last quarter-mile or so of the road to Theale is called Deadman's Lane on old maps, which suggests an old way. After half a mile of the main Reading road from Theale a zigzagging minor road, not so many years ago a country lane, climbs to the Tilehurst ridge between the Thames and the Kennet and so comes to Pigs Green and Prospect Hill south of Reading.

Ordnance Survey Maps

Oxford and Newbury. Sheet 158. 1 inch to 1 mile. 1940
Oxford and Henley-on-Thames. Sheet 105. 1 inch to 1 mile. Popular Edition, 1919
West Berkshire. Sheet 13. 1 inch to 1 mile. 1830

THE GREAT RIDGEWAY ON RODEN DOWN, BERKSHIRE
PHOTO: RODERICK STANDING

VIEW FROM THE GREAT RIDGEWAY ON SHILLINGSTONE HILL, DORSET
PHOTO: RODERICK STANDING

THE GREAT RIDGEWAY, FACING WEST TOWARDS BEAMINSTER, DORSET
PHOTO: MONICA HUTCHINGS

THE GREAT RIDGEWAY ABOVE OLD PARK COPPICE, DORSET
PHOTO: MONICA HUTCHINGS

3

SOME WILTSHIRE BRANCHES
OF THE GREAT RIDGEWAY

BARBURY CASTLE TO THE A 420

WHERE the Great Ridgeway comes to Barbury Castle on the Marlborough Downs two tracks, which begin as one and are never more than half a mile from each other, lead from the west end of the earthwork and go north-west to the escarpment which holds the Clyffe Pypard ridgeway (*see* page 149). Here, above Salthrop House, they unite again and continue down the scarp and across the fields to join the Swindon-Malmesbury ridgeway on the Swindon–Wootton Bassett main road (A 420) (*see* Map 10).

After about a quarter of a mile together the more westerly of the two tracks goes over Uffcott Down and through a ditch to pass east of the hamlet of Uffcott and then becomes a metalled byway to the Swindon-Avebury road (A 361). On the other side of the road, still as a metalled lane, it leads past Upper Salthrop Farm to the top of the escarpment, and then drops quickly down the steep slope between the woods and grounds of Salthrop House and Basset Down House to come in about two miles to the Swindon–Malmesbury ridgeway near Hagbourne Copse at a point about half way between Wootton Bassett and Swindon.

The other track from Barbury curves across the downs in a more northerly direction for about two miles and crosses the Swindon–Avebury road at Red Barn. From there it is a byway leading to Upper Salthrop Farm, but when this byway turns west to the farm, a track going north for half a mile and then a footpath west along the ridge brings it to the first track. When they have crossed the Avebury road the angularities of the byways they traverse to get to the crest of the ridge suggest the original line has been lost here. It is also possible that one of the two branches is of a later date than the other, though both, for the first mile from Barbury at least, have the appearance of being kin to the Great Ridgeway.

BARBURY CASTE BY SMEATHE'S RIDGE TO MARLBOROUGH

Approximately 7 miles

Another track leaves the Great Ridgeway from this same meeting-place on the west side of Barbury and goes south-east through the earthworks to become the trackway along Smeathe's Ridge (*see* Map 26). In three furlongs it is crossed by a track running south. This is part of the old coach road from Swindon to Marlborough, its northern continuation going off as a metalled lane over Burderop Down and along the west side of Burderop Park, and then as a footpath and lane which lead to Swindon Town railway station.

The section of the old coach road south from Barbury is a ridgeway above the valley of the Og. For the first three-quarters of a mile it goes south-east, and then keeps south to pass Four Mile Clump, a group of trees which always has the winds of this high open place tugging at its boughs, and which was a spot much beloved by Charles Sorley, the young Marlborough poet who was killed in the First World War. From Four Mile Clump the track begins to fall from its 800 feet, and in two miles, where it comes to a gaunt group of cottages known as Old Eagle, has dropped to 470 feet, though it can feel as bleak here as on its higher reaches.

About halfway between Four Mile Clump and Old Eagle, when the track was used as a coach road, the passengers would have seen on the slope of Rockley Down a white horse cut in the turf immediately below the summit of the ridge, a horse whose square-cut flowing tail suggested it was moving at speed. It is not known who was responsible for the cutting of this figure, but Morris Marples, in his book *White Horses and Other Hill Figures*, says it probably belonged to the late eighteenth century. Nor does it seem to have remained visible for long, for its presence was forgotten until the field was ploughed a few years ago and its outline, scarcely more than a shadow, revealed again.

At the Old Eagle crossroads the track joins the Wootton Bassett–Marlborough road (B 4041), which goes over Marlborough Common, and from Marlborough it could have linked up with other ridgeways south of the Kennet.

OLD EAGLE TO POULTON DOWNS

A branch leaves the coach road near the Old Eagle cottages to rise behind them and curve east as a minor road to Ogbourne Maizey in the Og valley (*see* Map 26), accompanied most of the way by a narrow belt of trees and hazel coppice, which suggests a road of greater width in earlier times. The wayside woodland with its wild bowers and hazel wands makes this a secluded way of much charm, particularly in spring. In about a mile it falls to the village as a steep hollow lane between high mossy banks which are topped with old woodland on the left. After crossing the Og—a stream as small as its name and often dry in summer—it comes to the main road from Swindon to Marlborough (A 345), beyond which it crosses the railway and winds eastward up the valley side to Poulton Downs and reaches a meeting-place of ways, including the Roman road from Mildenhall.

This meeting-place has altered in recent years since the downs about it were ploughed, but twenty years ago the tracks led into a wide area of rough pasture surrounded by blackthorn thickets, so that it was like a private, almost secret, went-way. It still holds the track coming south from Liddington Hill along the Upham ridge (*see* page 7) and past Bytham Farm, and which continues from the old cross-ways to pass Rabley Wood on its way to Marlborough. There is a 1779 reference to this track from Liddington Hill as being part of a well-used road from Bishopstone to Marlborough.

OLD EAGLE TO AVEBURY

Approximately 4½ miles

Another branch leaves the coach road about a mile below Old Eagle and goes north-west over one of the loneliest stretches of the Marlborough Downs (*see* Map 26). For its first two miles over Barton Down and Manton Down it is now hardly more than a footpath beside the training gallops of Manton Racing Stables. On Manton Down, not far from the mutilated Manton long barrow, the footpath divides into two. One continues to Old Totterdown and then becomes a track through Totterdown Wood and on over the downs to the Great Ridgeway at Glory Ann Barn (*see* Map 25), while the other goes across Clatford Down and Overton Down. Here the sarsen stones lie thickly in the old rough pasture, their rounded weather-worn shapes sunken in the tussocky grass and looking so like a flock of old grey sheep that no other name but Grey Wethers seems possible for them. On Overton Down the footpath meets an open trackway coming from the direction of Manton House and merges with it to cross the Great Ridgeway and descend first as a track and then as a drove-like lane past tumuli to the Avebury Stone Circle (*see* Map 10). The lane cuts through the great bank surrounding the Stones on its way to Avebury village. The O.S. map calls this lane 'Herepath' to just beyond the point where it comes to the Ridgeway.

TRACKWAYS BETWEEN THE GREAT RIDGEWAY AND SALISBURY PLAIN

Map 4 shows Salisbury Plain to contain a bewildering network of track-ways, many of which must be very ancient indeed. Yet when we notice how dense on all parts of the Plain are the traces and remains of ancient settlements and burial places, it is not surprising there should be so many. There are so few river valleys on the Plain that once the traveller reached these chalk uplands he was free to take any course which led in the right direction, so that on the whole the Salisbury Plain trackways are without the usual windings and deviations of other ridgeways. Travellers would, of course, tend to follow a way which was already visible rather than make a new one.

There are three special points to which many of the tracks lead: Stonehenge, Yarnbury and Old Sarum. Those to Yarnbury were kept in use later than the others because of the great sheep fair held there until modern times, while Old Sarum remained a focal point at least until the thirteenth century, when the cathedral and town within and round the earthwork were abandoned and a new cathedral and town built in the valley below.

In the north-west region of the Plain, the part west of the Avon valley and north of the Vale of Wylye, there are three trackways which stand out clearly as branches of the Great Ridgeway, one leading south across the Plain to Stonehenge, the other two leaving the Great Ridgeway farther west and converging on Yarnbury Castle, all three probably continuing to Old Sarum and linking up with other ridgeways there.

REDHORN HILL TO STONEHENGE AND OLD SARUM

Approximately 18 miles

Taking the more easterly one first, it is a continuation of the ridgeway across the west end of the Vale of Pewsey as well as a branch of the Great Ridgeway, which it reaches by climbing Redhorn Hill (*see* Map 23). This track is particularly interesting because it is part of the route along which R. J. C. Atkinson, in his book *Stonehenge*, suggests that the Stonehenge sarsen stones were hauled from the downs above Avebury, where even today the 'grey wethers' are numerous. From the Great Ridgeway at the top of Redhorn Hill, and with Urchfont Clump as a far-seen landmark on the right, the track runs south-south-east over Chirton Down and Chirton Gorse to Black Heath and Ell Barrow. This barrow stands where a number of trackways and parish boundaries meet. From Ell Barrow the track that becomes the road past the Bustard Inn to Salisbury is not the line of its further course, for this is a modern road, once the direct way from Devizes to Salisbury. The older way, as Dr Grundy suggests, probably lay a little east of this road, following parish boundaries on higher ground in a more serpentine course past Shrewton Folly and Blackball Firs to the Neolithic camp called Robin Hood's Ball on Alton Down, and thence to Stonehenge.

From Robin Hood's Ball the track probably followed a course which took it along the west side of Fargo Plantation to a point on the Shrewton–Amesbury main road three-quarters of a mile west of Stonehenge (see Map 4). It may then have turned south-west to Longbarrow Crossroads near the Winterbourne Stoke group of barrows and have taken the line of the Salisbury road past Druid's Lodge, where it is crossed by the Harrow Way coming from Stonehenge. About a mile and a half farther on it is crossed by the Old Barn Road from Stapleford to Woodford and Old Sarum. By turning roughly east at the junction with Old Barn Road it could have come to Woodford in about a mile and crossed the Avon there in going to Old Sarum; or by continuing south along the narrowing tongue of down on the line of the main road for another three miles or so it would come to Stratford-sub-Castle with Old Sarum standing up about a mile away on the opposite side of the river. There was a Roman ford at Stratford-sub-Castle and it is likely there was a ford at this crossing before Roman times.

Ignoring the smoothly tarred surface of the broad main road from Druid's Lodge it is quite easy to forget, when there is a lull in the traffic, that it is now a modern highway. It has all the characteristics of a ridgeway coming to its end on a narrowing ridge of downland between the Wylye and the Avon. It passes barrows, earthworks and the low banks of a field system, and in places broken, grass-grown hollow ways can be seen on each side. Across the valley to the west the wooded Grovely Ridge holding another ridgeway makes the skyline; on the east are the high downs between the Avon and the Winterbourne, and to the south, beyond Wilton in the valley, the ridge of downs traversed by the Salisbury Way. These distances are shut out as the road descends into Salisbury.

West Lavington Down to Yarnbury

Approximately 7 miles

The next of these three branches from the Great Ridgeway is the one which leaves it at the tumulus on West Lavington Down about five miles south-west of Redhorn Hill, and runs south-east across the Plain to Yarnbury Castle (see Map 22). One reason why this track has remained so well defined is because it became part of a coach road from Bath to Salisbury. It was also one of the green ways along which sheep were driven to Yarnbury Fair held within the banks of the earthwork. As a coach road it came to the foot of the Plain at Tinhead, where it climbed the scarp to continue along Coulston Hill and over Littleton Down to the tumulus on West Lavington Down about a mile east of Imber.

Leaving the Great Ridgeway here it goes on as a green track to the long barrows on Chitterne Down and then on past tumuli to Breach Hill where it crosses the track that is now the metalled road from Tilshead to Chitterne. The next reach winds on over the downs past Chitterne Barn to Chitterne Down where it crosses the A 344 road from Shrewton to Chitterne and then goes on to the meeting-place of trackways beside the small circular earthwork just north of the much greater earthwork of Yarnbury Castle. It passes along the east side of Yarnbury, where in the shaggy grass at the foot of the embankment is a coach road milestone which records above the date 1754 that it is 12 miles from Warminster and 10 to Sarum.

Bratton Castle to Yarnbury

Approximately 15 miles

Before following this trackway south from Yarnbury we will go back to the third branch from the Great Ridgeway because it, too, leads across the Plain to Yarnbury. This is the track which runs south from Bratton Castle to the Great Ridgeway about two miles west of Imber and coincides with its south loop as far as Bowls Barrow, where the long ditch runs parallel to it on Bishopstrow Down (*see* Maps 20 and 21).

From Bowls Barrow it continues past Knook Barrow and the sites of ancient villages and on along Breakheart Hill to the A 344 road at the west end of Chitterne (*see* Map 22). As the main road it passes above the head of Codford Brook and eastward through Chitterne village before turning south-east and continuing with the main road for about a mile to where the main road turns east over Chitterne Down to Shrewton. The track, however, continues its south-easterly line to the meeting-place of ways at Yarnbury, where it joins the previous track from West Lavington Down.

Yarnbury to Old Sarum

Approximately 10 miles

Yarnbury seems to gather the shallow hollows and broad undulations of the Plain round and up to its banks on all sides, although the camp is no higher than the surrounding ridges and summits of downland. The skylines seen from the tops of its banks are wide but not distant, giving no long views as seen, for example, from the Great Ridgeway between Broadbury Banks and Redhorn Hill. The farthest sweep is that to the south-west where the skyline is the long ridge with Crovely and Great Ridge woods on it. The open furzy area by the small camp to the north of Yarnbury Castle makes a meeting-place 200 yards or so across in most directions, with trackways coming to it through great expanses of corn and equally great sweeps of pasture and intersecting each other as green ways among the gorse thickets, separated by rough turf and patches of downland flowering plants grown tall in the tousled uncropped grass. Yarnbury Castle is banked along the skyline two or three hundred yards to the south, with a single broad trackway leading to it (*see* Map 4).

This is our two branches from the Great Ridgeway combined, going on past the east end of the earthwork as a broad fenced way made up of a chalky central band with tussocky grass margins as wide as the central way. As soon as it has passed the camp it crosses the A 303 road from Stonehenge in going south-east over Berwick Down, and in about a mile and a half crosses the Langford Way, beyond which it begins a gradual descent to Stapleford near the junction of the Till and Wylye. Here it coincides for about a quarter of a mile with the Wylye valley main road A 36, in crossing the Till. The main road turns south to keep along the riverside to Wilton, but the track continues east as the Old Barn Road and comes to the Druid's Lodge road, A 360, a quarter-mile beyond Down Barn.

East from the Druid's Lodge road the line is that of a byway to Woodford on the Avon. From there, after crossing the river, it swings south to Old Sarum, probably along the line of the byway through Newtown which becomes a footpath and is shown on the map passing above the woods at Little Durnford, and then by track and footpath to the meeting-place of trackways and Roman roads on the hill-saddle opposite the east gate of Old Sarum. During its period as a coach road it probably turned south beyond Down Barn to follow the Druid's Lodge road to Salisbury.

TRACK FROM IMBER TO PERTWOOD CROSS-WAYS

8 miles

Near a loose cluster of trees which makes a landmark between Bowls Barrow and Imber (*see* Map 21) a track branches from the southern loop of the Great Ridgeway and goes almost straight in a south-westerly direction across the downs to East Hill Farm on the edge of the Plain above Heytesbury. It is really another loop of the Great Ridgeway west from Imber, for after dropping into the Wylye valley and crossing the river, the direction it kept on the Plain is held over the downs south

of the river until it reunites with the Great Ridgeway a little to the north of the
meeting-place of trackways near Pertwood (*see* Map 19). Tytherington stands at
the edge of the valley bottom opposite Heytesbury, and here the track rises to the
downs again when it has crossed the valley as the modern road which bridges the
river. Formerly there were fords at and close to Heytesbury.

The track lifts to the west side of Tytherington Hill and is over 600 feet up
when it is passing the site of an ancient village. About a mile farther on it loses
height in dropping into and crossing Long Bottom, a steep-sided, flat-bottomed
dry valley, much of it now cornland, running east from Rook Hill. The track
mounts the opposite side at Redding Hanging and, reaching the north-east corner
of a triangular wood, leads along the wood's east edge to join the Great Ridgeway,
which converges on it within the west margin of the wood in coming south from
Sutton Veny. As a rough hedged lane the united tracks reach the Pertwood cross-
ways in another half-mile.

Ordnance Survey Maps

Marlborough and Devizes. Sheet 112. 1 inch to 1 mile. Popular Edition, 1919
Swindon. Sheet 157. 1 inch to 1 mile. 1940
Salisbury. Sheet 167. 1 inch to 1 mile. 1940
Salisbury. Sheet 167. 1 inch to 1 mile. 1959
Frome. Sheet 166. 1 inch to 1 mile. 1946

4

SOME DORSET BRANCHES
OF THE GREAT RIDGEWAY

BULBARROW TO MILBORNE ST. ANDREW

Approximately 6 miles

THE earliest O.S. map shows a through road from Bulbarrow south to Milborne St. Andrew which follows closely this suggested branch of the Great Ridgeway. From Bulbarrow Hill (*see* Map 16) a track, now a minor road to Ansty Cross, leaves the Great Ridgeway at the south end of Moots Copse and follows the line of this road for three furlongs. The road then swings south-west to Ansty Cross, but a track and then a footpath continue the southward line to join up with the road from Ansty Cross to Milborne about a quarter of a mile west of Hilton. It goes with this road along the ridge of Coombe Hill for over a half mile, but as it approaches Great Down Clump above Coombe Bottom the road turns south-east past Long Close Farm to Hewish Farm. The ridge road, however, continues to Gallows Corner, a meeting place of old ways. There are a bewildering number of lanes, minor roads and tracks in this region, many of which radiate from Ansty Cross or near it, winding about the hill-slopes, for the ground here is broken up into many small hills, none of them of any great height except Coombe Hill, which reaches 695 feet where the track crosses it.

South from Coombe Hill the track is on the watershed between the Devil's Brook and the Milborne stream. Past Gallows Corner it continues in the same south-south-east direction as a track and footpath to Bagber Wood and skins the east side of the wood and its tumulus in going to Milborne St. Andrew. From Milborne there seem to be several ways leading to the Piddle which the trackway would have to cross to link up with the ridgeways on the heathland between the Piddle and the Frome (*see* Map 1), and so come to the sea and the Dorset Coastal Ridgeway (Chapter 29). But today the connection, if there was one, has been lost. The minor road leading to Weatherby Castle and crossing the Bere Regis–

Dorchester main road to pass Double Barrow on its way south to Briants Puddle may have been the line, and there are several fords near by where it could have crossed the river.

Another likely continuation from Milborne goes on as a track past the west end of Weatherby Castle to Tolpuddle, and after crossing the main road and the stream continues past Southover Heath where it joins the ridgeway which runs west from Throop Clump and past Culpepper's Dish to Puddletown (*see* page **201**). There is also about a mile of track south-west again which joins the Wareham–Dorchester Ridgeway at Tincleton.

Nettlecombe Tout to Dole's Ash

Approximately 2 miles

From the south side of the earthwork on Nettlecombe Tout (*see* Map 15), across the little valley from Bulbarrow, a track leads south-west following the edge of the ridge above Lyscombe Bottom to tumuli on Plush Hill, and then goes south along the broad hill-shoulder to come to the Dole's Ash crossroads about a mile north-east of Piddletrenthide. This cosy little village in the narrow Piddle valley seems much more than a mile away in spirit.

Four green tracks and a minor road meet at Dole's Ash in the midst of an open, lonely plateau of farmland, which looks lower than its 529 feet above sea level because of the higher hills around it from which the tracks descend. The wind, however, can blow as sharply here as on the hilltops and it rarely knows the soft airs of the valley, for this small plateau is made up of large fields and few trees, with nothing of the lush wooded beauty of the Milton Abbas region and nothing of the wild strangeness of the broken chalk hills and deep coombs around Plush. The countryside of Dorset can change in a few hundred yards from one kind of remote landscape to another, and this particular stretch, though cultivated, has a bleakness which the two ash trees near the crossroads seem to emphasize. One is nothing but a gaunt skeleton of what was once a large tree, the other is so old that it has lost the poise and grace of a mature ash and stands stubborn and stiff, clinging tenaciously to a life from which the sap has nearly departed. It would be pleasant to see a young tree planted there to carry on the name of Dole's Ash.

The minor road which comes to the crossroads was once part of a coach road from Piddletrenthide going west to Cheselbourne along Streetway Lane and the miry, rutted and now overgrown lane which passes Gallows Corner on its way to Milton Abbas. Many of these Dorset crossroads, the meeting-places of many tracks and half-forgotten bridle paths, must have been more important in bygone days. Some were the junctions of trackways linking one ridgeway to another, others were the meeting-places of medieval roads which afterwards became incorporated into coach roads, as can be seen on the early maps of the county. Some led to the old village of Milton Abbas, which Joseph Damer, afterwards Earl of Dorchester, entirely demolished when the new village had been built out of sight of his mansion in 1786. As new roads came into being in the nineteenth century many of the older ones lost their importance and became green lanes and bridle paths serving local needs, and now that buses, cars, cycles and motor-cycles have made walking from village to village or market town unnecessary they are fast falling into decay. We think there must be more lonely and now unimportant crossroads in the heart of Dorset than in any other county, and the Dorset highways authorities acknowledge them in nearly every case by a distinguishing name on their signposts, a great help to the traveling stranger and a reminder of their former importance, if one likes to see it that way.

Dole's Ash Farm was the Flintcomb Farm of Thomas Hardy, where Tess worked in the great fields 'a hundred acres in one patch'.

Evidences of prehistory are thickly scattered on each side of this trackway from Nettlecombe Tout. Within the first quarter-mile it goes through a cross-dyke where the ridge is narrowing and beginning to fall. Dorset has many well-preserved examples of cross-dykes on its trackways and in nearly every case they cross shoulders of high open ground with their ends on steep slopes at the heads of coombs, often where one or two spurs holding branch ridgeways converge. Beyond the cross-dyke the track passes tumuli, a ditch and more tumuli in reaching Plush Hill, where the narrowness of the ridge ends. A small circular earthwork lies about a quarter of a mile east where the trackway is descending to Dole's Ash. About half a mile to the west and running roughly parallel to it a lower track, which may have been its summer way and is now a road from Mappowder to Piddletrenthide, crosses the Great Ridgeway beside the former Inn at Folly, and comes down past Plush and the steepness of East Hill round the edge of a coomb where a stucco-covered pigeon-house lies hidden amongst great chestnut trees in the grounds of the manor-house of Piddletrenthide.

From Dole's Ash the trackway may have gone along the line of the minor road west to Piddletrenthide, crossed the Piddle and its narrow valley, and on westward, keeping the line of a minor road which rises steeply out of the valley to come in about a mile and a half to a point near a tumulus where it meets the Old Sherborne Road. It could have joined up here with the Old Sherborne Road or continued across Black Hill by a track which curves above a field system, minor earthworks and a tumulus to the east side of Cerne Abbas. Here it would have to cross the Cerne and the higher springs of Sydling Water if it wanted to continue to the Great Ridgeway at Long Ash Lane near Folly Hill. A minor modern road takes that course today across the chalk ridges, going over Rowden Hill and Hog Hill and keeping to the north of the village of Sydling St. Nicholas to Peak End Hill and on to Stagg's Folly at Long Ash Lane. From Long Ash Lane it goes on west-ward beside Charity Bottom and round the north side of Castle Hill and its camp just north of Cattistock (*see* Map 14).

OLD SHERBORNE ROAD; SHERBORNE TO MAIDEN CASTLE

Approximately 17 miles

Three main chalk ridges connect the Great Ridgeway on the north with the Dorset Coastal Ridgeway and its branches on the south, and the trackways along them lead south to cross the Frome before reaching the Coastal Ridgeway (*see* Map 1). Taking them from east to west, there is first the ridge between the Piddle and the Cerne on which runs the Old Sherborne Road to Dorchester; the centre ridge runs between the Cerne and Sydling Water, holding a series of tracks and footpaths which were once continuous as the Furzey Down Road; and on the third ridge, between Sydling Water and the Frome, runs the Romanized ridgeway known as Long Ash Lane and which today is part of the A 37 road from Yeovil to Dorchester. South from the Frome they cross the Dorchester–Bridport ridgeway in coming to the sea.

The Old Sherborne Road has come about halfway when it crosses the Great Ridgeway at the south end of Little Minterne Hill (*see* Map 15). South from this point to Dorchester it is on the watershed between the Piddle and the Cerne, and is also the line of a far more ancient road than the coach road from which it got its name in the eighteenth century. It is being used more and more nowadays as a through route by travellers wishing to avoid the busy A 352 road from Sherborne to Dorchester, particularly in summer when the main road carries heavy holiday traffic to Weymouth and other seaside resorts near by.

Unlike the A 352 road the Old Sherborne Road passes through no villages on its journey south—a ridgeway characteristic—and the downs on each side of it have many field systems and settlements, minor earthworks and tumuli. This must have been a much more densely populated area in pre-Roman times. Its greatest height is 850 feet on Little Minterne Hill where it meets the Great Ridgeway, and with some minor undulations it falls with the ridge gradually all the way to Dorchester. It passes over the downs above Cerne Abbas leaving Giant Hill on the west, and goes along a narrow wood before coming into the open again on Buck Hill. Belts of woodland beside a track are also a ridgeway characteristic today; it was one way of using the extra width of a trackway when landowners wished to reduce the size to a normal wagon width.

From Buck Hill the track rises again to East Hill and then its descent becomes more rapid, for as it passes a little east of Charminster it has lost 200 feet or more. It crosses the Frome at Burton Mill to the east of Poundbury earthwork, which seems to guard the crossing of the river as well as the road at its foot. As the Old Sherborne Road it now comes to an end, and it is impossible to tell today the exact route a continuing track would have taken through the town, but it is likely it went approximately south-west to pass the western end of Maiden Castle (see Map 1).

Within a mile or so of Maiden Castle the metalled road from Victoria Park becomes a wide track with the large mound of Clandon Barrow conspicuous in a field on the right amidst tall pylons, while on the left arable fields rise to the foot of the outer ramparts of the earthwork. The track crosses the Winterborne, a stream which, as its name implies, is dry in summer, and near Ashton Farm it joins the B 3159 road from Bridport to Weymouth and follows this road for a mile or so, joining the Coastal Ridgeway on Could's Hill where it comes to the Bridport road just east of the pumping station.

In going north from the Great Ridgeway on Little Minterne Hill the Old Sherborne Road comes to the south-west end of Ridge Hill, where it forks to descend the scarp to meet the main Dorchester–Sherborne road (A 352), which has been roughly parallel to it up the Cerne valley. From near Tiley the line is continued by the main road to Sherborne and is no longer a true ridgeway. Numerous brooks and streams make this part difficult to follow.

To return to the fork on Ridge Hill, a track, now a minor road, goes north-east along Ridge Hill to Castle Hill at Duntish. About half a mile to the west past Duntish is Dungeon Hill Camp, a wooded landmark on a small shoulder pushed northward into Blackmoor Vale. From Duntish the road winds past the heads of streams through Pulham and Kingstag and on past Blackrow Common, where it joins the Sherborne–Sturminster Newton road (A 3030), a comparatively high road with water-meadows on each side (see Map 5).

What happened after passing Blackrow Common it is difficult to determine, but it may not be too fanciful to work out a route which could run, after many windings, to Penselwood, where there was a forest gap in early days. We have only the most fragmentary evidence of antiquity for this suggested continuation. After joining the Sherborne–Sturminster Newton road it could follow it north to cross Caundle Brook at Warr Bridge and come to Stalbridge. Winding generally north-east between the streams and over Prior's Down it would come to Cale Bridge and then to Fifehead Magdalen to follow the ridge between the Stour and the Cale. This would take it past Heart Moor and on to Tinker's Hill, where it comes to the county boundary. It could continue north with the boundary to the west of Bourton after crossing the Mere–Wincanton road (A 303), keeping north along the ridge to Penselwood and its meeting-place of trackways. Here it would not be far from the Harrow Way and another ancient track going to the Mendips.

TRACK FROM BATCOMBE HILL TO BLACK DOWN

Approximately 12 miles

A quarter of a mile west of the Cross and Hand on Batcombe Hill a track leaves the Great Ridgeway (*see* Map 14) and goes south-south-east over Gore Hill, where scatterings ofgorse in the rough pasture suggest that this may have been the reason for its old name. Ronald Good states in his *Old Roads of Dorset* that this track 'as late as 1765 appears as a complete road bearing the name Furzey Down Road—onnecting up with the road system of Blackmore Vale'. Like the Old Sherborne Road on the next parallel ridge to the east it has many settlements, field systems and minor earthworks in its six miles or so from the point where it leaves the Great Ridgeway on Core Hill to where it comes to the Frome at Grimstone. It also has the same gradual undulating descent with its highest point where it branches from the Great Ridgeway.

For the first three furlongs it is a parish boundary as well as a footpath; beyond that it is a clearly defined way to the river. In places the crest of the ridge leaves room for little more than a wide green rutted track, with fields falling more steeply on the Sydling side than the Cerne side. It goes over Wancombe Hill and past the west edge of the woods of Cerne Park, crossing a by-road from Cerne Abbas which there begins a steep winding descent to the village of Sydling St. Nicholas in its narrow valley. From this point the line of the track is a parish boundary to Ridge Hill. It makes a swing with the ridge south-south-west along Crete Hill, an odd name for a Dorset hill and one into which one would like to read more significance than it probably possesses. Here the track fans out into three, the middle one continuing the line through a ditch and then past Jackman's Cross and a settlement on Grimstone Down to Grimstone. From there it crosses the main road (A 37) and the river to Muckleford.

A minor road leads south-south-west from Muckleford and has many tumuli in sight all the time, including two long barrows on opposite sides of the road. Near another long barrow and a cluster of tumuli it meets the main Dorchester–Bridport road and coincides with it for a quarter-mile to North Hill. Here it leaves the main road to go south-west as a minor road with wide green margins which rises all the way to Black Down, where it first crosses the trackway coming from Eggardon Hill and then joins the Coastal Ridgeway (*see* Map 1).

TRACK FROM BATCOMBE HILL TO POUNDBURY

Approximately 9 miles

An ancient road called Long Ash Lane, and sometimes the Old Yeovil Road, leaves the Great Ridgeway (*see* Map 14) west of Batcombe Hill and goes south-south-east as the main road (A 37) to Grimstone, about four miles north-west of Dorchester (*see* Map 1). Although this is marked as a Roman road on the map and has the straight lengths we expect of one, it is also a ridgeway which has had its natural windings obliterated by Roman and modern road-makers. It is a good example of a road which has been in use in one form or another since pre-Roman times and which is today one of the busiest roads in Dorset.

It could have crossed the river at Muckleford in early times and followed the line of the lesser Roman road south of the river to Poundbury Camp, or by keeping for a short distance on the narrowing watershed between the Frome and the Cerne it could have crossed the river nearer to Dorchester, at Bradford Peverell or at Wrackleford, whose names suggest ancient crossing-places. From Poundbury it could have linked up with the trackway west of Maiden Castle and joined the Coastal Ridgeway on Gould's Hill.

TRACK FROM NEAR MAIDEN NEWTON TO EGGARDON

Approximately 3½ miles

From the more southerly possible line for the Great Ridgeway to take to cross the Frome near Maiden Newton a line leading south-west across the Frome valley would in three or four miles come to Eggardon Hill (*see* Map 1), a spur of the southern chalk ridge projecting into the western vales and holding Eggardon Camp on its summit. In Dorset this hill-fort is eclipsed in size and in the boldness and grandeur of its conception only by the more elaborate many-ringed Maiden Castle. Modern civilization, with its pylons, new housing estates and roads, is creeping up on Maiden Castle—a visit to it makes a pleasant evening stroll from Dorchester—but Eggardon stands up in a secluded countryside, a landscape of many winding streams, coppices, bracken-covered slopes and fields bountifully hedged with tall trees. Nor has Eggardon Camp received the same skilful and modern excavation as Maiden Castle, so that when we contemplate it the range of our imagination seems limitless. Its massive chalk bastions, ramparts and ditches still hold unrevealed the archaeological evidence which would tell us something of the kind of men who first built this hill-fort, and of the succeeding generations who lived and died there before it was left deserted and its banks and ditches folded into the natural contours of the hill. For those who know and love it Eggardon holds the very essence of Dorset's unique appeal, not only for itself but because the old tracks and roads to it make some of the best walking in the county, leading the imagination onward as well as the feet. They are all worthy of the climax which the final climb to the great banks of grey-green turf unbroken by shrubs or trees brings to the traveller, the view of the Channel beyond Bridport, the Chesil Beach, as well as the Dorset heights which make the skyline leading to the sea.

For the most direct route to Eggardon from Maiden Newton the track has to get on to the ridge west of Wynford Eagle, first crossing the Hooke at Tollerford west of the town, where traces of an old ford can still be seen south of the stream by a small modern bridge, though on the northern side a garden comes down to the water and its banks have been built up. A parish boundary rising from the narrow marshy valley takes the line up the hillside to the top of the ridge above Toller Fratrum, and then a footpath and a track which soon becomes a metalled farm road continue it along the ridge across high open cornland above Wynford Eagle, to come to Eggardon Hill. Seen from this ridge about two miles from Tollerford, from where a green track descends to Toller Porcorum, the Evershot ridge standing out as the northern skyline looks a very likely route for the Great Ridgeway to Toller Down Gate.

In the field it can be seen that the original line of the trackway has been ploughed out and that another track has taken its place for the easier working of the large fields, though as the summit of the ridge is nowhere very wide, except where it comes to Eggardon Hill, the diversion can only have been slight and in some places a mere straightening of its natural windings. One notices it, however, when instead of the metalled track making a gradual curve south-west with the ridge to come to the meeting-place of ways and the cluster of tumuli east of Eggardon camp, the farm road makes a right-angled turn through a gate to become one of these converging lanes. Once through the gate it soon leaves the arable fields behind and arrives at the open hilltop as one of the network of metalled tracks which run between rough pasture dotted with gorse and tumuli.

Taking the westward line the track soon reaches the south-east corner of the lowest bank of the camp and comes to an end. On all sides but the east the slopes of Eggardon fall precipitously from the earthwork to stream-threaded fields several hundred feet below, so that the great bluff projects into the valley and dominates it.

TRACK FROM BEAMINSTER DOWN TO EGGARDON

Approximately 7 miles

Another track to Eggardon leaves the Great Ridgeway west of the tumulus on Beaminster Down (*see* Map 13). It begins as two tracks within 200 yards of each other, one a wide grassy one, the other a lane hedged on one side. The hedged lane was once part of a coach road to Bridport which followed this trackway. The two converge southward and meet in less than half a mile at the minor road which goes south-west by Beaminster's Whitesheet Hill to the town. From this road a byway continues the line, following the ridge between Higher Langdon and Langdon Farm to Dirty Gate on the road to Beaminster from Toller Down by way of Storridge Hill (B 3163). Dirty Gate was once a crossroads on a coach route past Eggardon to Bridport, and the group of Scots pines there makes a striking local landmark, though Dirty Gate is no longer an important crossroads.

From Dirty Gate the continuation over Hackthorn Hill shows what can happen to an old coach road or hedged trackway when it is no longer used. Only a traveller on foot can make a way between hedges that have spread inward into thickets, while bracken and long grass hiding the deep old ruts make the narrow centre which remains open difficult walking. After about half a mile this disused lane joins the minor road which branched from the Beaminster road below Dirty Gate and goes with it, winding to Warren Hill in a general south-east direction and climbing gradually to Mount Pleasant, where there is a meeting-place of five roads and another group of Scots pines in a banked enclosure to distinguish it. Before the hedges of the five lanes grew so tall and shut out all but the immediate view along them, Mount Pleasant hilltop, with its triangular gores of waste land, must have been a magnificent five-went way. Today the minor roads dipping to Hooke, Kingcombe, Toller Porcorum and Poorton go off almost secretly to those delightful Dorset villages.

Three furlongs beyond Mount Pleasant the way forks; one fork meanders south-east to Toller Porcorum as a metalled lane, the other, the trackway to Eggardon, drops down southward as a charming lane edged with hazel copses to a lush little hollow. This hollow holds a brook and a railway line, though both are so hidden in greenery in the spring and summer that only the rich growth of water-plants betrays the brook and the occasional sound of a train the railway line. The track soon leaves the hollow and its woodland world and rises to pass a little east of Barrowland Farm and come to the high open plateau where the only bushes are ragged clumps of gorse, and here it joins the other tracks at the meeting-place by the east end of Eggardon Hill (*see* Map 1).

The main road from Dorchester to Bridport (A 35) (*see* Map 1) on the chalk ridge which runs north of the Bride is as much a ridgeway as any road could be, and in early times must have been a link between Eggardon Camp and Poundbury Camp, north-west of Dorchester, and the fords over the Frome near by. Its first four miles or so from Dorchester to Lambert's Hill is named Roman road on the O.S. map, and was evidently a trackway later used by the Romans as a route west from Dorchester. A suggested line of its continuation from Lambert's Hill keeps roughly a mile or so north of the Dorchester–Bridport road and runs in the same direction in a series of four straight lengths, the first and third keeping north-west and joined together by the second and fourth, which go west, so that on the map it looks as if it proceeds in two steps to reach the east end of Eggardon at Two Gates.

Along each side of the Dorchester–Bridport road are Standing Stones, tumuli, the remains of several long barrows, and earthworks of various kinds so close to each other that one feels this ridge must have been of the greatest importance in pre-Roman times.

South of Eggardon to Black Down on the Coastal Ridgeway the track must have skirted the head of the Askerwell valley, and a track today leaves Eggardon at Two Gates and goes first south-east and then south-west to meet the Dorchester–Bridport ridgeway near the earthen circle half a mile north of Litton Cheney. A line to the Coastal Ridgeway could have followed the A 35 eastwards for a mile or so and then branched south-east over Martin's Down, through a cross-dyke and along the ridge of Whatcombe Down, with tumuli thickly scattered about it all the way, to come to the by-road east of Little Bredy which in a mile leads south-east to Black Down. Thus any of these Eggardon tracks could link the Great Ridgeway in the north with the Coastal Ridgeway in the south.

Ordnance Survey Maps

Dorchester. Sheet 178. 1 inch to 1 mile. 1945
Taunton and Lyme Regis. Sheet 177. 1 inch to 1 mile. 1946

THE GREAT RIDGEWAY, FACING WEST PAST CHARTON FARM, DEVON
PHOTO: MONICA HUTCHINGS

THE GREAT RIDGEWAY APPROACHING THE MOUTH OF THE RIVER AXE, DEVON
PHOTO: MONICA HUTCHINGS

VIEW FROM THE FURZEY DOWN RIDGEWAY, DORSET
PHOTO: MONICA HUTCHINGS

VIEW FROM EGGARDON, DORSET
PHOTO: MONICA HUTCHINGS

5

THE ICKNIELD WAY

Approximately 23 miles

THE Icknield Way is part of an ancient road which was once a through way from East Anglia to the western part of the south of England. That it existed before Roman-British times and continued as part of the road system throughout the Middle Ages and well into the sixteenth century there can be little doubt, for from the Anglo-Saxon charters onwards many references to it can be found in old documents. Indeed, there is more mention of the Icknield Way in early times than of any other ancient road in Britain.

The earliest mention of Ikenilde Way and Icknilde Strete comes in the Anglo-Saxon charters covering the Berkshire and Wiltshire reaches of the road. As stretches of it were straightened and incorporated by the Romans into their own road system the reason for the word Strete is explained, though the evidence points to the fact that the Icknield Way was not originally a Roman road but in many places in Wessex, at least, a Romanized summer way of the Great Ridgeway. That it was only partly used by the Romans is shown by the 'Ikenilde Way' of some of the charters. Even today it is possible to distinguish some of the Romanized reaches by their characteristic straight lengths, though they, in their turn, have become modern roads.

In earlier times several widely separated Roman roads have been called Icknield Street, which has led to some confusion with the Icknield Way. One is the road in the Midlands that leaves the Foss Way at Bourton-on-the-Water and runs north through Alcester to Birmingham and beyond, though Codrington in his *Roman Roads in Britain* calls it Ricknild Street. In the fourteenth century it was mentioned by Ralph Higden as part of one of the four royal roads, the one going from St. David's to Worcester, Birmingham and Derby. It was as Ricknild Street in his native county of Warwickshire that the Elizabethan poet-topographer Drayton recognized this road from the south-west corner of Wales that 'on his midway did me in England meet'.

Although the course of the Icknield Way is now only to be guessed at farther west than Wanborough, a mile or two from the Berkshire-Wiltshire border, it could have linked up with this Icknield, or Ricknild, Street of the Midlands by means of Ermine Street—crossed on the very edge of the Wiltshire downs at Callas Hill close to Wanborough—as far as Cirencester, and then by the Foss Way as far as Bourton-on-the-Water. It could also have linked up with the supposed extension of the Midland road into South Wales by way of Ermine Street from Cirencester to Gloucester and beyond. Not far from the south, or Berkshire, end of Ermine Street are other roads that once had the name Icknield attached to them. Whether these links were continuous before Roman times it is impossible to prove today. 'It seems likely that Icknield, like Watling and Ermine, was a generic name for a road in ancient times', wrote Edward Thomas; and there we will leave it.

To return to where the Icknield Way enters Wessex (see Map 30), it is generally accepted that this road, like the Great Ridgeway, its companion along the Chiltern chalk, crossed the Thames at Streatley and that the Icknield Way followed the line of the Reading–Wantage road away from the river; but there is an alternative crossing between South Stoke on the east side of the river and Moulsford on the west, where a track runs west to join the Reading–Wantage road on Kingstanding Hill, although if this was its place for crossing it would have had to make an abrupt westward turn on Mile End Hill, two furlongs south of Icknield Farm, in following the line of the minor road to Stoke. This abrupt turn may, of course, be a modern rearrangement of the old road.

From Kingstanding Hill as far as Upton it keeps the line of the main road, and on the left, beyond the immediate fields, miles of downland, now mostly cultivated, stretch away to the skyline. It crosses the White Hollow Way of Aston Upthorpe about a mile before coming to Blewbury, with the strip lynchets on Blewburton Hill in view on the right, the olive-green of their turf steps looking much older and darker than the cultivated fields flowing up the hill.

From Upton, two miles farther on (see Map 29), the main road now becomes the modern version of another ancient road, the Port Way, which makes a shallow bow-like curve through its seven miles westward to Wantage; but the Icknield Way, like the string across the bow, goes more directly by keeping south of the main road as a track across the swell of Hagbourne Hill and on over the scarp-foot levels of Harwell Field to Aldfield Common and past Park Hill and Roundabout Hill to the east side of Lockinge Park. Here the track, which has flowed like a slow green river since leaving Upton, was lost when the grounds of the park were enclosed. Five villages—West Hagbourne, Harwell, East Hendred, West Hendred. Ardington—lie between Upton and Wantage, and whilst neither the Port Way nor the Icknield Way passes through any of them they are all nearer the Port Way.

Where the Icknield Way crosses the Abingdon–Newbury road (A 34) on Harwell Field half a mile or so of it lies within the grounds of the Harwell Atomic Research Station estate on the opposite side of the road. But it has not been lost, for the line has been preserved by a strip of newly-sown grass between a hedge of young thorns and with saplings behind the thorns which will one day make this short stretch run through a tree-shaded avenue. Looking down the length going through the Harwell estate one can see the Icknield Way rising out of the flat stretch of Harwell Field and disappearing over the skyline as a darker green track through a cultivated field. By the side of the road a post office and shop in a wooden building bears the name Icknield Way Post Office, an amenity which would have amazed earlier travellers on the old road.

In the five miles or so from Upton to Lockinge Park the track has kept between 320 and 400 feet up and has had to cross Ginge Brook in its little hollow of elm and ash trees, an insignificant though charming stream and no obstacle in dry weather. This reach is named Icknield Way on the O.S. map: it was called Ickleton Street in the eighteenth century, and local people today call it so from Aldfield Common onwards, the use of 'Street' suggesting traditional memory of a time when the ancient track still showed traces of having once been converted into a made way, possibly during the Roman period.

Though its line has been lost through Lockinge Park, and the line of its exit from the park obliterated by cottages and gardens, a byway going through West Lockinge and then turning north and then west to Round Hill, first as a footpath and then as a straight open track, suggests the line. It enters Wantage as the Port Way, not passing through the centre of the town but keeping a little south of the old part, though in recent years the town has expanded along it.

Earlier O.S. maps name its continuation westward 'Roman Way', but its characteristics are clearly those of an ancient summer way, for it keeps on a shelf between the rich fields and elm-shaded villages of White Horse Vale and the downland escarpment carrying the Great Ridgeway. Where the downs are embayed by hollow coombs it follows the curving footline across their entrances, and though short lengths may have been straightened by the Romans and by modern road authorities, its general aspect is that of a road winding and undulating with the lie of the land, flowing naturally in its half-way world between downland and valley. Except where it is rising from the Thames to the downs it never runs much below 300 feet, and west of Wantage usually keeps above 400 feet.

On this side of Wantage (see Map 28) only two villages, Letcombe Regis and Letcombe Bassett, lie between the Icknield Way and the downs. After the Letcombe villages five more are strung out close to the road but a little below it towards the valley fields, a sure indication that the spring line is below the road and that the course of the Icknield Way is where it always was, above the springs and so comparatively dry.

After passing Blowingstone Hill the Icknield Way skirts the valley-fronting steeps of White Horse Hill, beginning and ending with sudden inward and outward bends across the openings of two coombs in doing so. In between them the road first leads past Britchcombe Farm and then to the point where it is open to both the width of the Vale of White Horse and the upsurging slopes of the downland bastion that is White Horse Hill. Standing in front of and much lower than the main hill is Dragon Hill, an artificial-looking mound with a flat circular top, by the side of a chalk track winding in a slant up to the scarp and leading to a level of turf close to Uffington Camp. This is the most dramatic part of the twelve-mile stretch from Wantage to Wanborough. For not only is there the Uffington White Horse cut in the turf just below the hill-crest, but nature herself has carved and rounded one of the great downland coombs in the scarp under the White Horse. It dies away on the valley side of the road, yet there, although it contains a narrow wood hiding the source-waters of a brook, its scrub-dotted sides belong more to the hills than to the tamed and gentle valley.

The Icknield Way then winds along under Hardwell Wood in which the banks and ditches of a camp are far from easy to see and explore under the trees and a dense tangle of undergrowth. It is *Icenhilde Way* here in the charters outlining the boundaries of Uffington and Compton Beauchamp, and again in the Hardwell charter, but *Ikenilde Street* between Idstone and Ashbury where it keeps a straighter line. All the way fascinating valley country opens out rich in old churches and manor-houses, with cottages of downland chalk and thatch as well as of valley brick and of stone from the limestone country a few miles to the north-west. Deeply grooved tracks that seem even more secretive than the valley by-roads lead up to the downs, some with disused deeper ways beside them filled with thickets of thorn and brambles. Between Blowingstone Hill and Wanborough there are more of these tracks coming from the Great Ridgeway on the downs above the Icknield Way than in any other stretch in Berkshire and Wiltshire. Each of the original homesteads and parishes had its allotted strip of downland for corn and pasture as well as its valley meadows, and consequently a way leading to the downs; and though today some of these tracks have been transformed into metalled roads up the scarp and take the slope the easiest way, many steeper unmetalled ones remain, indelibly hollowed out by the passage of farm wagons and horses. Some of them date at least to Saxon times, for they are mentioned as boundaries in the Anglo-Saxon charters of this district.

Weather has also played an important part in deepening these sunken ways, for heavy rainstorms over the downs turn them into beds of foaming white torrents, which subside as quickly as they begin, but not before they and the small flints in the mixture of churned-up chalk and water have scoured the tracks a little deeper.

Throughout the years the tracks become more like rifts or clefts than roads, for the rushing water tears away the vegetation at their sides and leaves the soft chalk exposed, and then frost plays its part and crumbles the sides into a chalky debris that falls on each side and gradually makes the way narrower. When, in the past, a track was no longer negotiable a fresh width was trodden out alongside, so that a present-day track is often shelved alongside a defile that is like a subterranean passage because it is choked with thickets of bird-sown ash, elder, spindle and way-faring tree and hung with curtains of traveller's-joy, bryonies, bindweed and wild-rose briars almost terrifying in their urge to rise above the decaying litter of centuries of dead growth and reach the light.

The Icknield Way passes through the village of Ashbury and edges the hamlet of Idstone before crossing the border of Wiltshire (*see* Map 27). It then passes through Bishopstone, where we have heard villagers refer to it as the Ickleton road and the Ackleton road: Andrews' and Dury's map of 1773 names it Huketon Way. Rising a little, it makes a short turn away from the valley to crook itself like an arm round the downland side of Little Hinton village, and after a steep dip and rise across the mouth of a coomb reaches and crosses Ermine Street near the top of Callas Hill. It is now only half a mile from Wanborough. This last half-mile comes to the village in characteristic fashion as a shelf-road, and has wide green margins and tall thick hedges with the scarp-foot fields on the right dropping away to the damp brookland fields in the valley towards Swindon.

There seems to be no reason why it should have ended at Wanborough, though westward we have found no mention of the Icknield Way in old documents to provide a clue to its further course. The scarp turns south for three-quarters of a mile towards Liddington village, and the road, still keeping true to character, may have followed the line of the present road from Wanborough to Liddington and then on by Medbourne and Badbury south-west to Chisledon, where it could easily have joined the Great Ridgeway. There is also the possibility that it continued along the line of roads leading west from Chisledon to the outer scarp of the chalk at Wroughton, but where then—who can say?

Ordnance Survey Maps

Oxford and Newbury. Sheet 158. 1 inch to 1 mile. 1940
West Berkshire. Sheet 13. 1 inch to 1 mile. 1830
Oxford and Henley-on-Thames. Sheet 105. 1 inch to 1 mile. Popular Edition,
1919

6

THE HARROW WAY

Approximately 72 miles

THE Harrow, or 'Hard Way', is one of the oldest roads in Britain, and like the Great Ridgeway, its only competitor for the title, with the possible exception of the Icknield Way, crosses the country from east to west. The Harrow Way's eastern terminus is the Kentish coast near Dover, and it enters Wessex at the Surrey-Hampshire border, whilst the Great Ridgeway comes from East Anglia and enters Wessex after crossing the Thames at Streatley in Berkshire. The two great highways come together on the chalk downs of Wiltshire, and after that their routes intermingle at various points in Dorset and reach the same western terminus at the mouth of the Axe in Devonshire.

Through the ages confusion has arisen between them as to which is the Great Ridgeway and which the Harrow Way after the Wiltshire-Somerset border is crossed. It may be that tradition, or folk memory, has made out of the trunk and main branches of a great prehistoric coast-to-coast road two principal roads with separate identities. When one thinks of the configuration of the eastern and south-eastern uplands these roads had to traverse across Britain, the way they lead inevitably to the Wiltshire Downs and the great chalk plateau of Salisbury Plain, as well as the different kind of country and the distances in between the eastward ends of the branches, it is easy to realize how the separation came about. An ancient road—though it could be travelled along from one side of the country to another—was not originally planned to do this. It grew up out of various local trackways which became linked together as the need arose, and in its earliest days must have fluctuated until it finally settled into a definite route which long experience had proved to be the most useful. Once it became well established the natural conservatism of man would keep it in being. The name Ridgeway and Harrow Way must apply to practically the same kind of trackway, for all ancient roads had to keep to the higher ground of the watersheds. Both are generic names for highways which existed when the Saxons made their first settlements in the river valleys. We can only write of these roads as they have come down to us, with many reaches that the changes and chances of past centuries have obscured or obliterated.

From Dover the Harrow Way goes over the North Downs into Surrey, and for part of its way through Kent and Surrey is known as the Pilgrims' Way. Pilgrims travelling to the shrine of Thomas à Becket at Canterbury kept this section of the trackway alive in the Middle Ages, and since then it has acquired a sentimental value which has kept it from being ploughed out like some of the other trackways. Its Kent and Surrey reaches are certainly amongst the most charming parts of the Harrow Way.

Now as it goes west from Farnham and enters Hampshire and the Wessex of this book it ceases to be a green track and is on the line of minor metalled roads for most of its way across the county. Just within its first Hampshire mile (*see* Map 8) the Harrow Way passes on its right the coppice containing the earthwork called Barley Pound—the remains of a Norman castle probably constructed in the twelfth century—and in almost another mile and a half the earthwork in Penley Copse on the left of the road, the name Penley and the rectangular construction suggesting an ancient cattle compound. This brings the road to where, almost half a mile south-east of Well, it probably forked into two branches that come together again at Oakley, twelve miles farther west.

The left-hand branch is represented by the line of lanes running a little south of west to Sutton Common and then by the metalled road going south-west along the ridge and descending to the Golden Pot Inn on the Odiham–Alton road (A 32). Turning north-west the branch continues over Western Common as a footpath and then as a byway to Nash's Green, where it bends south-west as the minor road through Bagmore before turning north-west again to come to Ellisfield. From Ellisfield, still a metalled road, it winds and twists as well as undulates through Farleigh Wallop and on across the Basingstoke–Preston Candover road to the A 30 road from Basingstoke to Winchester, where tumuli stand just west of the crossing. It has been gradually losing height from 684 feet on Farleigh Hill to 550 feet as it comes to the main road.

Now making for Oakley, its course past the tumuli is lost, although the quarter-mile of parish boundary from the main road to the site of the Roman road from Silchester gives the direction and cannot be far from the actual line. Three furlongs beyond the Roman road a lane and a footpath to East Oakley may also be on the line, continued perhaps by the road through the village as far as the church and then by a path from the church to where the Basingstoke road is crossed by the railway a little west of Oakley station. When this road is passing the station it represents the end of the other branch of the Harrow Way coming from Penley Copse.

This right fork coincides with the road going north-westward through Well and Long Sutton to Four Lanes End on the Odiham–Alton road, and then on to Five Lanes End with a more westerly trend to Polecat Corner. Still keeping west, it is the minor road along the north edge of Hackwood Park, and after crossing the A 339 road joins the A 30 road for a mile and a half to the Stag and Hounds Inn beyond the junction of the two main roads, A 30 and A 33. The A 30 turns away south-west, but a minor road, known locally as Pack Lane (a significant name for an old road) keeps the line past Kempshott village and after crossing the Roman road goes to Oakley station. Somewhere near the station it is joined by the other branch and so completes the loop, though the actual place of joining is not clear today.

Professor C.F.C. Hawkes, in an article in the *Proceedings of the Hampshire Field Club*, 1925, suggests that the route through Ellisfield and Farleigh Wallop was the original line of the Harrow Way, and the Long Sutton, Polecat Corner route was its summer way which, being more direct, superseded the parent ridgeway and has now become known as the Harrow Way. This has happened to other ridgeways. As well as being more direct the Polecat Corner route is lower, keeping to an altitude of 300-400 feet, while the Ellisfield–Farleigh Wallop route keeps between 400 and 600 feet and in places ascends to 700 feet. The lower route is signposted as the Harrow Way on the Basingstoke by-pass.

The two branches now go on as one. From Oakley to beyond Andover the railway and the Harrow Way are never far from each other, though after being lost for a short distance by Oakley station and going along a byway for about two miles it becomes a track, mostly hedged, and makes a north-westerly swing to rise past Kingsdown Wood and then turn south-west again for half a mile to cross the Kingsclere–Overton road before beginning a fall that brings it back to the railway line again. This stretch from the Kingsclere–Overton road is marked Harrow Way on the 1-inch O.S. map. There is a Ridgeway Farm about half a mile short of the line of trees known as Caesar's Belt on the Roman road coming south-west from Silchester. This is a mile and a half north of the Harrow Way opposite Laverstoke, and we have wondered if there may not once have been a loop of the Harrow Way on the higher ground in this region, and if the line marked Harrow Way on the map was another reach of its summer way. There are many tumuli on these hills as well as a long barrow, and the country is open with large unhedged fields dotted with occasional small woods.

A minor road just west of Oakley station leads north-west from the Harrow Way—which is lost at this point because the railway has taken its place—and may be on the line of a track that once linked the Harrow Way with the North Hants Ridgeway. After about a half mile the line leaves the minor road to become a footpath and parish boundary along the edge of Great Deane Wood and then a path along the edge of Frith Wood leading to Freemantle Farm. It is continued by a footpath on For Down, and then by part of a track which comes east from Walkeridge Farm and turns sharply to come to and cross the line of the Roman road. Beyond the Roman road it is a track and footpath to the top of White Hill above Kingsclere, where it meets the North Hants Ridgeway at the crossing of the Kingsclere–Overton road.

Now passing north of Whitchurch, the course of the Harrow Way wavers in uncertainty before crossing the parallels of the Newbury–Winchester main road (A 34) and the railway line. After passing over the railway on a small bridge the track disappears, but a faint hollow trail across the next two fields past Cholesley Farm and Down Farm comes to a metalled lane which leads to Dirty Corner. Near Hurstbourne railway station the true line of the old road may be represented by a fold in the ground which is lost as it comes to the railway track, and was obviously obliterated when the railway track was made.

We next pick up the line of the Harrow Way on the south side of the railway as a metalled road bridging the Hurstbourne stream over firm gravel at Chapmansford Farm, a name which implies that there may have been an ancient ford here used by pedlars travelling the old road.

Near here, just north of the Harrow Way, are the Hurstbourne pit dwellings, said by Dr. Stevens to have been inhabited in Roman times because of a shard of Samian ware found when they were being excavated. According to O.G.S. Crawford, in *The Andover District*, two fragments of a typical cinerary urn with overhanging rim and the half of a perforated quartzite hammer of the Bronze Age were also found, as well as a gold British coin of the Early Iron Age.

For the next four miles the road runs less than a furlong south of and parallel to the railway. As it comes within a mile of Andover and crosses the Roman road slanting down from the north-west to go through Harewood Forest, the Harrow Way becomes a lane between high ragged hedges. This is not a green lane underfoot, for it has a covering of cinders. It has been much used by gipsies as a camping place.

The lane brings us to the main Newbury–Andover road (A 343) north of the town, and there the Harrow Way's continuation westward over the River Anton for the next mile of its course has been lost. The Anton is only a small stream here and a detour either to the north or south would not have led to a better crossing-place, so it seems likely that a fairly direct westward line was kept. It was at this point that a hoard of bronze implements was found in watercress beds in 1913, and it seems likely they were lost by a bronze-smith travelling along the Harrow Way.

A new Andover housing estate situated at the beginning of a broad hedged lane which turns west from the hill just past the hospital is sign-posted Harrow Way (*see* Map 7), and this lane continues for nearly two miles before coming into the A 303 road and going with it for nearly half a mile to reach Weyhill. Weyhill was once famous for its autumn sheep fair, which lasted several days, drawing shepherds, farmers and others interested in sheep from all over the south of England, and serving also as an open market and pleasure fair for the countryside around. Unlike Yarnbury and Tan Hill in Wiltshire, and Woodbury in Dorset, much cultivation of the surrounding area has obliterated the wide series of trackways and droves used by the shepherds and their flocks which must have led to it from all directions. Only the hedged lane from Andover remains, and this is being urbanized at its east end. The other tracks have become modern roads.

The Harrow Way must now become one of these, and when the main road at Weyhill branches into two it takes the left-hand fork and follows it to Thruxton about a mile and a half on. It leaves the main road here and becomes a minor road going to Quarley, parting from this road just before coming to the village and taking the line of the metalled lane north of it that passes Lains Farm. Quarley Hill, an isolated chalk hill crowned with trees and an earthwork, stands up out of the plateau and is a landmark for miles around. Because of this boldness of outline, and the many evidences of ancient habitation on and about it, Quarley Hill has become one of those landmarks one remembers and looks for, and has gathered about itself a special significance not easily described. It must have been a landmark also to those early travellers for whom the Harrow Way was one of the main roads to Salisbury Plain.

Rising to Cholderton Hill the track, at a point where it goes through an ancient ditch that runs for nearly two miles from Quarley Hill to Thruxton Hill, meets another trackway coming south from Scot's Poor. As a minor road and parish boundary from Lains Farm the Harrow Way leads south-west to the corner of the grounds of Cholderton Lodge, where it again takes up its westward line. This line, in about three miles, brings it through Cholderton back to the A 303 road left at Thruxton.

It enters Wiltshire before passing through Cholderton village and as the A 303 road continues to within a mile of Amesbury and then, leaving the main road, makes a swing to the right as a track going under the railway to come up to the Avon at Ratfyn, a little upriver from Amesbury and the site of an ancient ford. The traces of a ford are not visible today but here the water is shallow and it has a good firm bottom.

From the Avon the line of the Harrow Way would lead over the downs immediately north of Amesbury to Stonehenge, and this may have been its termination. Taking it on a route from Stonehenge might be the ancient south-west trackway over barrow-dotted Normanton Down (see Map 6). It leads across the angle between the A 303 and the A 360 roads meeting at Longbarrow Crossroads, and comes out on the A 360 road near Druid's Lodge racing stables. After going with the main road for about a furlong—a diversion probably due to the building of Druid's Lodge—the track branches off to the west over the downs towards the valley of the River Till which flows south to enter the Wylye below Stapleford. The track soon descends to join the valley road in bridging the river at the south end of Berwick St. James. The bridge, or an earlier one on the same spot, probably replaced a ford at this point, but in any case the Till is not a difficult river to ford unless in flood, for like most chalk streams its shallow waters cover a clean flinty bed.

There are no signs of a continuing track on the slopes of down opposite the bridge, but about 300 yards along the village street a chalk track on the left leads up from the little valley to a ridge it follows south-west to a point from which it drops to the main road at Steeple Langford in the Wylye valley. This track is known as the Langford Way, and where it leaves the road in Berwick St. James there are two large sarsen blocks, one at each corner, set up as if to mark the way as well as to protect the wall-angles from traffic on the turn.

After crossing the Wylye at Steeple Langford the track ascends a shoulder of down which lifts it from the river valley to West Hill on the long east-to-west ridge that is the watershed separating Wylye and Nadder. Most of this ridge has an altitude ranging from 600 to 700 feet and has the ancient woods of Grovely and Great Ridge along much of the skyline. The track is on the ridge as soon as it has passed between the earthworks of Hanging Langford Camp and Church-end Ring at the west end of Grovely Wood, where it turns west and for about two miles coincides with the Grovely Wood Ridgeway. The parting comes when the ridgeway veers west-north-west in leading to the A 303 road under Stockton Wood, whilst the Harrow Way, keeping to the line of the old coach road which was superseded by the A 303, goes on to join that modern highway at Chicklade Bottom at the foot of slopes rising to the woods of Great Ridge.

From Chicklade Bottom the Harrow Way coincides with the main road for the next five miles by way of Chicklade and Old Willoughby Hedge (crossing the Great Ridgeway on Two Mile Down) to Charnage Down. At this point the main road makes a south-west turn to Mere (see Map 5), and three trackways fan out north of the road, for this must once have been a meeting-place of trackways. One of the tracks goes north-east over Keysley Down, the centre one keeps north of Monkton Deverill, and the third goes north-west and then more west as Long Lane to White Sheet Hill and Kilmington Common. This is the continuation of the Harrow Way and of the old coach road through Salisbury to London.

Rising all the time from its 711 feet where it leaves the main road to 784 feet on White Sheet Hill, with the earthworks of White Sheet Camp on a spur of downs on the left and passing through an ancient ditch and by a cluster of tumuli, this is the most splendid and—in feeling if not in actual number of feet—the highest stretch of the Harrow Way, and one of the loneliest downland walks in Wiltshire.

Long Lane was a name often given to a stretch of road which country folk, in the days when they were obliged to travel on foot, horse or wagon, found exceptionally long and wearisome, but it has another meaning also, that of a road coming from

afar. Nowhere on its long journey from the Kentish coast does the pilgrimage of the
old road, its passage through county after county, seem so moving as when it comes
to this last ridge of Wiltshire chalk before entering what were once the fastnesses of
Somerset forest and marsh.

A spur brings the track down from the hilltop, and its next mile and a half is a gentle
rise that takes it across the Stourton–Maiden Bradley road at Kilmington Common.

Leaving Kilmington Common the Harrow Way mounts between high banks
wooded with beech and oak to the summit of Kingsettle Hill where, half hidden
in the trees, Alfred's Tower stands. It was erected by Henry Hoare of Stourhead in
1772 to adorn the highest point of his estate and perpetuate the memory of King
Alfred who, according to the inscription over the entrance, '… on this summit
erected his Standard against Danish invaders'. Alfred's Tower is famous not for
the quality of its architecture but because its position on the boundary between
Wiltshire and Somerset, nearly 900 feet above sea level, makes it a landmark for
these two counties and for Dorset as well. From many ridgeways in these three
counties the top of the tower and the woods surrounding it are visible on the highest
point of the skyline. One comes to have an affection for it as a feature of a familiar
and much loved landscape, so that one thinks of it not as a Folly but as a symbol
of the meeting of contrasting countrysides. Here the intimate homely landscape of
Somerset fields and orchards netted in winding lanes and winding streams, and the
austere beauty of Wiltshire downland with its vast unhedged arable fields and high
pastures, its hillside beech groves and clumps, come together and take on a stronger
individuality because of it.

From Alfred's Tower the road falls to come to Redlynch in about three miles.
This part of it is named Hard Way on the 1-inch O.S. map, and if Hard Way is
another rendering of Harrow Way the implication must be that this three miles is
a continuation of the road which the map names Harrow Way in Hampshire. Still
metalled, it continues south-west as a minor road to Shepton Montague, though for
the first mile from Redlynch the modern road may have been taken just north of
the line to avoid the grounds of Redlynch House.

At Shepton Montague it crosses a tributary of the Brue beyond which the line
continues south-west for about a mile until it turns south up Cattle Hill. The name
of this hill may commemorate the days when the road was used as a cattle way,
though it must be said that place-names seldom have so simple an interpretation.
But there is plenty of evidence that cattle were driven along the Harrow Way in the
eighteenth and early nineteenth century, and until recent years old men were still
to be found in the villages on the route who had driven fat cattle from Somerset to
London through Wiltshire, Hampshire and Surrey.

After crossing the Castle Cary–Wincanton main road (A 371) the minor road goes
along for another two miles to Knoll Hill, where it again meets the A 303, a main
road it has met, followed and parted from time and again since it began its journey

through Wessex. From Knoll Hill the course is south-westerly past Yeovil, but there is a southward alternative that could have been taken instead, one that seems to us to have more of the characteristic features of a ridgeway than the other, which traverses lower and stream-netted country. The alternative branch may represent today the line of a track used by early travellers from this region about Cadbury Castle or Camelot as a link with the Great Ridgeway and with other ridgeways in Dorset, its course as a loop of the Harrow Way being completed by the reach of the Great Ridgeway from Batcombe Hill to Toller Down by way of Evershot. It follows the series of ridges from Knoll Hill to Sherborne, the watershed between the Yeo and the Cale, and continues south from Sherborne to the Great Ridgeway on Batcombe Hill; and as it approaches the scarp it also sends off branches to Gore Hill near the Cross and Hand and to High Stoy.

Taking this southern branch first, it is now a metalled minor road to Sherborne and begins when, in a quarter of a mile, the Harrow Way has turned from the A 303 road at Knoll Hill, crossed a small feeder of the Cam on the west side of Blackford, and reached the corner where the wooded grounds about Compton Castle project into the angle between branching ways. Ours is the left branch going along the east side of the grounds and on to Hill Farm, rising all the time, and with the earthworks of Cadbury Castle a mile or so to the west. This is a high road avoiding the streams which meander about Sutton Mentis and the country beyond. From Hill Farm it continues a little west of south for about a mile to come to Wheatsheaf Hill after passing the village of Corton Denham in its valley on the right.

Midway between Hill Farm and Wheatsheaf Hill a track going off on the right along Corton Hill is a way to Cadbury Castle. The ridge of Corton Hill leads back north-west in that direction to the Beacon at its other end, where the Whitcomb gap makes a narrow pass between it and a smaller isolated hill. After keeping well behind the crest of the steep hillside above Corton Denham the track passes the Beacon and curves down into this gap to join a metalled byway that rounds the east side of the smaller hill, but instead of going on with it when the hill has been rounded, branches off to the north, leaving Sutton Mentis on the left and making its last half-mile a straight approach to the foot of the hill under the earthworks of Cadbury Castle.

On Wheatsheaf Hill, where the road comes to the county boundary and passes into Dorset, there are signs that this was once a meeting-place of several trackways. Our way continues south as a metalled road over Poynington Down and along Holway Hill to Red Post, where it begins a slow descent to Sherborne. It seems impossible to say today what line it took through the town or exactly where it crossed the stream, but the stream would not be a difficult one to cross.

We pick it up again at Dancing Hill south of the town as the main road to Dorchester (A 352) and follow this road for about two miles until, approaching Long Burton, it divides into two branches. Our line then becomes the minor road which forks right and is a loop of the main road, for the two come together again at Dogbury Gate above Minterne Magna. Keeping south-south-west for three miles it goes along the east side of the long narrow wood called Holm Bushes to come to Totnell Corner, and from this meeting-place of roads it could reach the Great Ridgeway in about three miles by taking either the south-east or the south-west line.

As the south-east road that leaves the Castle earthworks on its right, it would go by Three Gates and Stone's Farm to the foot of the High Stoy headland, where the line of a footpath up the scarp leads to a track which would bring it to the Great Ridgeway between High Stoy and Telegraph Hill, or else by continuing with the road under the hanging woods of High Stoy come to it at Dogbury Gate. The other line from Totnell Corner runs west of the Castle and Crocker's Knap and crosses the stream called Wriggle River to reach Newland's Farm and Batcombe village. Between the farm and the village a branch turns abruptly south-east and passes through the woods at the Priory of St. Francis, to end in a track climbing steeply up the scarp to Gore Hill a little to the east of a tumulus and the Cross and Hand. An alternative is to keep south through Batcombe village and on past the isolated little church to climb the steep, deeply sunken trackway which leads to the head of the great combe on Batcombe Hill. Where the fall is steepest this trackway looks more like a ravine between two shoulders of down than a road and has all the appearance of great age, though some of its depth must be due to the scouring of surface water rushing down it in wet weather. From this point the remainder of the loop would be the Great Ridgeway through Evershot to Toller Down (*see* Map 14).

Having taken this loop-branch into Dorset we return to where we left the main Harrow Way crossing the A 303 road just south of Knoll Hill. (It still has many more Somerset miles to cover before it also comes to Dorset, though it approaches fairly near the border at Darvole, south of Yeovil, where the line of the Roman road to Dorchester, now the A 37, has been lost for a short distance as it goes over the railway and Whistle Bridge.) South-west from Knoll Hill it has to cross the first windings of several streams flowing to join the Cam and the Yeo, and this must have made it a wet way in a rainy season.

It goes through Compton Pauncefoot as the village street leading on to South Cadbury, but at East End, just before the road comes to South Cadbury, a lane branches south to meet the village road curving south-east round Cadbury Hill and continuing to Sutton Mentis. The configuration of the country here, with its small broken hills and stream-threaded meadows, means that the Harrow Way must take an irregular course to keep as far as possible on the low watersheds between the streams.

South-west of Sutton Montis, Brian Vesey-Fitzgerald takes it by a chain of track, bridle path and footpath over the fields to the east side of Marston Magna, and from there across the fields by a footpath to the Yeovil main road about three miles north-east of the town. This may have been a shorter Saxon variant of the old track, but a higher line from Sutton Mentis, keeping well above the streams, and of course, a longer way round, would continue south from Sutton Mentis along Corton Ridge for a mile or so, turning west along the county boundary to Woodhouse Farm and then by a byway leading into the metalled road to Marston Magna. To avoid the water meadows between Marston Magna and Mudford it could have made a detour south-east from the village to White Post on the line of the B 3148 road and then have swung south-west below Rowbarrow to follow the line of modern road which goes over the railway, and from which it would diverge to cross the Yeo at Mudford, where it would join the main Yeovil road and keep with it to the town.

South of Yeovil it follows the Roman road to Dorchester (A 37) for about a mile and a half, then when the Roman road, or its modern diversion, bends east to cross the railway it takes the line of a footpath for three furlongs south to come to the modern road at Darvole leading to Sutton Bingham. Near Sutton Bingham the Harrow Way disappears into a new reservoir, and a pleasant new waterside road has been made. The reservoir lies in a shallow hollow between gently sloping fields, and at its Dorset end, at least, looks more like a natural lake and adds the charm of the ever changing sky-colour and ripplings of its water surface to the rather dull intermediate kind of countryside which lies on each side of it. As we did not know this region before the reservoir was made we can only say how it appears to us today.

Beyond the reservoir the road goes on to Halstock, keeping just above a stream flowing parallel to it on the left, and as it comes within half a mile of the village having a stream on each side of it. It is a wide drove-like road with shaggy grass margins which keeps its width as it goes through the village past the village green with its fine old tree. We leave this road, however, at the south end of Halstock, for the Harrow Way turns into a green track called Common Lane. This lies about half a mile west of the metalled road and above the stream which goes with the road from Sutton Bingham almost to Corscombe. In about two miles, rising slowly at first and then more quickly in passing over Wood Fold Hill, the green lane comes to Corscombe. It has been fenced in one place and a spinney is planted across it, but the track obviously goes on through the trees, though it may disappear if the right of way is not established. Travellers on foot will then be forced to keep to the modern road, and another length of the Harrow Way will be lost for ever.

As it nears Corscombe the track leaves the half-Somerset half-Dorset countryside it has traversed for the last few miles and the landscape becomes truly Dorset in character. The village lies at the foot of the escarpment and from it the way climbs to Corscombe Cross on the main road to Dorchester along the Toller Down ridge.

The track crosses the Dorchester road and continues south-west for three-quarters of a mile to Beaminster Down. Here in a wide shallow hollow of common land it meets the Great Ridgeway coming from Toller Down Gate (*see* Map 13). As one road the Harrow Way and the Great Ridgeway now go on together, and whether we call it the Great Ridgeway or the Harrow or Hard Way, or think of one as a branch of the other, matters little. Stephen Spender, in his autobiography, *World within World*, wrote: 'Travel is an art which has to be created by the traveller', and on occasions during this journey across Wessex one could agree with this statement. But perhaps the best moment comes when, standing on the cliffs above Seaton Bay with nothing but the sea stretching beyond the bay and the white cliffs of Beer, we know we have come to a road's end.

Ordnance Survey Maps

Salisbury, Winchester and Reading. Sheet 33. ½ inch to 1 mile. 1926
Winchester. Sheet 168. 1 inch to 1 mile. 1945
Salisbury. Sheet 167. 1 inch to 1 mile. 1960
Frome. Sheet 166. 1 inch to 1 mile. 1946
Dorchester. Sheet 178. 1 inch to 1 mile. 1945
Taunton and Lyme Regis. Sheet 177. 1 inch to 1 mile. 1946

7

BRANCHES OF THE HARROW WAY

Approximately 18 miles

WHERE the Harrow Way comes to Cholderton Hill after going through the Ditch which runs from Thruxton Hill to Quarley Camp, a track branches from it and, keeping with the Ditch, goes south-east, passing the west end of Quarley Camp as it runs over Quarley Hill (*see* Map 7). From the camp a traveller can see on a clear day and by looking in all directions a circle of other hill-forts and camps, for Beacon Hill (Burghclere), Ladle Hill, Tidbury, Bury Hill, Danebury, Woolbury, Old Sarum, Sidbury, Bevisbury and Walbury are all visible from its summit, so that one feels tempted to work out an ancient route which would include them all. Three however—Quarley, Danebury and Woolbury—can quite definitely be linked together by this track connecting the Harrow Way and the South Hants Ridgeway.

South-east of Quarley Hill the track crosses the Roman road and a trackway coming south to pass through the Winterslow villages to the New Forest region, and after a confused furlong or two, where it crosses the railway and takes the line of a modern road, it leaves the road near an inn and goes off a little south of east as a metalled byway and parish boundary over champaign country to come to the Salisbury–Andover main road (A 343). It goes south along the main road for about fifty yards before striking south-east across another fine open stretch of downs— now mostly arable—for about two miles and still a metalled road, and then, about three furlongs east of the remains of two long barrows, is an open track again. In less than a mile from this point it comes to a meeting-place of tracks at some tumuli half a mile east of Danebury Camp.

The three rings of the camp on the hill of Danebury, some 150 feet above the general level of the plateau, are thickly planted with beech and fir, with yews of a much older date making patches of a more sombre colour amongst them, and the rounded wooded hill strikes a dramatic note in this wide area of cultivated down. Lengths of broken hollow tracks can be seen east and north of the earthwork, but today none of them actually joins up with the main trackway from Quarley. Dr. J.P. Williams-Freeman in his *Field Archaeology* points out that all the tracks converge on the eastern entrance, and that numerous very deeply worn ones curve down the hill to the north and turn west to Quarley. He also mentions this track, which can still be followed across the Test to Woolbury some four miles or so to the east.

Soon after leaving the meeting-place of ways the line becomes an old lane known as Church Lane leading to the church at Longstock and the ford over the Test which, as its name implies, was used by the Saxons and marked out by them with stakes. There are also some Danish entrenchments close besides the fording-place, probably because the Danes used the river as a highway, but it is generally accepted that the name Danebury has nothing to do with the Danes but came originally from a Celtic word Dun, meaning hill or fort. On an eighteenth-century map it is called Dunbury.

On the other side of the river (*see* Map 3) a track over a golf-course brings it to Upper Sandy Down Farm, just north of Woolbury Ring. The track, as well as the eastern end of the earthwork, is lost here under cultivation, but traces of it can be seen as a deep hollow way a short distance south-east of the camp. Farther on it has again disappeared, but it is obvious that it did not stop here but must have continued to a meeting-place with the ridgeway running east and west across southern Hampshire.

It could have done this in several ways. It may have followed the line of the main Stockbridge–Winchester road (A 272) as far as Folly Farm, where it could have joined up with the trackway from Finkley Down Farm (page **95**) going to connect with the South Hants Ridgeway at Weeke near Winchester; or it could have reached the South Hants Ridgeway between Farley Mount and Pitt Down by taking the line of the road going south to Little Sombourne and continued by the metalled lane which winds south-east and then south-west to Ashley, and then going on, curving and undulating, as a series of lanes to the Roman road below Ashley Woods. According to Dr. Williams-Freeman, local archaeologists call this way to Woolbury the 'British road'. The footpath the 1-inch O.S. map shows from Little Sombourne to Ashley might be the remains of a more direct part of the course.

This region is one that was heavily occupied by the Romans, for evidences of their settlement can be found all about it. The South Hants Ridgeway itself was Romanized from Ashley Down to Winchester, so it seems probable that some parts of the old trackway were preserved by being taken over by the Romans, and later the Saxons embodied in their roads other parts which were useful to them.

Too many different layers of civilization, including the Norman, have covered this region for an ancient trackway to have kept its original line.

FINKLEY DOWN FARM TO WEEKE

Approximately 12 miles

A cross-track going roughly south from near Finkley Down Farm about a mile east of Andover is given by Professor Hawkes, in his article in the *Proceedings of the Hampshire Field Club*, as linking the Harrow Way with the South Hants Ridgeway at Weeke about a mile north-west of Winchester. He could find no traces of its first few miles, which is not surprising when one considers that this has been a cultivated area since Roman times, and begins his itinerary after the Test, just above its junction with the Anton, has been crossed at Fullerton (*see* Map 3).

A line which might represent the way it went to the river can be picked up on the golf-course south of Andover, where a track goes south, keeping for its first two miles roughly parallel with and about half a mile east of the A 3057 road and well above the Anton, which the main road follows without much deviation from Andover to Fullerton. The track, after a mile or so of open country, passes the west side of Upping Copse and comes to an end at the B 3420 road. There is now a blank of about a mile and a half, but it could have continued along Red Hill above the main road to where the railway, the road and the river come very close together at Fullerton.

Across the river a wide lane which follows a parish boundary takes it in about two and a half miles to the White Hart on the Stockbridge–Sutton Scotney main road (A 30), passing a field system on the left in the first half-mile of its course over West Down, and then a tumulus on the right as it comes to the main road. Opposite the White Hart two tracks lead off across the downs; one, continuing the parish boundary and accompanied by a narrow strip of woods, turns abruptly east on the line of the Lunway, but the west fork goes past Leckford Down Farm and on along the east side of a wood and through the woods on Windmill Hill before it descends to cross the Stockbridge–Winchester road (A 272) two or three hundred yards west of Folly Farm. On this stretch also there is a field system on the downs on the left of the track, and on the same side a long barrow near the point where it meets the Lunway going east.

After keeping with the A 272 road as far as Folly Farm—the hiatus in the linking up across the main road may perhaps be explained by the diversion of the track to serve the farm—the track then becomes a wide green lane on the line of a parish boundary. It edges a small wood on the left, beyond which there are tumuli. The parish boundary continues south, but the track turns east in about a mile from the Somborne–Crawley road and passes the western outskirts of Sparsholt village before it dips south-east to cross the ridge between the Test and Itchen valleys at its lowest point at Ham Green. Here Professor Hawkes found more hollow trails. As a lane and then as a metalled byway it continues its easterly line past the crossroads of Wyke Mark to come to Weeke, and there meets the South Hants Ridgeway coming from Pitt Down and Teg Down golf-course.

Ordnance Survey Maps

Salisbury. Sheet 167. 1 inch to 1 mile. 1940
Winchester. Sheet 168. 1 inch to 1 mile. 1945

8

THE INKPEN AND NORTH HANTS RIDGEWAY

Approximately 38 miles

WHEN the Great Ridgeway has crossed the Vale of Pewsey and ascended to the Plain above Broadbury Banks (*see* Map 23), a track leaves it near a tumulus on Wilsford Hill and continues east along the north edge of the Plain to pass Casterley Camp, or to put it another way, an eastern branch or continuation of the Great Ridgeway from Wilsford Hill can be traced across east Wiltshire and north Hampshire to Basingstoke and beyond into Surrey, to come finally to the Kentish coast. In Wiltshire and Berkshire—for it comes to the border of Berkshire at Combe—this trackway is known as the Inkpen Ridgeway, but Hampshire archaeologists usually refer to it, from where it enters Hampshire at Walbury Camp, as the North Hants Ridgeway. It is particularly interesting because of the number of major hill-forts it passes on its way, so that one might almost take it in stages, with small detours, from one earthwork to another (*see* Maps 7 and 8).

Its first mile and a half take it with a southeasterly swing over the Plain to the north end of Casterley Camp, and then it comes back to the easterly line again to descend to the Avon valley and the Devizes–Andover road half a mile south of Rushall. It goes east for about three furlongs along the main road, crosses the Avon and comes to the village of Upavon. Thus far it has been in the outer region of Salisbury Plain's War Department country, but although it belongs to the military the land is still used as rough pasture and arable by local farmers. It is a lonely and rather desolate part of the Plain, the combined occupation giving it the appearance of not really belonging either to the farmers or to the military. There are gaunt reminders of the Army in the iron posts, old wire and other military debris half hidden in the tangled grass, while the farming seems to have little kinship with the neat and pleasant farmsteads in the valley.

The next two or three miles pass through aerodrome country. First as a track and then as a footpath the line continues over the golf-course on the south side of Upavon Hill, where it meets a track and parish boundary coming south-east up the downs from Wood Bridge where the Avon is crossed by the Pewsey-Devizes road. In about a furlong a track from Manningford Bruce on the same main road comes into it near a tumulus. The part of this track from Bruce Field Barn to Bohune Down is called Heathy Ridgeway in an Anglo-Saxon charter, and is the south end of an ancient road from Marlborough which descends Oare Hill and crosses the Vale of Pewsey by way of Wilcot Creen and Manningford Bruce.

The three tracks continue as one and as a parish boundary for nearly a mile over Bohune Down to come into the main road to Lower Everleigh, and then, as the main road, it rises again to the high and lonely village of Everleigh. The downs behind the escarpment on both sides of the main road are traversed by many trackways, and are thickly scattered with tumuli, field systems and earthworks, so that it looks as if as many as possible had to be crowded into it before the eastern limit of the Plain blends into the more forested regions of the Wiltshire-Hampshire borderland. The downs about Everleigh are also War Department country and tanks have scored many a new trackway among the old ones.

From Everleigh there are at least two routes the trackway could have taken to reach the meeting-place of tracks at Scot's Poor on its way to the Inkpen ridge. East of Everleigh, after about two furlongs along the main road to Ludgershall (A 342), a minor road branches just beyond Lower Farm and goes over Gore Down and West Hill, and in less than a mile before coming to Collingbourne Ducis this minor road forks. The north fork, known as Chicks Lane, leads to a ford over the Bourne just north of the village. The Bourne flows only in the winter, and during the summer months is a dry channel overgrown with weeds and rank grasses. Still as a minor road the line goes east from Collingbourne Ducis to Cadley and, after passing the Shears Inn, becomes a track over Sunton Heath, an area of sandy soil and scattered scrub. A number of tracks spray out on Sunton Heath and go north-east, east and south-east through Collingbourne Woods. Our track, however, here joins the ridgeway coming down from Scot's Poor between Collingbourne Wood and Rag Copse and goes with it to the meeting-place of tracks at Scot's Poor.

An alternative route or loop leaves the Old Marlborough Road between Coombe Cottages and Marlborough Road Cottages on the north side of Everleigh by a track going first north-east for half a mile to a point where a number of tracks unite in a wide way called Mill Drove, and then goes east and north-east to come to the main road just south of Collingbourne Kingston a mile farther up the Bourne valley from Collingbourne Ducis. We cannot say exactly where the Bourne was forded, but a short metalled byway north-east to Brunton on the opposite side of the stream suggests the line. From Brunton it is possible that there were two ways forming a loop to Scot's Poor—an earlier, higher and less direct track going by the long barrow on Fairmile Down and past Tow Barrow on Wexcombe Down before coming down to the woods and scrub at Scot's Poor, and what may have been a later version, lower and more direct, eastward past Hill Barn and Tinker's Barn, thus completing the loop from Brunton as well as the much longer one from Everleigh.

Scot's Poor once had a lonely inn on the opposite side of the road to where the tracks come in and where the Romanized road bends south-east to become Chute Causeway, but today this inn is a pleasant red-brick thatch-roofed house which, because of its situation, looks as if it might be a gamekeeper's cottage. It stands alone on the edge of a wood, with a shady path going down through the trees on one side of it. In front of the house a hollow overhung by a willow suggests that there was once a small round pond here. Our tracks now continue north-east as the metalled Roman road to Tidcombe crossroads. As well as its continuation east as Chute Causeway above the great hollow of Hippenscombe in Haydown Hill this stretch of the Roman road north-east from Scot's Poor was a trackway before the Romans came. It is a beautiful stretch of road with a belt of tall beeches on the right and open downs on the left and traces of overgrown trails here and there beside it. The long mound of Tidcombe long barrow lies just off the road. On the other side there is a field system. Another feature of the steep slopes of the downs here are the many lengths of ancient ditches running at various angles so that today their different directions seem purposeless.

At the Tidcombe crossroads it is difficult to decide which way the main track went to reach the west end of the Inkpen ridge, for Saxon and later roads have confused the issue. Perhaps there were several ways up. The line north is continued by a parish boundary along a wide overgrown lane, with thick, free-growing hedges, which passes another long barrow before it comes out in a mile and a quarter on a minor road leading to the Hungerford-Salisbury main road on North Hill. The lane comes into the minor road a quarter of a mile north of the track going east over Rivar Down from Botley Down, so that today it does not lead naturally into the first mile of the Inkpen ridge. Another way to reach the summit of the ridge from Tidcombe crossroads is by continuing north-east with the minor road to Oxenwood for a half-mile to the Oxenwood crossroads and there taking the road which goes north-west to Botley Down, where the track leads east from the metalled road and begins the five-mile length along the scarp-crest to Walbury Camp. Another alternative would be the minor road from the Oxenwood crossroads which goes north-east past Oxenwood Farm to Rivar Hill, where the track can be seen going off through woods on each side before the metalled road makes its steep descent to Rivar village. All three ways mean a climb to the edge of the escarpment, though the ancient green lane has the easiest gradient. Whichever line it took, once the crest of the ridge has been achieved there can be no doubt as to its course for many miles. Now, indeed, it has become a high and dry way.

The first three miles of the ridge are in Wiltshire, the next two and a half are in Berkshire, so that it does not officially begin to carry a Hampshire ridgeway until Walbury Camp is three-quarters of a mile behind (*see* Map 8). This is one of the finest and highest stretches of chalk downs in Wessex, for at Walbury Camp at the east end of Inkpen it tops by a few feet the summit of Milk Hill above Pewsey Vale and the Win Green height on the Wiltshire-Dorset border. Without having to cross any streams or find a way across wet valleys the track can go on winding with the hills for sixteen miles or more from Botley Down to Cottington's Hill, almost everywhere undulating between 700 feet and 960 feet, and giving tremendous views over Berkshire, Hampshire and Wiltshire all the way. At first can be felt the influence of the Chute and Savernake forest region it is leaving behind. From Botley Down the eye ranges first to the isolated copses and then to the whole splendour of Savernake Forest spread out below.

At the end of its first mile along Rivar Down the track becomes a lane, first with a wood on its right and then with trees overshadowing each side. Then it goes as a high lane through woods until it crosses the road to Rivar and comes out again into the open on Rivar Hill. The scarp falls away on its north side: it is on the gentler slopes of the south side that the greater number of footpaths, tracks and roads descend from the ridge. The track passes the end of a cross-dyke where a metalled way goes off to the farms and cottages of Buttermere, a hamlet just behind the crest and which is one of the several high and lonely little villages in this region of the chalk uplands. The road from Hungerford through Ham village also cuts through the ridge at this point, and as it comes up the steep slopes to the summit the high banks show how great was the wear of weather and traffic into the chalk before the surface of the road was metalled.

Keeping along the crest the track begins to rise over Ham Hill to cross the county border and come to Inkpen Hill's 955 feet and the long barrow on which stands Combe Gibbet. The hill here is called Inkpen Beacon and a fire lit on this high place must have made a far-seen glow in a night sky.

Walbury Camp stands on the bare summit of Walbury Hill—the highest chalk hill in England—on the shoulder of the ridge just where it begins a swing to the south-east, the single bank and ditch of the camp following the contours of the hill and using its precipitous slopes as additional protection. On all sides of the earthwork the ground falls away steeply, particularly on the north. Northward the view is across the Kennet to the last ridge of the downs beyond Lambourn; southward the hills which hold the camps of Fosbury, Quarley, Danebury, Bury Hill and Woodbury can be seen on a clear day, as well as the white scars under Sidbury Camp on Salisbury Plain. The soil is sandy over the chalk and gorse grows freely. When the valleys are sweltering in summer heat this is a pleasant place to rest and enjoy the cool gorse-scented breezes and the wide sweep of the country below in its infinite variety of field shapes and colours accented with bands and patches of woodland.

The Ridgeway runs through the camp from the north-east corner to the south-west, and on the rise inward from the north-east entrance divides into several hollow ways. It was the old county boundary between Berkshire and Hampshire before the whole of the parish of Combe was given to Berkshire. 'For archaeological reasons', wrote Dr. Williams-Freeman of this new boundary line, 'we must simply decline to recognize it.'

Going south-east with the ridge and still very high, it enters a more wooded terrain as it approaches the 'Clere' country in coming to Three-Legged Cross on the Andover–Newbury road (A 343). There is a covering of clay here, and this becomes apparent in the drifts of rosebay willowherb and foxgloves as well as in the oaks and rhododendrons of the Highclere estate to be seen from the Ridgeway. From Three-Legged Cross the track curves east and then south past tumuli on Upper Woodcott Down before turning east again and skirting a coppice in a gradual fall to Seven Barrows, beside the Newbury–Whitchurch road (A 34) and the Winchester–Newbury railway line running close together in a narrow pass through the ridge.

About three furlongs north-west of Seven Barrows, below the footslopes of Beacon Hill, is Chapman's Dell, an old pit surrounded by a low bank and with sunken ways leading into it from east to west. This *Ceapmanna del* of a Crux Easton and Woodcott Saxon charter, says O.G.S. Crawford in *The Andover District,* 'is probably a pit still to be seen at the junction of the modern parishes of Crux Easton, Woodcott and Burghclere. It closely resembles the so-called "amphitheatres" which are frequently found near Romano-British villages. … Place-names compounded with "chapman" are almost invariably associated with prehistoric roads or earthworks'. We remember the Chapmansford the Harrow Way crosses near Andover, and in Wiltshire there is Chapmanslade, through which the West Wilts Ridgeway goes on its journey north to the limestone country about Bradford-on-Avon.

The Newbury–Whitchurch road which the track crosses at Seven Barrows is perhaps on the line of a salt way which came north from the salterns of the Hampshire shore. Remembering that the White Way on the Cotswolds is thought to have been a salt way from Droitwich, we have wondered if the names 'White Shute' and 'Whitway' on this part of the Hampshire road may be indications of its early use as a salt way. If it was so used some of the salt carried along it would be for the people of the hill-fort on the summit of Beacon Hill, a chalk outlier from the main ridge about a mile north of Seven Barrows and with a long spur leading down towards the Ridgeway. The track from Chapman's Dell keeps west of the hill, following a parish boundary which it leaves and turns round the hill's north end to pass Ivory Farm and reach the main road. The slopes of the hill leading to the hill-fort are so precipitous that only by approaching it by the south-east corner, where the single entrance is situated, can an ascent be achieved without strenuous climbing. A track probably led from this entrance to the Ridgeway below, but there is not even a footpath shown on the map today.

The next camp on the ridge is on Ladle Hill a mile to the east, the shallow little valley separating the two earthworks being like a gateway to the gap by which the main road and the railway pass through the downs to Whitchurch. From Seven Barrows the ridge swings north-east to Ladle Hill. The track goes with it to the camp, although the 1-inch O.S. map does not mark it again until it is leading away from Sydmonton Park after the ridge has turned east at Ladle Hill. To reach the camp it rises over Great Litchfield Down where there used to be gnarled old thorns and stunted, wind-twisted oaks, with open glades and thin scrub on the higher reaches. This is an area which medieval documents describe as forest—not meaning, of course, dense woodland, but good country for the hunting of deer.

Turning east with the ridge just north of the earthwork on the hilltop, and passing a scarp-slope belt of bushes and then tumuli at the south edge of Sydmonton Park, the track curves round the head of a coomb to come to Watership Down, beyond which it veers somewhat south of east over Cannon Down to come to White Hill on the Kingsclere–Overton road. Here it meets a track coming north-west from the Harrow Way at Oakley (*see* page 83), but the Ridgeway keeps on as a lane to Cottington's Hill, where it makes a southward turn to Freemantle Park Farm. King John had a hunting-lodge here and the continuation of the North Hants Ridgeway from this point to Basingstoke is still called King John's Road by older local inhabitants. Tradition also says that from Cottington's Hill he used to ride to another hunting-lodge at Cranborne in Dorset by way of the Ridgeway we have just followed.

From Freemantle Park Farm the course is that of a wide lane through and then along the edge of a wood and on to Hannington. For nearly two miles of this it is a wide drove across the downs, partly along the north edge of a coppice, to where it passes south of Ibworth and comes to a point at which, for about half a mile, the lane is lost and a footpath continues the line. It becomes a lane again for a mile as it goes north of Tangier Park and after another mile reaches the minor road to Sherborne St. John. Here there is a break for a quarter of a mile until the line is taken up by the A 339 road to Basingstoke immediately after it has crossed the course of the Roman road from Silchester to Winchester, and for the last mile or so into Basingstoke the main road, once known as Dyers Down Lane, is the obvious continuation of the whole Ridgeway as well as the continuation of the wide lane it has followed from Hannington.

About a furlong south of the main road, soon after it has crossed the Roman road, is Winklebury Camp, the last of the hill-forts the North Hants Ridgeway passes before it goes into Surrey. It does not look like a hill-fort today, for it has suffered much mutilation. No entrances are now recognizable and today no trackway leads to it. Whether, in going eastward from Basingstoke, the North Hants Ridgeway joined the Harrow Way passing south of the town, or whether it went on independently, we are unable to say.

Ordnance Survey Maps

Salisbury. Sheet 167. 1 inch to 1 mile. 1940
Winchester. Sheet 168. 1 inch to 1 mile. 1945

9

A BRANCH FROM THE INKPEN RIDGEWAY TO OLD SARUM

SCOT'S POOR TO EASTON DOWN

Approximately 15 miles

A TRACK along a parish boundary leaves the meeting-place of ways at Scot's Poor (*see* Map 7) and goes south-west into the Chute Forest region which covers much of the north-west borderland of Hampshire and Wiltshire. The broad, tree-lined track appears to have been gravelled at some time, but there is now a line of mossy green growth along the middle between the wheel-tracks.

Keeping close to the east edge of Rag Copse the track comes to Shaw Cross, where the parish boundary continues south while the track goes on between Rag Copse and Collingbourne Wood for nearly a mile as a woodland way to Sunton Heath, which today remains as a shallow hollow, dotted with thorns and self-sown trees from the woods, below the west margin of Collingbourne Wood. The side of the hollow rising away from the wood is a more open slope to cultivated fields on a ridge of downland between the heath and the Collingbourne villages. The woodland reach of the track is a broad green way along the rough and irregular clearing between the wood and the outlying trees and thickets on the edge of the hollow. It leads to cornfields on the nearer slopes of Wick Down, where it is lost at first, but continues a little west of the tumulus on that down and passes a south-west extension of the woodland to reach Widgerly Down and a railway line half a mile north-west of the castle mound of Ludgershall.

There is a break from the railway to the Everleigh–Ludgershall main road, and another short break south of the main road, but the track can be seen again on Windmill Hill Down. It continues over Pickpit Hill, crosses the Ludgershall–North Tidworth road and continues past Andover Clump to Ashdown Copse near South Tidworth. This is a densely militarized area of training grounds, rifle ranges and barracks, so that it is difficult to investigate this part of the track in the field.

The map shows no track or footpath continuing the line south for the next two and a half miles until, north of the Andover–Amesbury main road on Thruxton Hill, about a furlong of the track can be seen, which continues on the opposite side of the road over Cholderton Hill, where it crosses the Harrow Way. It goes on over Quarley Hill, past the west end of Quarley Camp earthworks to cross the Roman road from Silchester to Old Sarum. For this length of a mile or so it coincides with a branch of the Harrow Way which turns east near Grately railway station and goes across the downs to Danebury Camp (*see* page 93). Our track kept south, though it is now lost where the railway runs between the Roman road and Boar Knoll. At Boar Knoll it can be seen again making a long shallow curve west of Juniper Down Farm before going on to pass Martin's Clump and a long barrow and lead over Tower Hill to come to Easton Down.

A number of tracks come in to a meeting-place on Easton Down just above a small coppice, but we are still in Army country so that it is difficult to investigate them. But it looks as if our track divided here into two ways, one to the south-west in the direction of Old Sarum, the other keeping east of south as far as the main road from Lopcombe Corner and then winding south-west to the Pepperbox on the Salisbury–Southampton road (A 36), where it could have linked up with the Lymington Ridgeway and the South Hants Ridgeway.

Taking the latter fork, the track goes on for nearly a mile south-south-east to cross the Salisbury–Stockbridge main road and then becomes a metalled road winding roughly south-west through the Winterslow villages—East Winterslow, Middle Winterslow, and Winterslow. It leaves the metalled road at the last village by a straight piece of lane and track which seems to be heading for Pitton, but the direct line to the village is taken up by a footpath and the track bends east of the village to come out as a lane a furlong or so south of it.

It has come now to a region of large woods, coppices and plantations which was once part of Clarendon Forest, in the Middle Ages a royal forest, where the use of a through trackway would be discouraged. Later it became part of the Clarendon estate, so that it is unlikely that the original line of the track can now be found. One can only conjecture its continuation after the next quarter-mile of lane south-west from the Pitton–Farley road. It might be the branch which, following a parish boundary, turns south to wind along the east margin of a wood and then becomes the road between the woods of Clarendon House and Nightwood Copse and continues with the parish boundary to the north-west corner of Common Plantation. Here the line of a minor road could have brought it south-west to Alderbury. Taking this to have been its course, its further course would then bring it eventually to the Pepperbox, perhaps along the line of the Salisbury–Southampton main road for a mile or so to avoid the stream and the marshy ground about West Grimstead. At the Pepperbox it would meet the Lymington Ridgeway coming north from Redlynch across Barford, Standlynch and Witherington Downs (*see* Map 2).

The run of the other fork from Easton Down is obscure in the first two miles south-west over Porton Down, which is also War Department country. But three-quarters of a mile of track which can still be seen going along Thorny Down leads to the main Salisbury–Stockbridge road, and the line may then be that of the main road for the next mile or so, passing the end of a track from Figsbury Rings, to where the main road crosses the Roman road near Hillcrest Bungalow. The remainder of the course to Old Sarum—about two and a half miles—is on the line of the Roman road, which either overlies the older trackway or supersedes it. Today this stretch of the Roman road is metalled and there is no necessity to cross the Bourne by the ancient ford through the river.

Perhaps the most interesting feature of this trackway is that it passed over Easton Down, once a busy meeting-place of half a dozen green ways, where Dr J.F.S. Stone discovered in 1930 and excavated in 1931 and 1932 some prehistoric flint mines and the homes of the miners and their families. He also discovered there and excavated a burial ground in which graves in the chalk contained urns and cremated human bones. Until the mines and their workshop floors were revealed it was not known that flint-mining had been carried on in Wiltshire. All these remains show that Easton Down was probably a site of prehistoric activity from late Neolithic times to the early Bronze Age at least. Beads found in an urn in one of the graves—one segmented bead of blue faience, three of amber and four of jet—are evidence of trade contacts with regions far beyond the borders of Wiltshire.

Ordnance Survey Maps

Salisbury. Sheet 167. 1 inch to 1 mile. 1940
Winchester. Sheet 168. 1 inch to 1 mile. 1945

10

THE TRACK FROM WALBURY CAMP
TO TIDBURY RING

Approximately 13 miles

THE MAIN chalk ridges of Hampshire run east to west so that the ridgeways naturally cross the county in the same direction, but there are shorter, north-to-south, trackways which link up the major ridgeways and the major earthworks, though the geographical evidence is more involved and these are less easy to follow today. Apart from the fact that Hampshire has been intensively cultivated since Roman times, one must remember that much of the higher ground as well as the lowlands was once covered with forests. The Chute country, especially on the southern slopes, is still thickly wooded. Remnants of Chute Forest remain as Collingbourne Wood, Doles Wood and Harewood Forest, which are mostly oaks with an undergrowth of hazel and other shrubs. The clay-with-flints which covers the chalk in many places on the uplands is responsible not only for the larger woods but for the woodland aspect of the hedges and the patches of scrub on hillsides which even today give the impression that if the land were left uncultivated or uncropped the forest would soon march in and take possession.

Parts of the earliest trackways must have been obliterated when the forest first began to be cleared. Later on, when separate woods were enclosed, other pans would disappear, not only because of the felling and replanting, but also because once they cease to be in general use tracks through woods become overgrown and are finally lost. This can be seen happening today in many an old enclosed lane no longer used by farm traffic or villagers. Free-growing hedge trees and bushes grow towards each other and intermingle their boughs, making tunnels of dank shade, while the undisturbed deposits of dead leaves and other decayed vegetation make a forcing ground for self-sown and bird-sown seedlings. An old lane of this nature is often all that remains of a once open trackway, for during the eighteenth and nineteenth centuries a trackway was often defined by banks and planted with hedges, not for the benefit of those who used them but to enclose the estates and farmland on either side, so that cattle and sheep being driven along them, as well as coach traffic and other travellers, should not stray on to private land. It was an arduous job to get rid of this kind of lane-thicket by cutting down the trees and grubbing up the roots before the days of bulldozers and other mechanical aids, and farmers usually let them stand; but today it can be a quicker and simpler operation. Though this helps the farmer to achieve the large uninterrupted fields more easily cultivated by modern farm machinery, it makes the job of discovering the line of an old road more difficult, and may explain many of the gaps it is impossible to fill in today.

One of these cross-trackways, that from Walbury Camp, the hill-fort on the east shoulder of Inkpen Hill, to Tidbury Ring, four miles or so south of Whitchurch, is described in an article in the *Proceedings of the Hampshire Field Club,* 1924, by Christopher Burne, who worked it out with the aid of Dr. Williams-Freeman, the Hampshire archaeologist, who has done so much to keep interest in the old roads alive, and Mr. Arthur Burne, another enthusiast and authority on old roads.

From the east corner of Walbury Camp (*see* Map 8) a grass track begins to fall gently from the summit and goes south-east to meet the metalled lane coming south from Woodhay Down. After keeping south-east for about two furlongs it turns south and begins to climb again to 942 feet on Combe Hill, with Combe village about half a mile to the west under the shoulder of the hill which holds the great earthwork. Combe is as isolated a village as any in Wessex. The roads about it are high and lonely and its nearest neighbours scattered farms and small villages as remote as itself. It is shut in by hills on all sides except the south. On the north it is overshadowed by the high steeps of Walbury Hill and on the east by Combe Hill only a few feet lower. On the west are Summer and Sheepless Hills, and on the south an area of hill farms and large woods stretches away for miles, dissected by waterless valleys and the roads winding about them.

The view from Walbury Camp on a clear day is said to include six counties, Berkshire, Hampshire, Wiltshire, Buckinghamshire, Surrey and Sussex, and on exceptionally clear days Dorset and Somerset as well; so here would be the spot to see most of Wessex spread before one, but from Combe Hill the most continuously extensive views are southward. The ground on each side of the road falls away to reveal hill-slope after hill-slope and the general impression is of a way coming down out of the highest upland solitudes.

From Combe Hill this ridge road continues south through Faccombe and almost a mile beyond to Kimmer, where the metalled road turns south-south-west from the ridge to go downhill through Faccombe Wood and join the Netherton-Hurstbourne Tarrant road, whilst the trackway, now lost for most of the next two miles, went straight on with the ridge. Christopher Burne shows how it kept the line by crossing a field to Doiley Wood and then passing through the woods on the course of a ride to come out on the south edge. Doiley Wood is not named on the latest 1-inch O.S. map, but it can be found named on earlier maps as a south-east extension of Faccombe Wood. South of Doiley Wood for the three furlongs to the Andover–Newbury main road (A 343) there is again a blank, since this track formerly went through woodland grubbed up within living memory. On the opposite side of the Andover–Newbury road it is also lost, but Christopher Burne gives convincing evidence of its existence before the woodland which covered this area was also grubbed up. He spoke with an old man who had helped to do the job and who told him of two rides, one on the line of the track, which had crossed each other at right angles on top of the little hill to the south of Essebourne Manor. This is a good illustration of how reaches of ancient roads have been obliterated.

If one continues the line south-east over the hill it comes to a short length of field track leading to a minor road winding south along the ridge to the Stoke villages. This is our way until it comes to the Stoke–Binley road and continues on the other side as a green lane winding down to Gang Bridge on the Bourne Rivulet. The Bourne is often dry in summer at Gang Bridge, and at no time would present a formidable crossing. After crossing the stream the track keeps along the bank for about a quarter of a mile and then climbs out of the valley as an old, wide, deeply sunken lane to a meeting place of ways called Five Lanes End above St. Mary Bourne village.

The south-east continuation of the lane after coming to this old meeting-place of ways soon becomes a footpath, crossing the Roman road and then the main railway line from Salisbury to London by a farm-bridge, and after this the Harrow Way half a mile west of Chapmansford. Still keeping its south-easterly line, it continues as Apsley Lane past Apsley Farm to Hurstbourne Common, and more as a rough cart track than a lane comes to the Whitchurch–Andover road on Hurstbourne Hill. Beyond this road the cart track turns south-west, but to get to Tidbury Ring our line keeps on as a footpath along a parish boundary, though the path is not marked on the 1-inch map. First by the side of a hedge and then between cultivated fields it comes to the Hurstbourne–Longparish road and the River Test.

It could have crossed the Test near a footbridge where Christopher Burne says there is a fordable place. He also suggests that the water here may have been lower in the old days before it was held up by a mill two or three hundred yards below. Across the river a footpath leads to a byway which goes past Larkwhistle Farm and under the Newbury–Winchester railway line. In another mile and a half the footpath comes within a field's distance of Tidbury Ring before going on to Tidbury Farm and its meeting with the A 303 road to Andover.

Ordnance Survey Map

Winchester. Sheet 168. 1 inch to 1 mile. 1945

11

THE LUNWAY

Approximately 42 miles

THE Lunway goes east and west across central Hampshire between the Harrow Way on the north and the South Hants Ridgeway on the south, though it is nearer to the South Hants Ridgeway for most of its course and finally joins up with it. It seems to have acquired its name from the fact that it was once on a direct route to London, the name then being kept alive by the obstinacy of tradition against forgetting what was once important long after any reason remains for its continuance. Or it may be more correct to say that the name became rationalized in the explanation. Sixteenth-century documents, according to Dr. Grundy, name the road north-east from Alresford to Bighton 'The London Way'; its continuation through Alton is still the direct route to London today.

Where the Lunway touches the north boundary of Crawley parish, two or three miles east of Stockbridge, it is called the 'Lundun herepath' in a Crawley Anglo-Saxon charter, and in an Easton charter is the 'Lundun Weg' just before it comes to the Lunway Inn on the Winchester–Basingstoke main road, so that the name goes back to Saxon times. The fact that it keeps to the watershed between the Itchen and the Mitcheldever Brook and passes through no villages suggests it was in use before then and was afterwards used by the Saxons as pan of a through way to London from the west.

It runs east from Old Sarum (*see* Map 4) as a minor road over the downs between the convergent Avon and Bourne and crosses the Bourne and the A 338 road from Salisbury before joining, near Hillcrest Bungalow, the A 30 Salisbury–London road, which then takes it in less than five miles to where the A 30 road divides at Lopcombe Corner and sends off the A 343 road north-east to Andover. The main London road continues to Stockbridge, first crossing the Wallop Brook near Nine

Mile Water Farm, and this road must be more or less on the line of the Lunway to its crossing of the Test at or near Stockbridge, a more serious crossing than the one over the tiny Wallop Brook. It may have cut across the bend the main road makes to go round the small isolated Meon Hill, where there is still an old footpath.

Across the Test it passes very close to Woolbury Camp, which lies two or three hundred yards south of the A 30 road beyond Stockbridge. The camp stands on a high ridge of down which rises steeply up from the river on the west and falls less steeply on the east, and the track probably kept along the ridge until it falls to the general level of the plateau. The view from the earthwork has Salisbury Plain to the west, with Danebury standing up in the foreground and Quarley Hill beyond, all three camps visible from each other, while to the east Hampshire opens out. Having now left forest country behind, arable fields and downs can be seen far and wide to the horizon, the patches of woodland emphasizing its openness instead of concealing it.

An ancient track comes to Woolbury from Danebury (*see* pages 93-95), crossing the Test at Longstock, a mile or so north of Stockbridge, and Dr. Williams-Freeman, in *Field Archaeology*, mentions a worn track running east over the down from the camp. The latter may not be the Lunway but a branch from it that went to the camp. It is not possible to tell today how the Lunway passed Woolbury, for the track has been lost under cultivation. We pick it up again (*see* Map 3) going along the north edge of the woods around Philip's Heath House, and from there it comes in about a mile to a crossing-place of tracks near Leckford Down Farm, known in coaching days as Leckford Hut, for at this crossroads the old coach road from Salisbury to London, now replaced by the A 30 through Stockbridge, turned north-east to Sutton Scotney and Basingstoke.

The Lunway, however, as a ridgeway between the Itchen and the Mitcheldever Brook, continues east as a lane and a parish boundary to the Roman road from Winchester to Mildenhall—here incorporated into the B 3420 road—passing a long barrow, two field systems and a tumulus on its way. There is a short gap east of the B 3420 road, but a quarter-mile south along it a track following a parish boundary takes the line on for half a mile to the A 34 road. Taylor's map of 1755 shows the Lunway continuous across the Roman road. Still following the parish boundary to the south of South Wonston, it keeps east on a very straight length for a mile and a half to a byway coming south from Stoke Charity, the straightness suggesting it may have been Romanized to lead to some now unknown Roman site. At this point the track ends but the parish boundary goes on and indicates a line crossing the railway south of Waller's Ash Tunnel and along the north edge of Burnt Wood to the Lunway Inn on the Basingstoke–Winchester road.

At the Lunway Inn it is joined by the Saxon Drove coming from Barton Stacey which has run roughly parallel to and about three furlongs north of the Lunway and on the crest of the ridge for the past three miles. From the A 30 road to the A 33 road—a distance of about five miles—this drove must be one of the finest examples in the county of a Saxon way that has not been taken into the modern system of metalled roads, and it is easy to see why the actual line of the Lunway from South Wonston to the Lunway Inn has fallen into disuse and become confused with the Saxon way. The drove leads south from Barton Stacey to the A 30 and then swings south-east in a continuous stretch of over five miles. It is interesting to note that the Lunway keeps south of the ridge-crest while the drove keeps on the crest. One cannot help wondering why an entirely new Saxon road should have been evolved when there was one already existing for several miles of the way, unless the Lunway had already fallen into disuse when the Saxon drove was made. There are no geographical reasons to make one more acceptable than the other, and it is the Lunway which follows the parish boundary.

The drove coincides with the Lunway as it goes east for a mile after leaving the Basingstoke–Winchester road (A 33), where it is metalled, and then turns south-east again as a track over Itchen Stoke Down to come to Alresford. When the drove and the Lunway separate, at the north-east corner of Itchen Wood, the Lunway continues nort-east as a metalled road and crosses the Candover stream at Totford. 'Candover' is said to mean 'the beautiful stream', and it certainly deserves the name as it winds between woods to join the Itchen at Itchen Stoke. Professor Hawkes suggests in an article in the *Proceedings of the Hampshire Field Club* that in late prehistoric or Roman-British times a branch grew out from this part of the Lunway and went to join the Itchen at Itchen Stoke the road that in medieval times became known as the Pilgrims' Way from Canterbury, and that the Saxon drove took the same course as this branch from where it leaves the Lunway to the tumuli on Itchen Stoke Down, the drove then turning off to Alresford.

After crossing the river at Totford the Lunway could have taken either of two lines which come together on Herriard Common near Bagmore about seven miles to the north-east. One goes south-east as a parish boundary and then east as a green lane to Bogmoor, afterwards curving round the south edge of Godsfield Copse—in the coppice hollow tracks can be seen—and keeping south of Wield Wood and passing the south edge of Barton Copse before changing to a footpath to Wield village. A footpath between the villages of Wield and Lower Wield may continue the line. From Lower Wield it then goes on along the ridge to Burkham House by footpath and lane, the nature of the ground dictating its winding course.

The byway north from Burkham House points to Herriard Common, but there is a short break between it and the end of the track continuing the line across the west fringe of the Common, which is where the other branch from Totford meets it.

The second branch from Totford, which Professor Hawkes suggests may be a summer way of the Lunway, is now a green lane going approximately north-east without a break for about five miles across the downs, leaving Juniper Hill on the right and passing a tumulus on the left before it comes to a minor road from Preston

Candover to Bradley, about three furlongs north-west of Bradley. It goes on as a parish boundary and byway, now through wooded country, rising gently and passing over Bradley Hill to reach Herriard Common and the other branch of the Lunway.

From here the Lunway could have joined the Harrow Way a little west of Bagmore and continued to a meeting with the summer way of the Harrow Way at Five Lanes End (*see* Map 8). In Herriard Park, as it goes north-east to the summer way, the track is lost, but it can be picked up again going along Priors Hill, where it becomes one of the tracks leading to the meeting-place of ways at Five Lanes End.

A branch from Barton Copse to Four Marks is described in Chapter 13.

Ordnance Survey Maps

Salisbury. Sheet 167. 1 inch to 1 mile. 1940
Winchester. Sheet 168. 1 inch to 1 mile. 1945

12

THE SOUTH HANTS RIDGEWAY

FROM PEPPERBOX HILL TO BUTSER HILL

Approximately 31 miles

THE Ridgeway which runs east and west across southern Hampshire was once part of a trade route which spanned the whole south country. From Beachy Head across Sussex and Hampshire it comes into south Wiltshire and there, on Salisbury Plain, could have joined any of the routes to the ancient west country seaports as well as those on the south coast between Christchurch and Weymouth Bay. Although most archaeologists agree that there must have been such a through route (and the tradition of its existence is still strong), the direct line today must be eked out in many places with conjecture and imagination. It seems likely that long sections of the Roman road from Old Sarum to Winchester took the place of the pre-Roman trackway, so that its continuity was lost long before modern times. The Saxons, who preferred the river valleys, would use only such parts of it as were useful to them, while the medieval pilgrims and travellers followed the lower Saxon roads whenever possible because of the hospitality of the inns and religious houses to be found in the villages or beside the rivers. The line also runs through much wooded country and heathland, difficult country in which to trace an old road.

From the Pepperbox, on the A 36 road about five miles south-east of Salisbury (*see* Map 4), a track following a parish boundary goes north-east, with narrow woods first on one side then on the other, and rising gently comes to the long ridge of Dean Hill in about two miles. Keeping just south of the scarp-crest in true ridgeway fashion, the track continues east towards the county boundary, which it crosses about half a mile south of East Dean, and then runs along the edge of Deanhill Wood north of the boundary.

After it leaves the Dean Hill ridge and the county boundary the course of its first two miles or so in Hampshire can only be roughly plotted today. It has no distinct ridge to carry it on its way to the Test crossing, for this border country is much broken into small hills with byways winding about them, and the soil is gravel with some clay, so that in earlier times it was probably covered with woodland. A suggested route which avoids the Lockerley stream flowing to join the Test—though it also keeps a mile or so south of Lockerley Camp which is on the south bank of the stream—follows a parish boundary beside Brokes Copse and continues as a lane past Gambledown Farm and Tote Hill to come to Newtown. From there a footpath takes it to Kent's Oak, where a metalled byway brings it to Kimbridge and the river. As this is gravel country the crossing would not be a difficult one. Romsey, about three miles away, has been famous for its gravel for centuries, and the gravel pits at Awbridge, not far from Kimbridge, have been a hunting-ground for seekers after palaeolithic implements for many years. Not, of course, that these worked flints have anything to do with the men who walked the trackway and crossed the river here in pre-Roman times; they date from an age so distant that they seem to belong to the geologist rather than the archaeologist.

Having crossed the river the track probably followed the line of the modern road past the Bear and Ragged Staff to Michelmersh. Its line through the village has been lost, but north-east a lane running south of Stubb's Copse may be close to the way it went. An old map shows its continuation along the ridge covered by Parnholt Wood, and there are vestiges of an old track through the wood. It goes on over Farley Mount Down as a wide lane and joins the Old Sarum–Winchester Roman road in West Wood (see Map 3).

The Roman road now takes its place, keeping north of Pitt Down under West Wood, Shedden Oak Copse and Crab Wood. This is forest country, another reason why a trackway would tend to die out, if, indeed, it lasted beyond the time of the Roman occupation. The original trackway would probably have run a little inside the present-day woods north of the Roman road and have continued over Teg Down to Weeke and the Test ford at Winchester, but there is nothing to suggest the line except a footpath through Crab Wood. We can only follow the Roman road to Winchester.

South from Winchester a minor road, which is also the line of a Roman road, goes past St. Catherine's Hill to rise to Deacon Hill. This hill has many old trails, especially on its north side, which may be the last vestiges of the Ridgeway. A track, footpath and then a lane along Deacon Hill to Telegraph Hill may be on the line, for on Telegraph Hill there are traces of hollow trails to Cheesefoot Head on the main road to Petersfield, while in a coppice on the north side of the main road there are more old trails.

From Cheesefoot Head the modern road (A 272) takes it on to the north of Lane End Down, and here traces of an old road south of the modern road can be seen as a slight fold in a cultivated field, and this is marked on Isaac Taylor's map of 1755 as going south-east to Lane End Down. Passing a tumulus on the right, hollow ways descend the hill, gradually narrowing and fading out as they come to the foot of the hill. From Lane End, about a quarter of a mile east of Lane End Farm, the way coincides with the modern Winchester–Warnford road and in about a mile comes to the Fox and Hounds Inn crossroads. Here, about a tumulus called Mill Barrow, faint trails can still be seen. The Ridgeway continues along the Warnford road, now accompanied by a parish boundary, until it comes to a tumulus just north of Wind Farm. The Warnford road is broad and drove-like with grassy margins and overhung on the right with trees, while on the left it falls gradually to an area of fields and cultivated downland. It is a very pleasant, quiet road all the way to Warnford, margined with narrow fields and coppices on each side until it falls to the valley which holds the village and the River Meon, suggesting that it was once a much wider road.

The Ridgeway, however, leaves it near Wind Farm to keep on higher ground and take a more south-easterly course, first to Lomer along a line marked only by a parish boundary and then as a parish boundary and lane to Beacon Hill. There are very deep hollow ways down Beacon Hill which wind south and are lost in the fields. The line of one is taken up by a lane which leads to a ford above Exton. This crossing is the 'shallow ford' in an Anglo-Saxon charter. It is possible that the continuation of the road from Wind Farm to Warnford is a loop or branch of the Ridgeway. From the river crossing at Warnford and from the Exton ford there are tracks up to the ridge of the southern chalk range which leads into Sussex and which holds the finest reach of the South Hants Ridgeway left to us today, a reach where one can have no doubt as to the way it went.

From the Exton ford a parish boundary along traces of a path—the path is not shown on the O.S. map—leads to and up the west spur of Old Winchester Hill to the hill-fort on the summit and on to the lane that rises from Warnford between high wooded banks and passes near the east side of the earthworks. The banks and trees along this lane shut out the view on each side, so that when one comes to the top of the rise where the lane widens into what must once have been a broad drove skirting the summit plateau of Old Winchester Hill, there is a sudden revelation of spaciousness.

Old Winchester Hill is rightly one of the county's treasured hills, and as it is now in the care of the Nature Conservancy the extensive cultivation of all the surrounding countryside ceases at its foot, so that, standing up some 400 feet above the Meon valley and more than 650 feet above sea level, it still keeps its ancient turf dotted with juniper and thorns and other scrub. A yew wood makes a patch of sooty blackness, and the massive banks of the camp on the western extremity of the ridge-spur seem to have been moulded and smoothed into their oval rings to make a crown for this venerable place, a crown whose inner circlet is embellished with a cluster of green round barrows. There is a thin capping of clay and sand over its chalk in places and this gives it a particularly interesting and varied vegetation, for as well as the yew, juniper and other chalk-loving trees and shrubs, and the orchids, cowslips and small aromatic herbs of downland turf, it also has plants which prefer sandy and clay soils. A track makes a darker green band across the turf to the camp, and from both track and camp there is a southern view to the Isle of Wight, while northward the Medstead ridge keeps the eye in Hampshire. East Meon's grey little church under hanging woods looks very peaceful in its narrow valley, while four miles to the east Butser Hill stands up, the last great landmark before the traveller passes into Sussex.

As today's metalled lane the Ridgeway, in about a mile, comes to the neat modern crossroads on Teglease Down which has taken the place of an ancient five-went way. The tumuli once so plentiful about it cannot be seen now: they have been reduced by ploughing to a slight swell in the ground here and there. The Ridgeway here is open to the view, with arable fields on each side, though we did see some sheep, as was fitting, on Teglease Down. It has been narrowed in places to a meagre width by wire fencing where its marginal ground has been taken in for cultivation. We could not help remembering an old Welsh law which says: 'Sixscore pence is due to the Lord for ploughing up a road, but nothing is due for sowing it nor for harrowing it, since there is no penalty for improving it.'

Dr. Grundy mentions a track which branches north-west three-quarters of a mile past the crossroads and was called the White Water Way in a Chidden charter and Water Way in a Meon charter. Its beginning has been lost but its continuation from below the ridge can be seen as a lane going north from Coombe past Hole House and along the edge of the little valley west of Hen Wood. Dr. Grundy suggests that the name White Water Way came from the chalk-clouded water of the brook which rises at Seal's Spring south of Whitewool Farm.

In another half-mile a grassy track which can still be seen goes off over Wether Down. Here a slope too steep to plough has kept its old turf and a thin scattering of bushes, and noticing it one realizes how cultivation has changed the appearance of the downs since the days when they were open sheep-walks. By clothing them afresh each year, from the bright greens of springing corn through all the changing tones of ripening to the pale yellow of stubble, it has taken away that look of hoary antiquity which once emphasized the difference between the lowland and the upland world. But in spite of these changes and the narrowed width and wire fencing, this stretch of road from Old Winchester Hill to where it goes secretively under Hyden Wood is still a trackway which rides the ridge.

On the opposite side of the road, about fifty yards beyond the track over Wether Down, several disused hollow ways fan out as they descend a shallow coomb in the direction of Chidden and Hambledon, to fade away in the grassy bottom of the coomb and become a footpath. We have wondered whether this was once a 'salt way' coming from salterns on the Hampshire shore and continuing as the track over Wether Hill and Salt Hill.

Between Chidden Down and where the Ridgeway descends to cross the East Meon–Clanfield road, the huts and other buildings of a naval station line the road, and H.M.S. Mercury is proclaimed on a signboard near its entrance. But though the sailors have come to the Ridgeway the old road has still many miles to go before reaching the sea, yet from it the Solent and the Isle of Wight can be glimpsed at many points along these miles of its course from Old Winchester Hill.

The continuation of the Ridgeway across the East Meon–Clanfield road takes it along a narrow green lane under the north side of Hyden Wood. Looking back as one enters the lane the slope to the crossroads can be seen scored with old tracks long disused and spreading out in characteristic fashion as they fall to its foot. Although open on the left to the Meon valley the lane as it begins to rise is so deeply sunken below the level of the fields that the view is much restricted. Brambles and tall rank herbage also help to enclose it, and in places briars and shrubby growth on the low bank on the woodland side as well leave scarcely enough room for two people to walk abreast. The Ridgeway no longer soars, but creeps along, overhung by the tall old trees of the wood and shut off in its damp hollow from the world beyond. The woodland plants growing on the mossy right bank and the vistas between the trees can make it a very pleasant way in spring and summer, though not easy walking. At one time the lane has been roughly metalled, but the surface is now broken and overgrown by tussocks of grass and the usual tough weeds which grow on trackways.

Still rising, the Ridgeway comes to Tegdown Hill, where it leaves the woods. Ahead there is only the bare massive shape of Butser Hill to be seen, the details of its steep sides and complex of coombs and shoulders about the main summit plateau getting clearer with every step along the three-quarters of a mile to a branching of tracks opposite Oxenbourne Down, which is Butser's southward extension and itself no mean hill. On the other side of Butser is War Down, another great and steep hill of chalk, and between them the winding narrow pass through which the main road (A 3) goes south to Portsmouth. Continuing east from the north end of War Down is the scarp-ridge that takes the South Hants Ridgeway on past Sunwood Farm and across the county boundary to become a Sussex ridgeway; and to reach it the way must, of course, either have gone round the south ends of the two intervening hills or have passed over their summits.

At the branching of tracks on the shoulder west of Oxenbourne Down the right-hand fork takes the direction round the hills by leading south-east to Hog's Lodge and the main road, from the other side of which, but a little along it towards the hills, a track leads off north-east up the dry narrow valley at the foot of War Down to the top of the scarp near the lime works above Buriton, and there turns eastward to pick up the Ridgeway again. Yet the left-hand fork leading north-east and through entrenchments set across the neck of Butser's south spur was the course of the original track. This is made plain by Professor Stuart Piggott in his account of Butser Hill published in *Antiquity* in June 1930. Near the entrenchments the track sprays out into one or two branches, the main way being that which continues east along the edge of the summit plateau and then drops down a spur into the modern cutting traversed by the Portsmouth road. In coming down it divides into a number of deeply grooved and more or less parallel hollow ways such as are often seen where a trackway descends a hillside. Some of them must be old branches that were superseded by new when the wear and tear of use and the erosion of weathering made them too narrow, deep and rough. Beyond the cutting the way goes diagonally up the side of War Down and over the hilltop to where, above Buriton and joined by the hill-foot track from the south end of War Down, the ridge takes it along east-ward into Sussex.

Discussing the branches leading from the main Ridgeway on Butser, Professor Piggott gives evidence on which he suggests that a very sunken track going north from the summit and descending to the valley in the direction of Petersfield may be as old as the Bronze Age, and that it was the link between the Butser settlements of this period and an outlying one on Petersfield Heath three miles away, where there is a group of round barrows.

Ordnance Survey Maps

Salisbury. Sheet 167. 1 inch to 1 mile. 1940
Winchester. Sheet 168. 1 inch to 1 mile. 1945
Portsmouth and Southampton. Sheet 132. 1 inch to 1 mile. Popular Edition, 1919

The Harrow Way between Basingstoke and Andover, Hampshire
Photo: Monica Hutchings

The Harrow Way above Amesbury, Wiltshire
Photo: Monica Hutchings

The Harrow Way near Great Ridge Wood, Wiltshire
Photo: Monica Hutchings

The Harrow Way approaching Compton Pauncefoot, Somerset
Photo: Monica Hutchings

13

BRANCHES AND LOOPS OF THE SOUTH HANTS RIDGEWAY

Pitt Down to Merdon Castle

Approximately 2 miles

FROM the meeting-place of five tracks on Pitt Down (*see* Map 3), four miles west of Winchester and about a furlong south of the Roman road, a track leads south-west for half a mile and then turns sharply south to pass Violet Hill, where there are several hollow ways going in the same direction. From Violet Hill it curves south-east to pass above Southlynch Plantation, coming at the north edge of Hursley Park to Merdon Castle, an earthwork in which a Norman castle once stood inside the banks of a prehistoric camp.

Merdon, or Merdun, was the assembly place of a Saxon Hundred and the chief manor of the district, so its historic interest has been continuous from early times. The earthwork stands on a chalk ridge which in its natural state would be downland, and yew trees flourish there. The old road past Violet Hill goes between many yew trees which give it a processional air, as of a road leading to a very special place, though, of course, they must have been planted long after the prehistoric earthwork and the Norman castle were deserted and ruinous. On the banks of the camp itself there are several yews of great age and size. One of the largest grows on the main rampart of the Norman castle, so that it may have been growing since the early part of the twelfth century when the Norman castle was destroyed.

This short branch from the South Hants Ridgeway may be part of a track which linked Woolbury Camp near Stockbridge with the Merdon earthwork.

DEACON HILL TO TEG DOWN

From the angle made by the Roman road on Deacon Hill, a mile or so south-east of Winchester, a track branches from the South Hants Ridgeway and runs along the north edge of a belt of trees going approximately south-west to the golf-course on Twyford Down, passing a field system on the left and a settlement south of St. Catherine's hill-fort on the right. After about a mile it leaves the trees and turns south-south-west as a track and then a lane to come to the Portsmouth road just north of Twyford Lodge. It crosses the River Itchen near Shawford House and from Shawford on the opposite bank goes north-west and then north as a lane and track to Yew Hill, where there are many hollow ways and a cluster of tumuli. As a lane it runs along the west side of Oliver Cromwell's Battery, an earthwork which tradition says was thrown up by Oliver Cromwell to besiege Winchester Castle. As the castle was some two miles away this may be one of those traditions which show a confusion of folk memory, in which Oliver Cromwell became identified with an earlier warrior. Dr. J.P. Williams-Freeman in *Field Archaeology* says that 'it is more like the enclosure of some Bronze Age flockmaster'.

Following the lane on the west side of Oliver Cromwell's Battery it comes in less than half a mile to the Winchester–Romsey road (A 31), and, after crossing the road, a short length of track and then a break of two hundred yards or so bring it to the Roman road coming from Pitt Down. From the Roman road a footpath curving north-east over Teg Down and a final length of lane take it to Weeke to join up again with the probable course of the South Hants Ridgeway.

LANE END DOWN TO CHERITON

7 miles

CHERITON TO FOUR MARKS

In an article in the *Proceedings of the Hampshire Field Club*, 1925, Professor Hawkes traces a branch of the South Hants Ridgeway from Lane End Down, south of the Winchester–Petersfield road, to Four Marks. Signs of this route are even more difficult to find today, but a part of it runs so unmistakably along ridgeway country that it is hard not to believe that it once linked in some fashion, if not exactly as we shall describe, the South Hants Ridgeway, a branch of the Lunway, and the Medstead ridge north of Four Marks leading into Surrey.

From the summit of Lane End Down (*see* Map 3) this branch goes north-east to cross the Itchen at Cheriton. The first one and a half miles are obscure today, but a short length of the Owlesbury road to the main road and then a bit of open track and, after a gap, a footpath passing near Westfield Farm to Cheriton, may be the survival of the line. Across the Itchen, here only a tiny stream, a path through a timber yard leads up into the fields, and then a track and parish boundary take it to where it becomes a green road under the south edge of Cheriton Wood and continues as a lane past Old Park Wood and the north edge of Bramdean Common. This is the part which has ridgeway characteristics and is on the watershed between the uppermost reaches of the Itchen and the River Arle. East of Bramdean Common a footpath—on the line of a road called in Tisted charters the Way of the Pole— takes it to the West Tisted–Ropley road, and a short distance along this road there is a track and then a lane to Merryfield Farm.

To continue along the ridge the way has now to make a northward swing in the direction of Charlwood and Lyeway along a course that would bring it to Four Marks, where it could have joined up with a branch of the Lunway and thus continue to the Medstead ridge a mile or so north of Four Marks. As the crow flies the distance from Merryfield Farm to Four Marks is about three miles, but today's traveller must make sharp-angled turns through a criss-cross of metalled byways to come to it. How the early traveller got to Four Marks it is impossible to say. He would have a broad undulating ridge to follow, and perhaps the half-mile of road north from Plaindell Farm to Charlwood gives an indication of the line, together with the mile of footpath running north from the road near Willis's Farm to the main road in Four Marks. This would link up with the branch of the Lunway we have mentioned.

This branch leaves the Lunway near the south-east corner of Barton Copse half a mile south of Wield and is seen as an old lane going south from the Medstead road and into woods where it is lost. But the modern road from Heath Green to Hattingley and a footpath to Medstead continue the line. From there the likeliest course would first be that of the present road south-east over Roe Downs, west of Chawton Park Wood, and then a continuation to Four Marks.

SALT HILL TO WEST TISTED COMMON

West of H.M.S. Mercury on Wether Down a track branches north-east from the South Hants Ridgeway to go over Salt Hill (*see* Map 3), a name suggesting that it may have been on the route of one of the old salt ways coming from the salterns of the Hampshire shore. From Salt Hill the track drops down to Coombe Cross in the midst of an area of cultivated fields, an intersection of ways which, being named, was probably a more important route-point when the downs were open and the tracks across them carried not only local traffic but more general through traffic as well. From Coombe Cross our track goes roughly north to Henwood Down, where it is lost for the next mile or so through Hen Wood and in the grounds of Westbury House, though traces of a track can still be seen in Hen Wood. There is a short length of a way leading from the grounds of Westbury House which may point to the ford by which it crossed the River Meon, at this point a trickle of a stream less than a yard wide.

Beyond the river there are two branches, both going roughly north–north-east with only a quarter-mile or so between them. The more westerly of the two is a drove-like lane following a parish boundary for the first five furlongs and crossing the railway and the main Winchester–Petersfield road (A 272) before it comes to Stock Farm, this lane then continuing to Bailey Green. It is likely that this is a modern version of the old track which was lost when the railway line was laid down.

The other track from the river goes as far as Peak Farm as a footpath and then disappears, though a line north-west would take it across the railway to join the first branch where it comes to the main road. But there is evidence from an Anglo-Saxon charter that it continued north, and today, after a blank of nearly half a mile, it can be picked up beyond the main road as a footpath running north–east to Privett. A road going north-west from Privett Church, called Street in a Meon charter, takes it to Bailey Green. The true line, owing to the making of the railway tunnel, is probably lost here.

The two branches now continue as one, taking the line of the minor road north from Bailey Green to the main road (A 32). In a field immediately north of Bailey Green vestiges of an old track or former road running parallel to and just east of the modern road are visible. In almost half a mile the minor road comes to the main London road at a point where four very large round barrows, known as the Devil's Jumps, stand in a line. From this point the course of the old track is not clear. It may be represented by the wide lane that runs west of Privett station to Lane End at Brickkiln Farm, and then by the footpath over West Tisted Common to where it would join another branch of the South Hants Ridgeway near Merryfield Farm, the one that leaves Lane End Down near Winchester and crosses the Itchen at Cheriton.

Ordnance Survey Map

Winchester. Sheet 168. 1 inch to 1 mile. 1945

14

THE LYMINGTON RIDGEWAY

Lymington to Redlynch

Approximately 23 miles

A HAMPSHIRE Ridgeway begins close to Lymington (*see* Map 2) and runs north-west across the New Forest to Redlynch on the Wiltshire border, its twisting course still followed by modern main roads for most of the way. It begins on the watershed between the Avon Water and Lymington River, going through Woodside and Pennington as a modern minor road, and not until it leaves Durns Town and the mile-long straggle of houses north of Durns Town does it get away from houses and come to the open heath of the Forest. At the north-east corner of Set Thorns Inclosure the road from Durns Town—which has all the appearance of a track that has been surfaced—comes into the road which runs across the New Forest from the Lymington–Lyndhurst main road to Picket Post and to that point is part of the Ridgeway. On the left it is at first overhung by the trees of Set Thorns Town, can be seen broken trails and shallow hollows which may once have been part of the original trackway. The trails and the main road keep to the ridge, while on a lower level the green of Long Slade Bottom, one of the grass-sown 'lawns' of the Forest, accompanies the road for nearly a mile, brilliant as a narrow jade-green lake in the swarthy covering of heather surrounding it. On all sides stretches the undulating dark moor patched with solid shapes of massed woodland, while woods fringe most of the sky-line and seem to quench the light which nearer Lymington comes from the sea as well as the sky.

Just before it reaches Wilverley Post, where it meets the main road from Lyndhurst to Bournemouth (A 35), our way passes the Naked Man, a skeleton tree-trunk enclosed by a railing on the north side of the road. However this came by its name, its blanched, naked appearance fits in well with the landscape, for on occasion this has a wild desolation, and at almost any time could serve as a scene for a melodrama in which benighted travelers encounter ghostly visitants who give them horrid warnings of evil to come. There are tumuli not far from the road. Because these mounds are made of the gravelly soil of the heath they are less shapely than the round barrows of the chalk downs, so that one never feels certain at first glance if they are tumuli or just large overgrown heaps of dumped earth and gravel.

The Ridgeway continues through Burley to Burley Street on the low ridge taken by the modern road to avoid the small streams and marshy ground on either side. As it comes to Burley Street the road curves through a small eastward bulge to avoid the lower slopes of Castle Hill which stands on its line, and it seems likely that the old track also avoided these slopes. There does not seem a sufficient flat width of ground on the slopes along which the track could run. Here the road is deeply sunken between wooded banks and holds the wet in rainy seasons, but in less than a furlong it begins to rise and leave the streams behind, coming to Picket Post in about a mile and a quarter.

From Picket Post it is on the watershed between Lymington River and the Wiltshire Avon, making a north-easterly turn to keep above the heads of the streams flowing into the Avon, and following the main road to Bratley Plain, where there is a six-went way of four tracks and the two arms of the main road from Ringwood to Cadnam (A 31). A tumulus stands on the left side of this meeting-place where the tracks radiate as dark green ribbons of fine turf winding through gorse and heather. The main Cadnam road goes on to Stoney Cross, but the Lymington Ridgeway leaves it at Bratley Plain to take the line of a byway winding a mile or so north of the road it has just left and passing Milkham Inclosure and Slufters Inclosure, and after one mile or so it turns eastward. There are tumuli here and there along it. After about three miles in which it is rising to Fritham Plain this byway is lost in the concrete runways and squares of a disused aerodrome, though it can be seen as a track with parallel trails vanishing into the aerodrome margin and can be picked up again a mile or so to the north where it approaches the Cadnam–Downton main road on Bramble Hill. From here, and for a mile and a half north-west to where it reaches its highest point at Telegraph Post, there is a tremendous view over the Forest on all sides. Far to the south-west are the Purbeck Hills, on the south-east the waters of the Solent and Southampton Water sparkle at the skyline on a sunny day, while the view west is over the Avon valley to the pale downs where the dark beech-clump on Clearbury Rings is very conspicuous.

The Forest now sheds some of its sombre colour, for there are woods margined with a clear green turf nibbled to a lawn-like closeness by the forest ponies, and green vistas between the tree trunks as well as open glades set about with clumps of bushes to break up the browns and dingy purples of its heathy ground-covering. There is much gorse-yellow to catch the sun, and the wind which nearly always blows on this high plateau gives light and movement to the leaves of ash, beech, oak and birch trees making up the mixed woods. Only about the conifer plantations are the gloomy static tones of the heathland intensified.

At Telegraph Post a well-defined track leaves the Lymington Ridgeway and goes south-west along the Hampton Ridge to the edge of the Avon valley at Frogham, a distance of about four miles. Here it becomes the minor road winding down the valley side to Fordingbridge. Across the Avon it ascends to the downs on the other side of the valley and comes to Whitsbury Down, where it joins up with a number of Wiltshire ridgeways. That this was an early route across the north-west corner of the New Forest there can be little doubt, for it passes many tumuli on its way and, when it has crossed the Avon and climbed to the downs on the other side, it goes very near to Whitsbury Camp before it finally comes to the open plateau holding the meeting-place of ways. It must also have been much used in Roman-British times as one of the routes along which the New Forest ware made in the potteries just below the Hampton Ridge was carried, for old tracks wind up to the ridge from the sites of the potteries, in places with broken trails accompanying them. These old trails have a rather ghostly look, for their sunken surface usually consists of the grey and white pebbles of the Forest gravel packed so hard into the barren ground that only an occasional pallid tuft of thin grass grows amongst them.

The Hampton Ridge lies above the marshy bottoms of Latch more Brook and Ditchend Brook, its treeless slopes covered with heath and low creeping gorse. North of it, between Ditchend Brook and more streams flowing into the Avon, another ridge of moorland leads away from the Avon valley and holds a ridgeway which is now part of the main road from Fordingbridge to Southampton. It and the Hampton Ridge track unite at Telegraph Post. The many tumuli along Hampton Ridge, however, suggest that its track was the more important route in earlier times.

From Telegraph Post this minor ridgeway first goes west-south-west to Picket Corner, where a number of green tracks come in, and then, after passing a large tumulus called The Butts, it goes along Cooper's Hill, close to the woods of Islands Thorns Inclosure, Amberwood Inclosure and Sloden Inclosure, all on the left. It then passes a tumulus between Long Bottom and Latchmere Bottom in coming to a branching-place of ways at Windmill Hill. This is the end of the ridge and most of the tracks descend to the river valley. Our track becomes the gravelled way leading west through a scattering of bungalows and houses half hidden behind conifers and gorse and bramble clumps to Frogham village, and from there is the minor road descending to Fordingbridge a mile and a half away.

Traces of the ford used before the first bridge was built can still be seen at Fordingbridge in a dry season. Immediately below the bridge the river, though wide, is shallow and has a gravelly shelving shore on the side away from the gardens behind the main street. A road called Green Lane, which until recent years was a green lane in fact as well as name, leads away north-west from the river and the Salisbury main road at the bridge end of the little town, winding past some old cottages to come into the drove-like road which leads over the railway to Radnall Wood and Tinkers Cross. From here the metalled road continues north-west to and through Whitsbury, having the wooded banks of Whitsbury Camp on the right at the north end of the village, but it seems likely that the original line of the trackway was several hundred yards east of and therefore higher than the modern road, where a track along the margin of a belt of woodland follows the crest of the narrow ridge and comes to the east side of Whitsbury Camp. North of the earthwork the track would enter the wide plateau of downland between the Avon and its feeder the Allen River, and there, on Whitsbury Down, would link up with several Wiltshire ridgeways.

But to return to the Lymington Ridgeway which, as it continues its way from Telegraph Post along the line of the main road from Cadnam to Downton, has passed to the watershed between the Avon and the Test. At Windyeats Farm, about halfway between Telegraph Post and North Charford, the Saxon Way, which O.G.S. Crawford named the Cloven Way, joins it after coming west from No Man's Land and mounting the steep wooded slope from Pound Bottom. About half a mile short of North Charford a lane branches west and joins a minor road leading down to Hale House in the Avon valley and to the ford below it, a lane which has all the appearance of an ancient track.

At North Charford itself a second lane goes off west and in a quarter of a mile divides into two branches, one leading a little north of west to Lodge Farm and the other keeping west and becoming a track which is open to fields on the left and has a narrow belt of woodland on the right. This track is reminiscent of other ridgeways about to make a descent to a valley bottom, and it looks as if it may represent a branch from the Lymington Ridgeway to the downs on the other side of the Avon. When it comes to the end of the first field it begins its fall to the valley, going past Searchfield Farm to come to the fords opposite North Charford Manor House. In recent times the river has been deepened by several feet and it would be impossible to ford it here now, but the wide, shallow trackway leading to it suggests a continuation beyond the river, while on the opposite side a lane leads up to cross the Salisbury–Christchurch road and then rise past North Charford Down Farm to Gallows Hill on Wick Down above the Avon valley, where it is joined by a track leading up from the ford below Hale House. It leaves Callows Hill through a gap in Grim's Ditch and continues over the downs to link up with the Ox Drove, the Salisbury Way and other ridgeways in south-west Wiltshire.

Returning again to the Lymington Ridgeway, it has now come to within a mile of Redlynch. As a Hampshire ridgeway it may be said to come to an end at Redlynch, where the main road it has followed from Bramble Hill makes an abrupt left turn to descend to Downton in the Avon valley. It has also come to the end of the New Forest and entered chalk country, which is evident not only from the lighter tones of the landscape but by the smooth swell of the land before it. It has now to link up with Salisbury Plain, and it does this by going north, first as a short stretch of metalled byway which goes on as a track over Barford Down. This is a typical chalk track sunken between high banks as it falls by some old wayside quarries and then rises to the open country beyond. Here it illustrates the truth of the statement that old roads wear in, not out. On the gravels of the New Forest, as on any heathland, this fact is not so evident, for the nature of the ground prevents them from wearing in so deeply.

The line goes on over Barford Down, Standlynch Down and Witherington Down, still as a track and open for most of the way. Not so many years ago these downs were sheep-walks, but today they are mostly arable fields or enclosed cattle pastures. Just north of Witherington Down the track meets the Salisbury–Southampton road (A 36), and near the Pepperbox joins the South Hants Ridgeway coming along the ridge of Dean Hill. At or near this point it was once joined by another track coming south across the Plain through the Winterslow villages and Pitton, a trackway which became lost in Clarendon Forest but which obviously once continued south to meet the other two ridgeways. It must also have linked the Channel coast with several routes from Salisbury Plain as it does today.

The Lymington Ridgeway, and its branch along the Hampton ridge which lies just above the sites of the New Forest potteries, must have served as a route along which the products of the potteries were distributed in Roman-British times. An article on Sorviodunum by Dr. J.F.S. Stone and D.J. Algar in the *Wiltshire Archaeological Magazine* for December 1955 suggests a possible way to Old Sarum from the New Forest potteries area by Downton and Petersfinger, which crossed the Bourne at Milford and then went north along the top of Bishopdown to Old Sarum. About a mile of this track leading south-east from Old Sarum still exists, though the development of the Paul's Dene housing estate on the southern slopes of the hill makes it less obvious than it was some twenty years ago. When, in 1953, a refuse dump of Roman-British date was discovered about 500 yards south-east of the east gate of Old Sarum the fragments of pottery dug up turned out to be almost entirely from the New Forest potteries.

At the Lymington end of the Ridgeway, from Buckland Rings, an earthwork a mile north of Lymington and overlooking the Lymington River, an old road called Silver Street passes the west side of the camp, and from its north-west corner goes direct to New Milton and thence to Christchurch. The area about Buckland Rings is now built up: there is even a bungalow and garden inside the camp itself, but beeches, oaks, birches and tall ragged bushes, with mounds of brambles and a ground-covering of bracken, keep it isolated in a woodland enclosure. From its east side a short lane leads down to the Lymington River and is a reminder that the camp guarded both the old road and the waterway.

Ordnance Survey Maps

Lymington. Sheets 179 and 180. 1 inch to 1 mile. 1945
Salisbury. Sheet 167. 1 inch to 1 mile. 1940

Two views from Sir Richard Colt Hoare's *Ancient History of Wiltshire*, 1812-19:
The Wansdyke on Tan Hill; Trackways near Stonehenge
Reproduced by permission of the Wiltshire Archaeological and Natural History Society

PURBECK FROM THE DORSET COASTAL RIDGEWAY
PHOTO: MONICA HUTCHINGS

THE GROVELY RIDGEWAY EMERGING FROM GROVELY WOODS, WILTSHIRE
PHOTO: MONICA HUTCHINGS

15

THE NORTH-WEST BERKSHIRE RIDGEWAY

A RIDGEWAY serving the north-west area of Berkshire and leading into North Wiltshire, where it could have linked up with the ridgeways coming from the Marlborough Downs, Salisbury Plain and the Cotswolds, crossed the river at North Hinksey near Oxford. The modern roads from Oxford were completely altered by the making of the turnpikes, and the crossing at Botley taken by the main road today does not seem to have been used for through traffic in pre-turnpike days. This eastern end of the north-west Berkshire Ridgeway, and of the pre-turnpike road to Cumnor and Faringdon, abuts on the river at North Hinksey, and for its first mile or so is a path to Chawley Brickworks. It reaches Cumnor from there as a stretch of minor road which is the north side of a triangle which it forms with the Wantage main road (A 420) and a road from Cumnor to Abingdon.

Continuing south-westward the modern road from Cumnor to Appleton is only partly on the line, for the old road went straight to Appleton instead of making the abrupt turn west for 200 yards or so towards Baton before continuing south-west.

On the 1820 1-inch O.S. map this line is still shown as a footpath. South-west of Appleton the modern road through the woods of Appleton Lower Common and Appleton Upper Common follows the line, and the name Street given to this part in an Anglo-Saxon charter suggests that the Romans adopted it here. Just beyond the woods the modern road goes abruptly south for two furlongs before continuing westward, probably to avoid marshy ground, for there is a Marsh Farm off the road close to the line it would have taken had it kept its direction; it seems likely that the trackway also made a curve southward at this point.

Still keeping on the ridge between the Thames and the Ock the road goes on a little south of Longworth and then along the south-east margin of Hinton Waldrist, but where the modern road turns south to join the main Faringdon–Abingdon road near Wellmore Farm a short length of track and footpath keeps the line to join up with the same main road farther west in Pusey Common Wood. From here the next four and a half miles of main road to Faringdon is a ridgeway and must have been the line the trackway followed.

A number of ridgeways and cross-ridgeways now represented by modern roads meet at Faringdon. Of the six main roads which radiate from the town in all directions—including the Highworth road which branches from the Great Coxwell road half a mile south of the town—the one going north-west to Lechlade appears to be least like the course of an ancient trackway. The line of the Ridgeway beyond Faringdon follows the Highworth road (B 4019), leaving Ring Clumps on the left and the camp in the woods of Badbury Hill on the right in its first two miles. It crosses the River Cole and the Wiltshire border on the west side of Coleshill and then rises to the little town of Highworth on its hill.

About half a mile south-west of Faringdon a branch probably made a link with the Great Ridgeway on the escarpment overlooking the White Horse Vale six miles or so to the south. To do this it was necessary to go south-west along the low watershed between the Ock and the Cole and above the damp meadows in which they run. This is the line of the Faringdon–Swindon road (A 420), which, as far as Shrivenham, is a ridgeway well above the streams on either side. After Shrivenham, however, the route is more difficult to determine. It may have turned approximately south to reach the foot of the downs at Ashbury or maybe Little Hinton, and thus could have joined the Icknield Way (*see* Map 27), but the many brooks in this part of the Vale would have caused miry going in wet weather. Even today the roadside fields are often patched with standing water after heavy rains or when the snows begin to melt.

Ordnance Survey Maps

Oxford and Newbury. Sheet 158. 1 inch to 1 mile. 1940
Swindon. Sheet 157. 1 inch to 1 mile. 1940

16

THE SUGAR WAY

Approximately 13 miles

A TRACK which once served the undulating belt of downland leading from the chalk uplands of north-west Berkshire to the Marlborough Downs can still be traced running roughly parallel to the Great Ridgeway between White Horse Hill to the east and the Upham ridge to the west. This track keeps between a mile and a half and three miles inward from the scarp over-looking White Horse Vale, and can be linked up with the Great Ridgeway by several cross-tracks over the downs which, before motor transport became common, were used by shepherds, drovers and wagoners taking their flocks, herds and corn to town markets and hilltop fairs. The memory of these days is still fresh in the minds of the older countryfolk, and we have been told many stories of adventures and mishaps which befell wagoners and drovers on their journeys through what was then a very lonely stretch of downs. Today, in spite of modern roads across them, they still feel very remote from the valley world.

We are calling the whole of this track the Sugar Way, from the name *Shuger Waie* which the O.S. map gives to it between the Upham ridge and Sugar Hill. The name is a rationalized form of *Scocera Weg* in the *Perambulations of Aldbourne*, 1591, and has been translated as the 'Way of the Robbers', a romantic sounding name today but which no doubt had a sinister meaning when it first came into use. Whether it took its name from the ridge called Sugar Hill, whose flank rises like a green wall on the left-hand side of the main road from Wanborough Plain to Aldbourne (A 419), we do not know. The hill, because of its long smooth shape, is a distinctive feature of this region, and the Sugar Way begins to cross it about three furlongs south of Liddington Warren Farm. The hill-ridge also has its own short trackway, which rises steeply out of Aldbourne as a rough hollow lane and for a mile or so continues as a definite track until it comes to four round barrows set in a row. Its continuation along the top of the ridge beyond the barrows used to be one of those green ways closely covered with wide-open daisies when the sun shone but showing up as a ribbon of darker, shorter turf in grey weather. Nowadays either fences or cultivation make it difficult to follow to the long barrow at the other end of the ridge and the line is no longer clear.

The Sugar Way (*see* Map 27) branches eastward from the track which goes south along the Upham ridge from Liddington Hill to Marlborough (*see* pages 26 and 57), leaving it near a tumulus half a mile north-east of Lower Upham Farm and opposite the head of a downland hollow called Shipley Bottom. It descends to the hollow and passes along it to reach tumuli beside the Aldbourne main road, which it crosses, and is soon a very deeply-grooved way up the side of Sugar Hill. It continues across Sugar Hill and along the edge of a beech plantation south of Popplechurch to cross first another road to Aldbourne and then Ermine Street on Peaks Downs. Popplechurch is thought to be the site of a Roman posting station. A parish boundary has followed the track all the way. For the next quarter-mile or so the Sugar Way looks as if it may have coincided with Ermine Street before continuing its course roughly eastward between Russley Park and Goorlane Farm, where it changes from a surfaced byway into a track going on past Botley Copse and over Fognam Down to the Ashbury–Lambourn road (B 4000) at Fognam Farm (*see* Map 28), and then east along this road past the strip lynchets on the side of Row Down to Upper Lambourn. On the slope of down above Fognam Farm there is a great white scar of chalk quarrying, and separate coppices and small woods are like outriders of the thick line of Ashdown woods; but both the white scar and the dark woods only help to emphasize the great expanse of unhedged cultivated fields on both sides. The road itself has broad green margins where woodland flowers grow tall and mingle with the downland wayside plants in the long grass, and is open on each side except for wire fencing.

Northward from Upper Lambourn several ridges of down fan out narrowly and lead to the escarpment overlooking the Vale of White Horse between Wayland's Smithy above Compton Beauchamp and Hackpen Hill above Sparsholt, and each of these ridges has its track leading to the Great Ridgeway. The most westerly of these, passing above Knighton Bushes, leads along Knighton Down to Knighton Barn and the Ridgeway a little east of Wayland's Smithy and above the wood containing Hardwell Camp. The next ridge is followed by the track which passes Hangman's Stone near Upper Lambourn and, lifting in an easy rise all the way, traverses Woolstone Down, where it passes Idlebush Barrow, and then Uffington Down in coming to the Ridgeway behind Uffington Camp. Idlebush Barrow is a Bronze Age tumulus about which a story used to be told locally to explain its name. A traveller, seeking direction from a shepherd boy lying in the shade of a hawthorn tree, could get no speech from him, only a sleepily lifted foot to point the way. The story is almost forgotten now and the track is fading out through disuse.

Another track goes by the Hangman's Stone on Wether Down, a stone which is a reminder of the days of poverty and hardship in the countryside when sheep-stealing was rife. The tale is one which is also associated with similar isolated stones in other sheep-rearing countries, of the sheep-stealer who was strangled by the cord with which he had tethered the sheep to the stone while he rested. From Wether Down the track goes to Longacre Farm and joins the metalled road running through a cluster of tumuli known as Seven Barrows—though there are more than seven—and on northward to the Great Ridgeway at the top of Blowingstone Hill. From the road-angle among the barrows another track continues north-east for about half a mile to join and follow the line of another metalled road from Lambourn which comes to the Great Ridgeway at a tumulus above the head of the Devil's Punchbowl, a tremendous bare coomb hollowed behind the beak of Hackpen Hill.

Metalled minor roads have almost superseded the old trackways in this area. On higher stretches many of the tracks have been cut by fences or lost in cultivation, and often it is only when they begin to fall to lower ground as sunken ways that their line can be picked up again. The dark rigidity of conifers planted as windbreaks and to seclude racing establishments make the downs about the Lambourns rather sombre. They lack the light and grace given by beech, ash and thorn.

Ordnance Survey Maps

Oxford and Newbury. Sheet 158. 1 inch to 1 mile. 1940
Swindon. Sheet 157. 1 inch to 1 mile. 1940

17

THE ROMANIZED RIDGEWAY FROM SPEEN

THE first fifteen miles or so of the Roman road north-west from Speen to Gloucester is a Romanized ridgeway following directly the ridge of the water-shed between the Kennet and Lambourn rivers. The rivers join on the east side of Newbury, and Speen stands on the narrowing tongue of the watershed about a mile north-west of the town. The road as a ridgeway ends at Fox Hill near Wanborough in North Wiltshire, a mile or so before the chalk scarp begins to fall steeply to the Swindon valley. It is now a minor metalled road all the way (B 4021).

From Speen the line of the trackway and the Roman road which superseded it heads for and crosses Wickham Heath. There are no obvious traces of the Roman road or the original trackway to be seen for the first four and a half miles, that is until it has left behind the gravel-covered tertiary beds and entered chalk country beyond Wickham. In a Boxford Anglo-Saxon charter a road corresponding to the line is called Herepath, and in a Boxford Tithe Award it is called Ridgeway Road. Only two short parts of the whole road form parish boundaries.

When it has left the heath behind, the road passes through no villages until, eight miles on, it comes to the hill village of Baydon on the Wiltshire border. Here it reaches 764 feet and is still rising, its highest point, 788 feet, coming a mile farther on at Peaks Downs (*see* Map 27). Membury Camp in its woodland lies about half a mile south of the road two miles before it comes to Baydon. From the top of Baydon Hill a wide lane changing to a green track, which has the appearance of great age, winds flexibly along the ridge of Green Hill and then descends its shoulder to reach the main road from Aldbourne to Hungerford in the valley. As the road climbs higher to Baydon hilltop and Peaks Downs the valley world is left behind and the view is all downland, with dark clumps and groves of beech trees accenting the flow of curves that make up the great shallow bowl of downs about Aldbourne and the Liddington and Upham ridges beyond, while on the Lambourn side also the downs stretch to a far horizon.

On Peaks Downs the road becomes the Ermine Street to Cirencester and Gloucester. The 1828 edition of the 1-inch O.S. map shows a track going roughly parallel to the metalled Ermine Street from Peaks Downs along the ridge of Hinton Down and meeting the Great Ridgeway between Charlbury and Totterdown, more generally known today as Fox Hill. The later maps show this track only as a footpath. This footpath through rough pasture and then cultivated downland is rarely used today and is fast becoming lost. Its beginning is seen as hollow trails in the field on the right where it leaves Ermine Street on Peaks Downs opposite the gap in the beech woods through which a track over the downs from Bishopstone— known there as the Aldbourne road—passes to descend to Aldbourne.

At Fox Hill, some two miles farther on, this footpath and Ermine Street are still only a quarter of a mile apart, Ermine Street continuing to Callas Hill where it drops steeply to the Swindon valley and goes on through Stratton St. Margaret to Cirencester and Gloucester. The footpath crosses the Great Ridgeway, but is now lost for the quarter of a mile which led across the angle between the green road and the road down the scarp from Fox Hill to Little Hinton. Beyond this byway the line is soon made clear again by a rough, well-worn track which descends into the large, irregular, thicket-dotted coomb that lies immediately west of Little Hinton village. It goes along the nearer side in coming out to the Icknield Way beside Hinton Post Office and not far from the field of the Seven Springs in the mouth of the coomb. After this the line probably coincides with the Icknield Way going east to Bishopstone at the foot of the scarp, but in about half a mile it leaves the Icknield Way and continues north to Shrivenham as a minor road.

At Shrivenham it joins the main road from Swindon to Faringdon, which would take it on to meet the North-west Berkshire Ridgeway.

Ordnance Survey Maps

Oxford and Newbury. Sheet 158. 1 inch to 1 mile. 1940
Swindon. Sheet 157. 1 inch to 1 mile. 1940
North Wiltshire. Sheet 34. 1 inch to 1 mile. 1828

18

THE RIDGEWAY BETWEEN AVON AND THAMES

THE modern road from Swindon to Malmesbury, which begins as the A 420 and after about five miles goes into the B 4042 near Coped Hall and continues to Malmesbury, is on the line of a low watershed between the Bristol Avon and the Thames. Its highest point, 447 feet, occurs when it becomes the B 4042 road, its average height being about 300 feet. All the way on each side there is a bewildering network of tiny streams running into larger brooks which in their turn go to swell the waters of the two rivers. The windings of the road have been made to keep it above these waters and the damp meadows they intersect, and it is unlikely that the line of the old road could have differed very much from the modern one. There are no traces of tumuli or earthworks along its course except for the earthwork on Cam's Hill near the Avon crossing at Cow Bridge south-east of Malmesbury, but all traces of prehistoric remains, if any existed, could easily have been lost, for this well-watered region between the upper Thames and the Avon has been in continuous occupation at least since Saxon times.

The road runs through an indeterminate countryside, making a kind of passage-way between the chalk of the North Wiltshire Downs and the limestone country of the Cotswolds, limestone walls and buildings predominating as it gets nearer to Malmesbury. It may have linked up with the main Cotswold Ridgeway coming from Bath on its way to the north Cotswolds and which passes eight miles west of Malmesbury, but there are no indications today of how the connection was made. All we can suggest is that it may have joined the Cotswold Ridgeway more or less along the line of the Malmesbury to Tetbury main road, and from Tetbury went to Chavanage Green, once a meeting place of trackways.

Two branches led off from the Swindon–Malmesbury Ridgeway at the crossroads some five miles west of Swindon where the A 420 road turns sharply south-west to go to Wootton Bassett. One branch went north and then turned away to wind north-east to meet the North-west Berkshire Ridgeway at Highworth, the other taking the line of the Wootton Bassett road to get on to the chalk escarpment above Clyffe Pypard and follow it to the downs on the north side of Pewsey Vale and so link up with the Great Ridgeway and the Wansdyke Ridgeway (*see* Map 10).

WOOTTON BASSETT CROSSROAD TO HIGHWORTH

Approximately 12 miles

Tracing the branch to Highworth first, it goes for a mile and a half as the B 4041 road north to Lydiard Green, where it turns east as a minor road to Lydiard Millicent. From there it continues to Common Platt, an interesting place on the route because the 6-inch O.S. map shows a Ridgeway Farm near it and because Ridgeway Mead is a field name in Purton parish whose west boundary touches this point, while there is also a record of a Ridgeway Mill near Purton on the west bank of the River Ray. Almost a mile on from Common Platt the road rises to the low ridge which now holds the outlying northern suburbs of Swindon—Moredon, Rodbourne Cheney, Pinehurst and Upper Stratton—passing them in this order. It crosses Ermine Street at Kingsdown beyond Upper Stratton and in about a mile joins the main road from Swindon to Highworth and continues with it for the last two and a half miles to Highworth.

WOOTTON BASSETT CROSSROADS TO CLYFFE HANGING

Approximately 4 miles

To return to the Wootton Bassett crossroads and the branch leading south-west. This follows the A 420 road to Wootton Bassett, an ancient town whose importance decayed as Swindon grew into a large industrial centre. The line of the trackway leaves the main road at the bridge over the stream about a mile below the town, and follows a minor road south along a low watershed to pass over what was once Greenhill Common to come to Greenhill Farms. Here the road makes a slight turn west and rises to Breach Lane, and then, swinging a little east of south, goes on to Bushton and the charming old village of Clyffe Pypard lying under the steep slopes of the scarp. The track probably mounted the scarp on the line of the sunken metalled lane which zigzags up through the beeches of Clyffe Hanging to the top of the ridge, a ravine-like road overshadowed by its tall banks all the way as well as by the trees of its upper part.

Ordnance Survey Map

Swindon. Sheet 157. 1 inch to 1 mile. 1940

19

THE CLYFFE PYPARD RIDGEWAY

AT WANBOROUGH the outer scarp of the North Wiltshire downs becomes evident below the inner scarp, the shelf of downland between the foot of the inner scarp and the crest of the outer becoming wider each mile to the souths west. From Wanborough the run of the outer scarp is south to Liddington and then west by Chisledon and Wroughton to Bassett Down, then south-west above Clyffe Pypard to Cherhill, Morgan's Hill and Roundway Hill above Devizes. The outer scarp, like the inner, had its ridgeway, but unlike the inner scarp ridgeway—the Great Ridgeway (*see* Map 26)—which there is no difficulty in finding and following, the one along the crest of the outer scarp is not easy to find and follow today, although it undoubtedly existed in the past. There is a possibility that its former existence may help to elucidate the problem of the course of the Icknield Way west of Wanborough, for it offers a characteristic line for this road as far as Wroughton at least. But apart from the problem of the Icknield Way's continuation, the outer scarp ridgeway was a natural line of communication between the Wanborough and Chisledon district and the west end of Pewsey Vale, with a continuation into the north-west corner of Salisbury Plain.

The present road from Wanborough to Liddington village must be on the line, continued south-westward by the road through Medbourne to Badbury, where it curves round the head of a deep wooded coomb to cross the Marlborough main road (A 345) and come to the north side of Chisledon, the line being taken up again by the road west above Hodson and along the south edge of Burderop Park to its south-west corner. From here, instead of going sharply right and then even more sharply left with the present road to Wroughton, it would have been more natural for the line to have continued past Overtown and above Clout's

Wood and Marcum Bottom to Red Barn on the Avebury road (*see* Map 10). The byway past Overtown House may be on or near it, but beyond this the R.A.F. station between Overtown and Red Barn makes investigation very difficult. It is possible of course that the line went through Wroughton and up Wroughton Hill along the outer lip of Marcum Bottom to Red Barn, as the Avebury main road does today. From Red Barn a byway leads to the top of the ridge above Salthrop House.

This ridge road, on the watershed between the Bristol Avon and the intermittent head waters of the Kennet, must have continued along the edge of the steep scarp and behind Quidhampton Wood and Bincknoll Wood to Broadtown Hill, with the broken mounds of Bincknoll Castle half hidden amidst trees and scrub. The reason why there are no traces of a track above Bincknoll today may be explained by the geological make-up of this part of the scarp, which has caused landslips throughout the centuries. In an article in Volume I of *Wiltshire Notes and Queries* one of these landslips is mentioned as destroying the rear portion of the old manor-house. The writer, T. Story-Maskelyne, a local squire and antiquary, did much to preserve a store of local historical and topographical material which might easily have been lost to us.

At least two cross-tracks from this ridge lead to the Great Ridgeway on the Hackpen reach of the inner scarp which runs roughly in the same direction but is separated from it by several miles of downland plain. The area between the ridges is intersected by the infant Kennet flowing south to Avebury, here a winterborne stream, as the names of the villages on its banks indicate. One track now goes from Broadtown Hill as that part of the road from Wootton Bassett to Marlborough which passes through Broad Hinton and along Fiddlers Hill to reach the Great Ridgeway by climbing the flank of Hackpen Hill at the White Horse. Another, from above Clyffe Pypard, leads as a byway past a stone circle to Winterbourne Bassett. Today this stone circle is far from complete. According to Stukeley, it consisted of two concentric circles of stones with a stone in the centre and another west of the circle standing by itself. From Winterbourne Bassett a track over the downs and up the steep side of Hackpen Hill joins the Great Ridgeway about a mile north of Glory Ann Barn.

At Broad Town the track along the ridge crosses the Marlborough–Wootton Bassett road (B 4041), to continue above the hanging woods of Clyffe Pypard to Clevancy Hill, where the latest O.S. map shows it ending as a footpath. But there is evidence on Smith's map of 1884 that in his time it continued in rather angular fashion to Highway Penning. From here it goes first as a footpath and then as a track to cross Juggler's Lane, but south from Juggler's Lane to where it comes to the Beckhampton–Calne road the track has been lost, though a parish boundary gives the line, and on Smith's map it is a continuous track named Devizes Road. Across the main road a track and footpath take it over Cherhill Down, keeping just east of

Oldbury Castle and passing over Calstone Down to the Roman road, where on the latest O.S. map it comes to an end. Andrews' and Dury's map of 1773 shows that it once went on to join the Wansdyke Ridgeway at Old Shepherds' Shore, which was the gap made in Wansdyke by the old and now disused road over these downs to Bath.

Ordnance Survey Map

Swindon. Sheet 157. 1 inch to 1 mile. 1940

20

THE WANSDYKE RIDGEWAY

Approximately 22 miles

WE ARE calling this way along the downs of the north edge of Pewsey Vale the Wansdyke Ridgeway, not because we think that the Wansdyke and the track originated at the same time, but because the track follows Wansdyke for much of its course, and it is more convenient when writing about a road to give it a name. Its east end comes close to the Old Marlborough Road Ridgeway on Leigh Hill at the south-west corner of Savernake Forest, and no doubt it continued east of this road and into Berkshire to join the Inkpen Ridgeway. In an article on 'The Anglo-Saxon Boundaries of Bedwyn and Burbage' in the *Wiltshire Archaeological Magazine* of June 1921 O.G.S. Crawford sets out the evidence for the existence of very ancient roads in this region when the charters were inscribed. But the post-Conquest forest laws did not favour the survival of the earlier trackways: strangers were unwelcome on ways through royal forests, and whenever an ancient road ran through one it tended to fall into disuse and not be remembered when the area was disafforested.

Tracing the Wansdyke Ridgeway westward we pick it up at Hat Gate at the south-west corner of Savernake Forest, where it then goes west as a series of tracks and lanes to Clench Common, a place rapidly losing all claim to its name as more of its gorse and rough scrub is grubbed up and the common ploughed and enclosed. Here the track leading up to Martinsell Hill is called Martinsell Ride and goes along the edge of a strip of old woodland, with many broken furrows and low banks inside the wood accompanying it all the way. There is also a large round tumulus covered with trees inside the wood. Rising all the time the way passes under the north side of Martinsell Camp and along the edge of Rainscombe, from where one can look down into the great hollow with its beech-wood fleece and beyond the coomb to a breath-taking view over Pewsey Vale to the northern scarp of Salisbury Plain. Then a short path through a field brings it to the main road at the top of Oare Hill. For some years this part of the path was not obvious, but now a sturdy new stile in the hedge shows the way.

Martinsell is a high, massive, steep-fronted bluff at the north edge of the Vale of Pewsey. On its summit plateau is a large camp and other prehistoric earthworks. The track passes between the back bank of the camp and Withy Copse. Here, about a hundred yards from the track, was discovered a low mound that when excavated proved to be the rubbish dump of a wealthy household settled there in the Roman-British period. As well as many fragments of both native and imported pottery the finds included such objects as bronze tweezers, bronze and iron brooches, an iron arrowhead, door-keys, nails, a chisel, a bone scoop or spoon, pot spindle-whorls, a portion of a strainer and the remains of various other domestic objects, as well as a great number of fragments of animal bones, chiefly of sheep, pigs and oxen.

At the stile, turning one's back on Pewsey Vale, the Marlborough Downs, Liddington Hill and Barbury come into view, bringing to mind that the Great Ridgeway traverses these high, lonely downs on its way to Pewsey Vale and the Plain. When following the old trackways there are many high places where one becomes more conscious of the pattern they make, not so much individually but as the strands of a vast interlocking system of routes converging on Salisbury Plain and then fanning out again to cover the whole of upland Wessex and beyond. At the top of such hills as Oare Hill and Martinsell this awareness becomes heightened, perhaps because they gather about them on all sides some of the most spacious and beautiful downland and valley prospects in Wiltshire.

The main road drops down steeply between high beech-wooded banks on its way to Pewsey, but the trackway keeps to the ridge, and after crossing the road goes on past the earthworks on Huish Hill (see Map 10). It crosses Huish Hill and keeps north of Gopher Wood to go on over Draycott Hill and then Golden Ball Hill, never dropping much below 800 feet in its undulations. Beyond the Vale and the Plain the spire of Salisbury Cathedral can be seen on a clear day and near it the dark green hump which is Old Sarum. After passing behind the Neolithic camp on Knap Hill it comes to the gap between Knap Hill and Walker's Hill (see Map 24), and in this gap is joined by Workway Drove, an ancient road slanting up the scarp from the direction of Wilcot and Pewsey. The name 'Workway' is the form in which the road's Saxon name—*Weala Wege*, meaning Welsh (i.e. British) way—has survived. In this gap between the two hills the Wansdyke Ridgeway also crosses the Great Ridgeway coming to the Vale from East Kennett.

The Wansdyke Ridgeway goes on behind Walker's Hill and comes to the Wansdyke itself behind Milk Hill. An ancient pond, Oxenmere, mentioned in an Anglo-Saxon charter, lies a quarter of a mile south of the point where the track comes to the Wansdyke. The track continues westward with the Wansdyke along the lip of Milk Hill coomb to Tan Hill. Before the sheep fair held yearly on Tan

Hill was discontinued in 1932, this high ridgeway across the downs had its crowded days, but now the only flock of sheep one sees there today will be grazing on the steep slopes of the Milk Hill coomb, looking very small on the vast expanse of down as they feed. Behind the scarp much of the downland has been ploughed and stretches away to the Kennet valley as large fields, and there is much plough land on the lower slopes falling to the Vale also, so that the Wansdyke bank, covered with old turf that often looks more grey than green, is an outstanding feature as it winds and undulates over the hills and far away.

Going on from Tan Hill the Wansdyke turns a little away from the Vale of Pewsey and passes behind Easton Hill and over Roughridge Hill to come to the New Shepherds' Shore on the Beckhampton–Devizes main road (A 361). Still keeping with it the track crosses the old Bath coach road at Old Shepherds' Shore and within the next mile they both reach Morgan's Hill.

At Morgan's Hill the track turns south to pass over Roundway Hill and come to Roundway village, its last mile being a metalled road through the village to the Devizes–Beckhampton road. On the other side of the road it coincides for half a mile with the road to Coate and then goes off on the right as a drove along the divide between the west end of Pewsey Vale and the valley of the Bristol Avon. This track crosses the west end of Etchilhampton Hill and joins the Devizes–Andover road passing between Stert and Etchilhampton. It follows this road—here called the Lydeway—for nearly a mile and a half to Lydeway Farm, where it turns south as a minor road to Foxley Corner, an unimportant crossroads today but once the meeting-place of the Studfold Hundred. By taking this route across the western end of the Vale the track avoided the once waterlogged area of Canning's Marsh. From Foxley Corner the track, now a metalled way, goes straight to the foot of the Plain and climbs Redhorn Hill where, just over the top of the hill, it meets the Great Ridgeway (see Map 23).

Ordnance Survey Maps

Swindon. Sheet 157. 1 inch to 1 mile. 1940
Salisbury. Sheet 167. 1 inch to 1 mile. 1940

21

THE OLD MARLBOROUGH ROAD RIDGEWAY

OLD SARUM TO RAM ALLEY

Approximately 22 miles

A RIDGEWAY on the high ground between the Avon and the Bourne goes north from Old Sarum across Salisbury Plain to Ram Alley, a small but interesting hamlet a mile or so north of Burbage in the Savernake Forest area. The coach road known as the Old Marlborough Road, which was on the line of this ridgeway, then continued to Marlborough; the trackway, also, may have gone on in the Marlborough direction to link up with other trackways north of the Kennet. By turning east through, or just south of, Savernake Forest there would be nothing to prevent its getting on to the Inkpen ridge which carries the South Hants Ridgeway, and on its way over the Plain it crosses other trackways going east and west, including the Harrow Way.

For the first three and a half miles from Old Sarum (*see* Map 4) the Salisbury–Amesbury main road (A 345) is on the line, but soon after the main road leaves High Post traces of a parallel track can be seen on its east side running along a golf-course and gradually veering north-east until finally, a mile beyond High Post, the main road takes a more northerly line and leaves these traces to become an independent track. The main road goes on to Amesbury, but the track keeps its north-easterly direction through Porton Firs and a ditch to where, near a tumulus, it crosses a road coming norths west from Porton. The track continues over Earl's Farm Down and past many tumuli to cross the A 303 road—which here is on the line of the Harrow Way—and beyond the A 303 becomes a metalled road. In a quarter of a mile it crosses the A 3028 road going west to Bulford village.

This road, which crosses the Avon at Bulford, is the modern version of the Packway, an old east-to-west track across the Plain to Shrewton and beyond. After bridging the Avon at the site of the ancient ford it keeps just north of Durrington Walls earthwork in crossing the valley main road at Stonehenge Inn and continues west through the army camps on Larkhill and Durrington Down. This is War Department country and its maze of tracks going in all directions from various meeting-places of ways on the high plateau is difficult to disentangle today, but this particular track would be important in ancient times because of the river crossing.

North from the A 3028 road (*see* Map 7) the Old Marlborough Road for the next mile or so goes through Bulford Military camp, not becoming a track again until it has left the camp buildings well behind. It crosses the Nine Mile River, a tributary of the Avon and a very small stream, at Sheep Bridge, and is then named on the map 'The Old Marlborough Road'. On Brigmerston Down, two miles farther on, it passes through a star-like meeting-place of tracks and ditches where many tumuli are dotted about, and continues to rise over Haxton Down, Weather Hill and Everleigh Down to come to the high woods of Everleigh. All the way on each side are Celtic fields, ditches and a network of other trackways. On the right, as it comes to Haxton Down, the summit of Sidbury Hill with its hill-fort stands up above the plateau, the blanched scar of a modern firing range at its foot. North of Sidbury is Snail Down, a Bronze Age burial field where many round barrows are clustered together and every type of round barrow is to be seen. Snail Down had its later inhabitants also, for there is much evidence on the ground of a Roman–British settlement, including an old road which excavators recently uncovered.

Here the area on each side of the Old Marlborough Road has been scored and re-scored by trackways belonging to all periods of prehistory from Bronze Age to Roman, and in our time has been scored over again by the tanks of the modern army in training, so that even if one could get permission to wander freely over it the unravelling of these tangled lines would be an almost impossible task. Antiquity broods heavily over these downs, and at times they can take on a loneliness which makes even the Bronze Age burial mounds a reassuring confirmation of man's reality.

The progress of the Old Marlborough Road as it goes north from Everleigh over Summer Down and Hog Down to Aughton Down can be clearly followed. Probably its use as a coach road preserved it, as the need for coach roads preserved other ancient trackways in Wessex by keeping them in use during the late eighteenth and early nineteenth centuries. It is metalled for its first mile from Everleigh; but the metalled road makes an abrupt turn north-west to go past the woods of Everleigh Ashes and on over the downs to Pewsey, while the track continues west of the hill holding Crowdown Clump and Godsbury earthwork, to wind past the east side of Easton Clump on Easton Hill before becoming the steep rough track, bitten deeply into the chalk, that leads down to the south end of Easton village. At the foot of Easton Hill the track passes two rushy ponds, once considered to be the chief source of the Salisbury Avon, and though the stream they feed is but a tiny trickle in a muddy ditch, ancient travelers probably found this a marshy part of their journey.

The track goes through the half-mile of village street, a wide street with half-timbered and thatched cottages as well as more modern dwellings on each side of it. There are farmhouses and farm buildings also, and at the lower end, opposite the small plain church, is a meadow containing some grassy mounds and banks which tradition says was the site of a Trinitarian priory founded in the thirteenth century by Stephen, Archdeacon of Wiltshire. This remained, though not always in a flourishing condition, until the Dissolution. The chief work of its members was the provision of hospitality for poor travellers, which suggests that the road through the village remained more than a byway until the middle of the sixteenth century at least, and probably continued to be so used until the end of the nineteenth century by travellers and drovers crossing the east end of the Vale of Pewsey.

The present edge of Savernake Forest is some three miles from Easton, but early in the twelfth century it came much nearer so that the actual line of the track's continuation from the north end of the village is uncertain. After crossing the Pewsey–Burbage road it could have taken the same winding course as the metalled road does today, or, missing the village altogether, have taken another track, now lost, which left the main track on Easton Hill before it comes to Easton Clump and went north following the line of a parish boundary past Bowden Farm and so to Ram Alley. There is evidence in the Anglo-Saxon charters of Burbage and Bedwyn of a 'Boundary Way' which followed this line. Beyond Ram Alley the Marlborough-Andover main road (A 346), going past Leigh Hill Copse and then over Leigh Hill just within the Forest, seems its natural conrinuation to Marlborough. The 1-inch O.S. map shows a short length of track—which it names Trackway—east of the main road and going in the same direction, which is lost as it leaves the scrub of Leigh Hill and comes to a more densely wooded part of the Forest.

Ordnance Survey Map

Salisbury. Sheet 167. 1 inch to 1 mile. 1940

22

THE WEST WILTSHIRE RIDGEWAY

Kilmington Common to Biddlestone

Approximately 36 miles

FROM the crossroads at Kilmington Common, a mile or so east of the Wiltshire-Somerset border, a succession of ridgeways and the possible links between them can be traced winding north from the Harrow Way to join up with the Cotswold Ridgeway beyond Grittleton on the north-west border of Wiltshire. At Kilmington Common the Harrow Way is going west from Long Lane to pass over Kingsettle Hill into Somerset (*see* Map 5). Dr. Grundy, in the *Archaeological Journal*, 1918, has named this route to the Cotswolds the West Wiltshire Ridgeway.

Its progress, though aiming at the limestone country, the Midlands and perhaps Wales, is not a simple northward flow, for it makes many detours to keep on high ground and avoid streams, and in some cases almost winds back on itself. Since it can only be followed today as a series of modern roads made to serve villages and towns, with some short stretches where there is no road, track or footpath, there are occasions when one has doubts if such a route ever existed, though the usefulness of one in ancient times seems obvious.

All the way it has to traverse border country. At its southern beginning it must pass through part of the ancient forest of Penselwood, and it also impinges upon two great estates, Stourton and Longleat, which makes it likely that in the eighteenth century, when the principal enclosures took place, parts of it were diverted to go round instead of through these grounds. From this forest region it has to curve eastward to avoid the Frome basin and make for Chapmanslade, where the belt of clay narrows, and then must zigzag along the watershed between the Frome and the Biss. If this was a pre-Roman route from the south-west corner of Wiltshire chalk to the north-west limestone uplands it is seldom far away from the menace of forest and marsh in its middle section. As it comes to Bradford-on-Avon, and for many miles beyond, the going is still indirect though there is limestone under-foot, for here the ridges are fretted into many steep spurs and gullies. These would make progress tedious for a traveller if he had to climb up and down them, so that a wide diversion following somewhat lower ground would give easier and quicker going. All these things make it an interesting way to trace.

Two minor roads leave the Kilmington Common crossroads, either of which may represent the original line of departure. One goes north to Yarnfield Gate and from there follows the county boundary, first along the ridge above the woods of Witham Park and then through Tyning Wood and Penstones Wood to Gare Hill. There are several trails and tracks in the woods running roughly parallel to the metalled road. At Care Hill the metalled road makes an abrupt north-west turn to descend to the stream-threaded Frome valley. From this point there is no track through the woods ahead, but the county boundary, continuing north-north-east through the woods, probably marks the line as far as the road from Frome to Maiden Bradley, which it reaches opposite a turning leading east to Horningsham. Here we are on a hard road again, for this turning takes us along its zig-zagging course south of the Longleat estate to Horningsham. The enclosing of the Longleat estate and subsequent landscape gardening on a grand scale, including the making of artificial lakes and diversion of streams, probably accounts for the erratic behaviour of the road as well as its abrupt turn.

The alternative to this first six or seven miles is the line suggested by Dr. Grundy. It takes the more easterly of the two minor roads and goes from Kilmington to Maiden Bradley by winding north to Grange Farm, then north-east to Manor Farm, where it swings in a half-circle round Mapperton Hill before coming to the village, but a footpath and lane cutting across the hill makes a short route for foot passengers and is perhaps the earlier line. From Maiden Bradley the road winds for about one and three quarter miles north-east past Baycliff Farm to where a track from Bidcombe Hill about half a mile south of the road comes into it.

This track from Bidcombe Hill, an eastward spur of a high, narrow chalk ridge along the side of the Wylye valley between Maiden Bradley and Brixton Deverill, is interesting since it suggests a link by means of the West Wiltshire Ridgeway with the country to the north; just as the green track along Brimsdown Hill, the spur at the west end of the ridge, appears to be heading for the Mendips, though the line is not clear today and only a parish boundary carries it along from the tumulus at the tip of the spur. This steep wooded ridge has many tumuli and earthworks, particularly on the part called Cold Kitchen Hill. The track leading east from this hill along the ridge passes a long barrow and tumuli before it goes through a ditch, and winding north-east with the ridge then descends to cross the Wylye at Brixton Deverill. On the other side of the river it quickly ascends to Little Down and, still rising, turns south for 200 yards or so to get on to a ridge which takes it eastward over the Warminster main road (A 350) to continue to meet the Great

Ridgeway, or one of its loops, about a mile and a half north of the meeting-place of tracks near Upper Pertwood (*see* Map 19). Two ways—marked as footpaths on the 1-inch O.S. map—branch south from the green track along the summit of the Brimsdown ridge. One goes through a ditch before coming down to the Kingston Deverill–Maiden Bradley road near Whitepits, the other, when the ridge has curved east round Bushcombe Bottom, comes down by tumuli to join the lane which leads to a ford over the Wylye at Monkton Deverill. On the north side of the ridge, however, there is only the one track we have mentioned as joining the West Wiltshire Ridgeway.

At this point the West Wiltshire Ridgeway branches as a lane, which is also a continuation of the Bidcombe Hill track, for about a quarter of a mile, then joins the byroad that brings it back to the alternative way just east of Horningsham. The course is now north with the road past the village of Newbury and on through Longleat Woods, gradually swinging north-east past Park Hill and across Redway Plain to come to the Warminster–Frome main road (A 362). So far it has not dropped below 600 feet in all its windings and undulations. After following the Frome road for about a quarter of a mile west it turns north as a track to climb over Cley Hill, and from Cley Hill Farm, north of Cley Hill, the line can be followed as foot-paths and lanes to Chapmanslade. From the Kilmington crossroads this line has taken it along the watershed between the Wylye and the Frome.

It now follows the modern road west-north-west over Lodge Hill to Lambsgate Farm, along the ridge between Rodden Brook and Berkley Marsh. From Lambsgate Farm a minor road takes it to Hill Corner and then a lane brings it to a point about a third of a mile north-west of the railway. It then turns sharply north-west along another lane heading for St. George's Cross, but after a third of a mile the lane comes to a sudden end, there being no further track or path to complete the remaining three furlongs on the line to St. George's Cross. This zigzagging along the watershed between the Frome and the Biss Brook is determined by the necessity to avoid the brooks and streams on each side, and its angled turns by the making of modern roads, the only ones we can follow in this part of the route and which suggest a piecing together of old and new to suit modern needs.

From St. George's Cross, now an unimportant crossroads, its line becomes very involved, yet there seems no other way it could have followed to avoid wet country. First it goes north-east along a byway to the Warminster–Beckington road (A 36), following this through Beckington and then branching along the Trowbridge road past the remains of a barrow called the Devil's Bed and Bolster to come to Rode Hill and the B 3109 road to Bradford-on-Avon.

It now enters a clear stretch of about five miles on the line of the B 3109 to Bradford-on-Avon and then crosses the Avon to come to Maplecroft north of the town. It has left the clay and reached limestone country, but the line it may have followed from Bradford has been too much overlaid by later phases of civilization, from Roman to modern times, to make the last miles of its route any easier to follow than the others.

From Maplecroft it goes north-west on the line of the main road to Farleigh Wick. Although this is not a very high road it takes the easiest line, avoiding the higher riverside country to the west which is much broken up into steep slopes and narrow bottoms. Monkton Farleigh is the next place on the itinerary, and it is difficult to say which of the several footpath-ways going north from the main road at or near Farleigh Wick is on the natural line.

From Monkton Farleigh a metalled byway leads north-north-east for a mile or so, keeping away from the river and the wooded steeps immediately east of it between Bathford and Kingsdown. It seems likely that as the trackway came near to the Avon it may have been superseded by the Foss Way for the rest of its journey to join up with the Cotswold Ridgeway coming east from Tormarton. By crossing the Avon at Bathford it could continue by the Foss Way along Banner Down and west of North Wraxall to Fosse Gate, and make a link with the Cotswold Ridgeway there instead of a mile east at Crittleton, where the West Wiltshire Ridgeway comes to an end.

Dr. Grundy's itinerary from Monkton Farleigh takes the minor road north-north-east for just over a mile, and then, after 200 yards of footpath have brought it to a byway on the golf-course, it meets the A 365 road about a quarter of a mile west of Wormwood Farm. Here there is an abrupt turn to the north to follow the B 3109 road from Bradford-on-Avon, but this is left soon after it has passed over Box Tunnel and the way becomes a lane going north to Rudloe. This keeps to the edge of parkland and comes to Rudloe and the Bath main road (A 4) in half a mile. The course now lies through the extensive grounds of Hartham Park and is lost for a mile or so, but it must have made a north-easterly swing above the valley running into Hartham Park from Boundary Brook and then swung back to the line to come into the lane entering Biddestone from the south-west.

Beyond Biddestone it goes north along the line of the modern road to Yatton Keynell and then on to Grittleton, where it turns west to Fosse Gate. It could have linked up with the ridgeway going to the Cotswolds by continuing generally west through Littleton Drew and Acton Turville to Tormarton. Although this seems at first sight to be going a long way round from Biddestone, as well as keeping on lower ground, it might prove in the end to be the easiest and quickest way.

The country between Biddestone and Tormarton is intersected by several streams including the By Brook and the Broadmead Brook, but this is limestone country which drains quickly and the streams themselves would not be difficult to cross. A more serious obstacle is the high ground fretted into spurs and bluffs and cut by narrow coombs on both sides of the By Brook, which would have to be negotiated to get to the open country on the west. This would entail much laborious climbing up and down to cover a short distance, whereas the road from Biddestone through

Yatton Keynell has a gently undulating flow, and when the line turns west from Grittleton to Fosse Gate it is comfortably north of the streams and broken hill country.

It is difficult to come to any decision about the route as a through-way. There were times in the field when we were convinced that a continuous line once existed. On other occasions, particularly when studying the maps, we seemed to be picking a way on the most tenuous of evidence. We have included it, however, in the hope that others with a more intimate knowledge of the ground it covers may be able to add to our findings, or subtract from them, as the case may be.

Ordnance Survey Maps

Frome. Sheet 166. 1 inch to 1 mile. 1946
Bristol and Stroud. Sheet 156. 1 inch to 1 mile. 1946

23

GROVELY RIDGEWAY

Ditchampton to Kilmington Common

Approximately 27 miles

THREE roughly parallel east-to-west ridgeways of south Wiltshire converge upon the downs to the south of the hollow in which Salisbury lies, and which is the meeting-place of Salisbury Plain's five rivers—Avon, Nadder, Ebble, Wylye and Bourne (*see* Map 4). On the west side the Wylye and Nadder meet at Wilton and flow on as one to join the Avon coming through the Plain from the north. On the east side the Bourne comes from the north-east. The Ebble, south of the Nadder and coming from the west, enters the Avon at Bodenham about a mile and a half below Salisbury, the Avon flowing on southward to Christchurch. The converging rivers are all separated by high chalk ridges which the trackways follow.

It must be remembered that Salisbury—New Sarum—did not exist before the thirteenth century, when the church and town at Old Sarum on its hilltop overlooking the hollow were abandoned and the present cathedral and town were founded. Evidence of ancient fords exist today in the names of certain riverside villages, such as Ugford, Stratford-sub-Castle and Stratford Tonoy used by the Romans, Milford, Longford, Britford and others, where traces of fords can still be seen on the river banks. Moreover, these rivers could be more properly described as chalk streams and would not prove impassable barriers except when in flood, their beds being usually composed of flinty pebbles and their waters clear and shallow.

The most northerly of these three ridgeways is on the watershed between the Wylye and the Nadder, and was once part of a through way beginning at the Kentish coast and coming eventually to the Mendips and the Bristol Channel. Much of it has been lost, and the exact line of other parts is doubtful, but there can be no doubt that a trackway once traversed this watershed. It is interesting that coal from Somerset has been found in a British settlement near Stockton earthworks, confirming the continuation of the track west from the Wiltshire border. On the O.S. map it is marked as a Roman road going through the west part of Crovely Wood and through Great Ridge, but it was an ancient trackway before the Romans took it over as part of their route to the lead mines of the Mendips. Perhaps because its passage through Grovely Wood afforded poor pasturage for cattle being driven to and from markets and fairs it fell into disuse earlier than the Ox Drove and the Salisbury Way, though its enclosure in a private estate would also hasten its decline as a through road.

After crossing the Nadder at Ditchampton the Grovely Ridgeway ascends Grovely Hill on the line of an old road called in a Ditchampton charter 'Way of the Wood' and by local inhabitants the 'Hollows'. Both names well describe it. After going through two ditches it follows more or less the line of the Broad Drive through the wood to come in about two miles to a meeting-place of tracks. These tracks fan out and give off other tracks across the downs to the various fords and villages on the Nadder and Wylye. The 6-inch O.S. map records that an old Saxon boundary stone, the Powton Stone, stood at this point. The Roman road and its accompanying track go on in a westerly direction through the wood for another two and a half miles and come out at Dinton Beeches. Never more than a mile from the track are numerous earthworks and entrenchments on the spurs of down overlooking the Wylye—the small ring of East Castle, the double and triple banks of Bilbury Ring with the smaller Church-end Ring half a mile south of it. This upland area, holding two main trackways, one leading to the Somerset lead mines and the other to the tin mines of Cornwall, must have been well-populated in prehistoric times.

At Dinton Beeches the track is joined by the Harrow Way coming along West Hill from Steeple Langford, and it continues with it above Teffont Down, where for about a mile and a half it used to be known locally as the Ox Drove. Although the name Ox Drove survives only for this mile and a half of the track, it must at one time have been applied to its direct continuation east and west. Edward Thomas, in *The Icknield Way*, tells how, some forty years ago, local farmers questioned as to its subsequent route usually replied that it was the way along which cattle were driven from Somerset to London.

The Grovely Ridgeway coincides with the Harrow Way for nearly two miles and then turns north-west to follow the line of the main road, A 303, under Stockton Wood on Chilmark Down for a mile or more, with Stockton earthworks less than half a mile to the north of the wood. It leaves the main road to go north-west as a parish boundary through Great Ridge for half a mile before joining the Roman road, here lost for the same half-mile, and continues through the wood, more or less on the line of the Roman road, for another two and a half miles, coming out of Stonehill Copse at the west end of Great Ridge as a wide tree-lined rutted lane. In about half a mile this lane comes to the meeting-place of tracks about five furlongs north-east of Pertwood, where it joins the Great Ridgeway. At this meeting-place the Roman road can be seen going on west-north-west over the downs to just beyond the Shaftesbury–Warminster road (A 350), where it is lost again.

The Grovely Ridgeway now appears to follow the Great Ridgeway south-west, passing a hundred yards above Pertwood before coming to the Warminster road at Upper Pertwood Bushes (*see* Map 19). It takes the line of the main road for half a mile before going across Keysley Down and past a long barrow to join the main Chicklade–Mere road (A 303), thus cutting the corner between the two main roads. From here it again coincides with the Harrow Way on the line of the Mere main road past Old Willoughby Hedge as far as Charnage Down, where—with the Harrow Way—it leaves the main road to go over White Sheet Hill and follow Long Lane over the downs to Kilmington Common (*see* Maps 6 and 5).

The country west of Kilmington was forest land in prehistoric times and was still forest land in the early fourteenth century, according to the *Perambulations* of the Royal Forests of that date. When, in later centuries, the bulk of the forest was cleared, the old trackways would tend to disappear as small hard-won fields replaced woodland and scrub and new roads evolved to serve the farms and hamlets. Where Long Lane comes to the Kilmington Common crossroads the track leaves the Harrow Way and branches north-west to Druley on the Somerset border along a belt of woodland. Now that it has left the chalk ridges of downland and come to a region of more isolated summits, many streams and smaller hedged fields, it is not so easy to follow the line; and that there are different soils underfoot is evident from the predominance of oaks and hollies, and from the bracken and gorse on roadside banks and the reeds and rushes in damp hollows. But there are definite traces of an old road between the woods at Druley and Hicks's Park Wood in a wide sunken lane winding between low mossy banks with parallel broken trails on each side of it. This grassy hollow way, after crossing a field of ancient pasture, comes into a wide metalled byway which is its obvious continuation.

From there it probably followed the line of modern roads to Upton Noble, and then to the south-east corner of Dungehill Wood by the present road and track, and on through the wood by a footpath just inside its southern edge. After this its course becomes involved and broken. It is possible that the Roman road to the Mendips superseded the ancient track. Now, in its turn, the Roman road has become disused and lost in many places. There is a Cold Harbour Farm—always a suggestive name—about a mile or so north-west of Dungehill Wood, and a camp and a tumulus on Small Down Knoll about two miles west of the wood. Following modern roads and foot-paths roughly north-west the line comes in about five miles to the Foss Way, and after crossing the Foss Way makes for Maesbury Camp, where it picks up the Roman road again and follows it to the Mendip lead mines and on to the Bristol Channel. Much of this part of the Roman road consists of Romanized ridgeways. Beyond the lead mines a ridgeway on the watershed between the Yeo and the Axe goes over Bleadon Hill to the north side of the Axe, and so leads to the south-east corner of Weston Bay behind Brean Down.

Ordnance Survey Maps

Salisbury. Sheet 167. 1 inch to 1 mile. 1940
Frome. Sheet 166. 1 inch to 1 mile. 1946

24

THE SALISBURY WAY

16 miles

THE trackway on the ridge of downs south of the Nadder, the watershed between the Nadder and the Ebble, has become known as the Salisbury Way (*see* Map 4). Of the three south Wiltshire east-to-west ridgeways it is the best preserved, and is without a break from where it mounts to Harnham Hill, on the south margin of Salisbury, to the end of the ridge at White Sheet Hill at the head of the Ebble valley above Berwick St. John. Being a more direct route between Salisbury and the Dorset border than the river-side roads which wind from village to village in the Nadder and Ebble valleys, it served a useful purpose until the coming of the railways and motor transport. This may be the reason why, unlike many other ridgeways, it does not seem to have had periods of disuse long enough for it to have been forgotten.

The earliest mentions of it occur in various Anglo-Saxon charters giving the boundaries of the villages along the two rivers. It is the 'broad highway' in an Ebbesborne charter, 'herepath' in the Burcombe, Swallowcliffe and two Fovant charters, while the tumuli and ditches along its course once had Anglo-Saxon names—where they touched boundary lines—to distinguish them. One can well imagine that during the Middle Ages and until the Dissolution it was used by religious pilgrims as a route between Salisbury, Wilton Abbey and Shaftesbury Abbey, and when the flow of pilgrims ceased in the middle of the sixteenth century it was kept alive by travelers on horseback as a through road to escape from the valley mire.

The Salisbury Way was also the first fourteen miles or so of the coach road from Salisbury to Shaftesbury during the coaching era. After crossing the medieval Harnham Bridge, it left Salisbury by the old steep road ascending Harnham Hill which is now superseded by the modern A 354 road. On Andrews' and Dury's map of 1773 the mileage from Salisbury is marked by trees instead of milestones, beginning with *1 Mile Tree* on Harnham Hill and ending with *8 Mile Tree* east of Chiselbury Camp, after which it seems to have reverted to ordinary milestones.

Something of the urbanity of the eighteenth century still lingers about the Salisbury Way and about the spacious landscape on each side of it. Although raised high above the lovely villages which lie beside the river in the narrow valleys it does not seem aloof from them in spirit. Prehistoric remains usually give the impression of belonging more to nature than to man, but the Salisbury Way has been used so continuously that it has become part of the broad Wiltshire landscape man has fashioned through the centuries. Even today it is not forsaken, forlorn or forgotten. It still serves the farmers whose fields slope down to the rivers on each side, and one can seldom walk along it without seeing cars using its grassy rutted surface as a through upland way, or parked for the enjoyment of a picnic and the beautiful prospects it offers.

As an ancient track the Salisbury Way could have linked up with other trackways going north-east, north, and north-west over the Plain as well as into north Hampshire by crossing the Avon at Harnham Bridge. This bridge was built by Bishop Bingham in 1245, and a fifteenth-century document quoted by Canon Wordsworth in his book on St. Nicholas Hospital says it was 'made to supersede a ford'. A track undoubtedly crossed the Avon here in Saxon times, for a Saxon cemetery has been found on Harnham Hill as well as other evidences of Saxon occupation. The Salisbury Way could also have linked up with the southern and central Hampshire ridgeways by an extension crossing the Avon at Britford, a mile or so south-east of Salisbury, and then leading to them by way of Dean Hill and the Pepperbox. The name Britford suggests an early route. There is still a green drove running back from Britford and crossing the downs between the junction of the Ebble and the Avon below Salisbury. It goes roughly westward to cross the present Salisbury–Blandford road (A 354) and join the Salisbury Way at the top of Harnham Hill. The old road coming up from East Harnham also meets it here, and from this point its course is a smooth westward flow until it comes to where the escarpment makes a shallow bay, taking in the one and a half miles from Burcombe Ivers to Chiselbury Camp just north of the track. After passing Chiselbury Camp the ridge swings south-west to White Sheet Hill and the trackway follows it.

For the first mile or so from Harnham Hill the surface of the Salisbury Way is roughly metalled. It edges the racecourse accompanied by a narrow belt of trees on the left and then passes along the edge of the woods south of Wilton Park, with Neale's Barrow hidden in the trees. As it goes through woodland shade, and with flowery margins on each side of the metalled centre, this is the most charming part of its course, though it seems to belong more to the valley than the hills; but after it reaches a wide embowered lane it begins to rise higher and the influence of the Wilton estate is left behind as it comes to the open downs. On each side tracks drop down steeply to the villages, some of them Saxon ways mentioned in charters as boundary lines. Sometimes on the right, sometimes on the left, it is enclosed by tall hedges, but there are many gaps where the parallel ridges holding the Grovely track on the north and the Ox Drove on the south come into view, and always the Salisbury Way can be seen journeying onward like an uncurled snake across the light greens and buffs of the downland fields on each side of it.

In this gentle meandering, however, it has its dramatic passage as it comes to Swallowcliffe Down, where the drop to the valley has the swoop of a swallow's dive as it falls in swift descent. The track passes through a ditch at both ends of Swallowcliffe Down, with tumuli in between and the site of a prehistoric village at its west end on Middle Down just south of the way.

As it comes to White Sheet Hill, after passing the minor road that crosses the ridge from Alvediston to Ansty, a track which branches off to the north-west may have been a link with the Great Ridgeway, coming to it either at the meeting-place of tracks near Upper Pertwood Bushes or else continuing for a mile or so north-west of that meeting-place to a point on the Warminster–Shaftesbury main road. The first few miles of this track may have had their course altered when the Wardour Castle and Fonthill Abbey estates were originally laid out. Most of it is now only a series of very minor roads and lanes. After crossing the A 30 road half a mile south-west of Ansty it goes roughly north-north-west along the edge of and then through the woods east of Wardour Park to cross the River Sem and continue north-west to Newtown.

From Newtown the line of a high minor road going north takes it through woods over Beacon Hill to Hindon. North of Hindon it continues to Hawking Down Farm where the metalled road goes north-west, but keeping its northward line the track crosses the A 303 readjust east of Knoyle Down Farm and goes through the shrubby area of Upper Pertwood Bushes to come to the meeting-place of tracks five furlongs north-east of Pertwood. It would meet the Great Ridgeway here as well as the trackway coming through Grovely Wood and Great Ridge (*see* Map 19). Beyond the meeting-place a track and a parish boundary which might be its continuation go north-west over Rook Hill to come to the Warminster–Shaftesbury main road at a high point about two miles south-east of Warminster, where there is a cluster of tumuli, and where another trackway branches westward on its way to Brixton Deverill and the ridge holding the summits of Cold Kitchen Hill and Brimsdown Hill.

To return to the Salisbury Way, the last mile and a half of its course along White Sheet Hill before it comes to its western end is its highest reach, culminating in 795 feet just before the track has passed through a well-marked ditch. It now begins its descent, winding past the scars and startlingly white debris of chalk quarrying and becoming more deeply sunken as the slope steepens. At the foot of the hill it meets the Salisbury–Shaftesbury main road (A 30).

To join up with the Ox Drove coming along the watershed south of the Ebble, and to go on with the Great Ridgeway into Dorset it must now turn south-west. No direct line is obvious today, though the route could not have been very far from the line of the main road for the first half-mile or so from Sands Farm to Whitesand Cross. Here a minor road branches south-west to lead to the metalled Roman road, which soon rises to the open downs, where once more the view opens out and it is an upland road again. On the left just below the summit a track leaves the road and goes winding almost secretively past some turf-covered hollows—probably old chalk quarries—to Win Green. This is the western end of the Ox Drove. In another quarter-mile the road meets the Great Ridgeway coming across Charlton Down after climbing Breeze Hill, though in earlier days before the Zigzag was made the old road took the steepness of Breeze Hill in its stride, as it were, without deviation.

Ordnance Survey Map

Salisbury. Sheet 167. 1 inch to 1 mile. 1940

25

THE OX DROVE

GREAT YEWS TO WIN GREEN

14½ miles

VARIOUS trackways from east Wiltshire and Hampshire, having crossed the Avon at Downton and the fords north and south of it, rise to the plateau consisting of Wick Down, New Court Down, Whitsbury Down and Odstock Down which is bounded on the north by the River Ebble, on the east by the River Avon, on the west by Coombe Bissett and Rockbourne Downs and on the south by the Allen River flowing through Damerham to Fordingbridge. As well as having several long, broken lengths of Grim's Ditch, the region is also criss-crossed with a bewildering number of minor trackways—though it is impossible to tell today which were once the most important—leading by earthen long barrows, the yew woods called Great and Little Yews, and the camp of Clearbury Ring. This tree-covered earthwork overlooking the junction of the Avon and the Ebble is a landmark for miles and can be seen from many places on the east Wiltshire and New Forest trackways. From the summit of Clearbury high ground on the right bank of the Avon as far as Christchurch is visible on a clear day.

Three of these trackways across the plateau meet at the south-east corner of Great Yews and continue north-westward as one track to become the Ox Drove (*see* Map 4), which is the name given to the track which follows the fourteen miles or so of the ridge on the south side of the Ebble from between Little Toyd Down and Coombe Bissett Down to Win Green on the Wiltshire-Dorset border. The most northerly of these three trackways comes up from the river at Matrimony Farm, north of Charlton, and passing Clearbury Ring goes south-west along the south boundary of Nunton parish to cross Grim's Ditch and continue to the meeting-place of tracks at Great Yews. It then strikes north-west as an open track for half a mile before crossing another stretch of Grim's Ditch, and in another mile crosses the angle formed by the branching of the Rockbourne road from the Salisbury–Blandford road (A 354). It then coincides with the Blandford road, passing New Farm and crossing the Wilton Way coming south from Stratford Toney. Opposite Toyd Clump it leaves the main road and goes west as a wide stony lane.

The track soon begins a gentle rise, and in about half a mile comes to a small cluster of houses and a cross-way of tracks half hidden in trees. One track goes to Bishopstone in the Ebble valley, the other leads back to the main road.

Leaving the houses the Ox Drove narrows and now looks as if it is seldom used. There is no hedge on the left for a short distance, bringing the long flank of Pentridge Hill and Martin Woods into view, with a dark wooded skyline beyond. In one place it is almost impassable, waist-high with nettles and bramble trails, but it soon comes out of the tangle to an open green space where another track winds down to Bishopstone. After passing this track the Ox Drove becomes less tunnel-like between its ragged hedges. For a short distance it keeps to the edge of a wood but soon after the wood is left behind it crosses the Roman road, a low hump in the ground seen on the left going across a field in the direction of Badbury.

As with the Salisbury Way, the ridge holding the track becomes higher as it goes from east to west. In another mile the Ox Drove crosses the minor road coming up on the left from Martin and on the right dropping down to the village of Broad Chalke through a beech avenue. From the gap at the crossing the dark mound of Badbury Rings can be seen in the farther distance with the Purbeck Hills making a shadowy ridge-line on the horizon.

As the Ox Drove goes westward it is accompanied on the right by a narrow coppice of oak, holly, maple and hazel, suggesting that this woodland was once part of its width. After a hundred yards or so the left side as well becomes enclosed by forest trees, for this small area is now signposted as State Forest, making the track a hidden way where only the birds disturb the silence. It comes into the open again on Cow Down, passing a field system which air photographs have shown once covered the track itself, so that if the track existed before the field system was made it must have lost its original line here. The presence of a number of cross-dykes a furlong or so south of the track, however, made us wonder if it did not go through them originally instead of north of them as it does today. In the *Wiltshire Archaeological Magazine*, June 1949, it is recorded that in 1944 a hoard of bronze bangles and a bronze torque were found on Elcombe Down in the parish of Ebbesborne Wake not far from the track. These were said by Professor Hawkes, who examined photographs of them, to be known types of the late Bronze Age. To quote the writer of the article, Mr. H. de S. Shortt, F.R.N.S., F.S.A., describing this find: 'As all the ornaments were complete when lost or hidden, it is unlikely that they form a founder's hoard. They more probably represent a part of the stock of a travelling jeweller. Their position suggests accidental loss.'

As the Ox Drove comes to Trow Down it is outlined for a mile or so by tall conifers which give a rather unnecessary dramatic note to the top of the ridge. Almost at the end of this tree-line a track runs north to Winkelbury Hill and Camp, continuing below the camp as a steep winding hollow way to Berwick St. John. The old turf covering the banks and ditches of the earthwork makes them look as if they had been moulded out of a more ancient substance than the cultivated downs round them.

Still rising, the Ox Drove goes on along Monk's Down, where it has been metalled, but as it nears Ashcombe the metalled road swings steeply down-hill to the valley and the Shaftesbury road, while the Ox Drove becomes a green track again and curves round the rim of the great coomb, with the downs on each side falling away. On Monk's Down it reaches 839 feet, but after rounding Ashcombe to come to Win Green the height is nearer 900 feet. It has such an extent of downs and valley spread before it that the spire of Salisbury Cathedral far in the east looks no larger than a toy. One feels that the whole of Wiltshire can be seen from this last half-mile; and not only Wiltshire but the limits of Hampshire as well, for, on a clear day at Win Green, behind the most distant ridge of the New Forest a dim blue shape that is the Isle of Wight rises from a sparkling iridescence which is the sea. Dorset lies only a few yards westward, but the Ox Drove and the Great Ridgeway come together on the Wiltshire side of the border.

Ordnance Survey Map

Salisbury. Sheet 167. 1 inch to 1 mile. 1940

26

THE WILTON WAY

ALTHOUGH the Wilton Way is considered to be a road of Saxon origin much of it includes a trackway going over the downs south of Wilton and leading through Cranborne Chase into Dorset; this trackway probably existed before Saxon times (*see* Map 4). It may have derived its name from Wilton Abbey, not only because it began there but because it led to distant estates owned by the Abbey, or it may have been first called the Wilton Way in the days when Wilton was the capital of the kingdom of Wessex. When, in A.D. 827, Egbert created the kingdom of England by joining the states of the heptarchy into one, he founded a Benedictine priory at Wilton which King Alfred later converted into an abbey. Wilton Abbey was much favoured by royal and noble families before and after the Conquest, and the borough itself, before the cathedral and town of New Sarum came into being, was an influential religious stronghold with its thirteen churches, the Abbey and the Priory of St. John of Jerusalem. This must have meant much travelling to and from Wilton, not only on business connected with the manors and other lands owned by the Abbey in the surrounding country-side, but because it was customary for the heads of religious houses to make pilgrimages and visit each other. We know from old documents that it was used as an hotel and guest-house for noble travellers as well as for humble ones. From what we know about the state of lowland roads in medieval times it is only natural to suppose that travellers on horseback or on foot would rise to the uplands as soon as possible, incorporating into their route any lengths of trackways useful to them.

North of Wilton, after fording the river below the junction of the Nadder and the Wylye, the Wilton Way would come to the well-defined ridgeway between the Avon and the Wylye which leads across the Plain and past Druid's Lodge to Stonehenge, and which is now the A 360 road.

At its Dorset end the Wilton Way has now been lost. We pick it up between Martin and Damerham, but it must have continued from there for at least as far as Cranborne, though it is likely that it originally went on to Wimborne Minster and Christchurch. Between Martin and Damerham a wide drove known as Martin Drove is now the metalled road between the two villages, and is accompanied for most of its way by the Allen River, which rises at East Martin and flows on to join the Avon near Fordingbridge. About halfway between these two villages almost opposite North Allenford Farm a tree-shaded lane branches north from the road and comes to a crossing of the Allen River in its first few yards. The little river is usually dry in summer in these upper reaches, though the remains of wooden sluice-gates in the meadow on the right suggest that there were occasions when the meadow could be flooded.

The old stone clapper bridge over the narrow channel has given way to a modern concrete footbridge about three feet wide with a wooden handrail, but four great slabs of stone remain which once spanned the two blocks of masonry half hidden in a shaggy tangle of coarse vegetation. The centre of the lane dips to a wide shallow hollow which is the ford. In a normal summer the stream which feeds the ford dries up.

Soon after, the Wilton Way leaves the shade of the lane and comes into the open. On each side are the slopes of the downs, those on the right patterned with lynchets that curve up a shallow coomb. The track goes on as a foot-path through large arable fields, and in less than a mile crosses Bokerly Dyke and goes on across a great area of upland cornfield passing first Grans Barrow and then Knap Barrow. Both of these are earthen long barrows over 130 feet long.

The track then crosses the old coach road coming from the Salisbury–Blandford road and over Rockbourne Down to Cranborne. The remains of this old road can be seen as a ribbon of darker green traversing the plateau and ascending straight up the hillside.

After passing Grans Barrow the original way seems to have suffered diversion through ploughing and now goes round instead of across the angle of a field. This is an area of farming on prairie scale in which the line of the track has been lost.

We next pick up the line at Toyd Clump just south of the Salisbury–Blandford road. North of the main road it continues over Throope Hill to Stratford Toney and the Ebble, where there was an ancient ford, and here it comes to an end as a ridge road. Just before it comes to the river the track is called White Way in an Anglo-Saxon charter.

For most of its course the Wilton Way has had a straightness which suggests a made route rather than one which developed out of the lie of the land, though across the wide plateau of downland between Bokerly Dyke and Toyd Clump there was no reason for it to wander unduly from a straight line.

Ordnance Survey Map

Salisbury. Sheet 167. 1 inch to 1 mile. 1940

27

TRACKS FROM THE BADBURY DISTRICT

BADBURY RINGS, the tree-crowned earthwork which lies about three miles north-west of Wimborne Minster, is far better known as a junction of Roman roads, so that one sometimes forgets that it must have been a focal point for travellers on their way to and from the south coast long before the Romans came to Britain. Three Roman roads met at Badbury, one going north to Ashmore, another coming up from Dorchester and going through Badbury on its way to Old Sarum, and a third which went roughly south to Hamworthy near Poole. The Roman road to Ashmore survives in only a few broken stretches on the northern half of its course, and is an example of how an old road can disappear in a region which has been intensively cultivated for hundreds of years, so that one may well ask what chance an older trackway had of surviving—at least so that it can be recognized as such—when a road made with Roman thoroughness has been mostly lost.

That the Romans incorporated parts of older tracks into their roads from Badbury is not unlikely, for they did the same thing elsewhere, just as in their turn lengths of Roman roads have become incorporated into modern highways. It makes a fascinating if insoluble problem to try to disentangle this intricate weaving of old and new road patterns. In this part of Dorset, and in Cranborne Chase, there is little evidence in the field, so that one can only suppose that in most instances Roman roads soon superseded the old trackways where they did not actually take them over, and then they themselves lost their continuity when Saxon roads between settlements took their place. Also we must remember the region's proximity to the coast, so that it would have been overrun and then occupied by waves of invaders and immigrants from prehistoric times onward, and in modern times has suffered much development.

We may get a clue how the trackways came and went to Badbury from the great meeting-place of tracks still to be seen on King Down about a mile east of the earthwork. Until the Second World War this was an area of open downland, with tracks going off freely in all directions, but it is now broken up into large arable fields and enclosed cattle pastures, and many of the tracks have been lost, diverted or remain only in part where they serve a farm.

The meeting-place of tracks, though diminished, still shows vestiges of hollow ways fanning out in all directions, though it is impossible to determine major or minor ones in the surrounding fields. One track more continuous than the others goes north from Lodge Farm on the Wimborne–Blandford road (B 3082)—itself a ridgeway between the Stour and River Allen and also a Roman road—and goes north-north-east across King Down as a well-defined track (*see* Map 1). It passes Bradford Barrow in about a mile and a half and then makes a turn towards the north-west past Bradford Farm, meeting the Roman road a quarter-mile east of East Hemsworth. From there it goes on as a lane to Witchampton. The line now becomes lost for a mile or so. The track may have disappeared when the grounds of Crichel Park were first laid out. Its course is also complicated by the brooks flowing into the Allen, which the track would have to circumvent to come to the long ridge of chalk downs between the two valleys and their streams holding Long Crichel on the left and the Gussage villages on the right. There is much evidence of prehistoric man on this ridge—tumuli, dykes and minor earthworks—and the metalled road which runs along it must be on or near the line of a ridgeway.

In a little more than three miles the ridge comes to the Blandford–Salisbury road (A 354), and the further course of the track north or north-west of this road would bring it to Cranborne Chase, but it is impossible to tell if the minor road to Farnham leading to Minchington Down was the way it followed, though on Minchington Down there is a bewildering number of tracks, rides through the woods which may be old trackways, tumuli and earthworks of various kinds. Cranborne Chase was a royal forest closed to all but local travellers in the Middle Ages, though this may have preserved some of the trackways and the later Roman roads from the plough. The track must have gone on to the Chase, and from there it could have linked up with the Great Ridgeway via the Ox Drove on Charlton Down near Win Green.

Another track branching eastwards from the meeting-place on King Down, its first mile now lost, is picked up as a byway through shrubby woodland to cross the Allen and the Cranborne–Wimborne road (B 3078) at Clapgate. As a minor road called Smugglers' Lane—a significant name—it comes to Colehill, rising to the low watershed between the Allen and Moors River. It follows the watershed between the Stour and Moors River as it keeps a south-easterly line, going as a metalled lane through woods to come out on the Wimborne–Ringwood main road (A 31) above Little Canford. It has now left the chalk behind and come to heath country. The present line of the trackway follows the main road east for a furlong before branching south to the river, where obvious remains of an old ford can be seen leading to the water. The track, however, does not cross the river but keeps on along the line of the modern road (B 3073) between the river and the edge of the heathland, passing several tumuli on the left which have a rough covering of ling and moor grasses and stand on ground that is reedy and often waterlogged.

Dudsbury Camp, on the right just off the road, is hidden from view by the tall trees on its banks. On the river or south side the footslopes of the bluff on which the earthwork is situated rise out of the water-meadows of the meandering Stour to make a natural defence, for we were told that these water-meadows are often flooded in a rainy season. It is likely that in earlier times floods were more persistent, making a southern boundary of impenetrable marsh.

For the next two and a half miles to Hurn the road is practically in a built-up area and becoming more so as new bungalow estates are being put up. With houses and bungalows and their gardens lining the road it is impossible to look for traces of the old trackway. The area about Hurn is now an airfield and has become a vast plain of concrete and grass; but the continuation of the track must have been south-east after it had crossed the Moors River to follow the ridge of St. Catherine's Hill in the narrowing divide between the Stour and the Avon, and so coming to Christchurch. If one can imagine the road without the evidences of modern civilization which have reduced it today to a monotonous drabness, this stretch of the trackway from Clapgate to Christchurch must have been both difficult and desolate for earlier travellers, either setting out from the port of Christchurch or coming to it after a long journey across the downs and through the forest of Cranborne Chase, a stretch which, with its menacing river, marsh and moorland, they would be glad to leave behind. One must remember, though, that the Stour and the Avon may have been navigable much farther up in those times and that the road may not have come into general use until later than the tracks over the downs farther inland.

From the west side of Badbury Rings a wide track, with traces of older tracks on the left spraying out as it comes down the slope, follows the line of the Roman road south-west and passes several large round barrows close together before coming to the Wimborne–Blandford road (B 3082). This road for the next mile north-westward becomes a splendid avenue and the tall old trees and its generous width give it an air of distinction in a district where the local roads have more utility than beauty. Passing several tumuli it comes to the Tarrant, an inconsiderable stream often dry in summer, and crosses it. It then curves round Ashley Wood and over Keynston Down to come to Buzbury Rings, and continues from the earthwork for a quarter of a mile to where it is joined by the lesser road from Tarrant Rawston.

On the opposite side of the road there are vestiges of a track going north over the golf-course, but a well-defined track a little west of these traces goes north-west past a long barrow and Down Wood to Snow's Down, where there is a meeting of tracks at the corner of a coppice, one of which goes south-west as a metalled road to Blandford. Earlier maps show a rather different arrangement of these tracks. Our track, however, goes north along a ridge and on the east side of a small wood, passing between a pair of tumuli, and in about a mile goes through a cross-dyke. After crossing another shorter cross-dyke and leaving a settlement and two long barrows on the right, it arrives at the Blandford–Salisbury road (A 354) near Pimperne Long Barrow.

It continues beyond the main road and goes north to Hinton Bushes. Here it is lost in the grounds of Gunville House about a mile from the village of Tarrant Gunville. A lane which keeps outside the western edge of Gunville House grounds may be a diversion made when the grounds were enclosed, but where the track went from Hinton Bushes it is impossible to say today. It may have eventually become the Roman road to Ashmore and have joined the Great Ridgeway on Ashmore Down. This is Cranborne Chase country, and, between the high downs around Ashmore, remains of pre-Roman and Roman times, including the Roman villa discovered just south of Cunville House, are scattered thickly in the woods and on the downs.

Where the trackway from Badbury comes to Buzbury Rings another branch may have continued along the line of the present modern road from Buzbury Rings to Blandford, crossed the Stour there and, west of the town, followed a lane along the south side of Bryanston Park. From there a byway continues west, going north of Normandy Farm and under Field Grove Wood to come to the byway from Okeford Hill at Hedge End Farm. From this point a metalled track rises to Houghton North Down to meet the road coming up from Winterborne Stickland.

It continues on the line of this road, mostly a woodland way, with woods first on one side and then on the other and rising all the time to run for its last half-mile just inside the north edge of Delcombe Wood. It comes into the open on Woolland Hill and there joins the Great Ridgeway coming to the summit of Bulbarrow Hill (see Map 16).

The Blandford–Salisbury main road (A 354) (see Map 4) has many of the signs of an ancient highway, though modern road-makers have probably altered the original line in many places. It traverses an open countryside, now cultivated, where many prehistoric remains can still be seen in spite of centuries of cultivation. It has to cross two tiny streams—both of them often dry in summer—the one which rises half a mile north of the road below Chettle and the other at Cashmoor, with the Long Crichel ridge between them. It keeps west of Pentridge Hill where there are prehistoric settlements and burial mounds, and rises gradually to pass Woodyates Inn, once a well-known coaching inn, for this road was a coach road from Blandford to Salisbury, and many of the eighteenth-century milestones can still be seen on its margins. The Roman road, here called Ackling Dyke, which has run as a raised bank over the fields for many miles from Badbury, comes into it and seems to be on the line of the Blandford–Salisbury road for a mile or so before reaching Woodyates Inn. The Roman road continues its north-east line past the woods of Vernditch Chase to ascend to the ridge south of the Ebble valley which holds the Ox Drove, but the Blandford–Salisbury road goes on past Martin Drove End, cutting through Grim's Ditch at Swaynes Firs and on past Toyd Clump. Here it could link up not only with the Wilton Way but with the many tracks that meet on Whitsbury Down. In another mile the road turns north over Coombe Bissett Down and then falls to the narrow Ebble valley. Vestiges of old tracks in between the Salisbury–Blandford road and the track to Tottens, which is on the Ebble just east of Coombe Bissett, suggests that the line has been lost here, and that the original track crossed the river at the ford at Tottens and went on to Harnham Hill over the end of Homington Down. Below Harnham Hill it could link up with the Salisbury Plain ridgeways by crossing the river by Harnham Bridge, where there was once a ford, or meet the Hampshire ridgeways by way of Britford or the other Avon crossings in the vicinity.

From the gravel road going east from the meeting-place of tracks on King Down a branch leads north-east to cross the Allen and come to the village of Hinton Parva. An old name for this village is Stanbridge, and there is evidence on old maps that an early coach road from Wimborne crossed the river at this point on its way to Cranborne after coming up from Wimborne on the west side of the river, thus avoiding the wet heath and marshy land immediately east of it. It is probable that the bridge at Stanbridge replaced an earlier ford, in which case this may have been the route taken by a trackway coming from the Badbury–Wimborne district to reach the Horton ridge on its way to the Wiltshire Downs north-east of Cranborne Chase.

At first sight the Wimborne–Cranborne main road looks very much as if it might be on the line of the Ridgeway. It is a broad open road with wide green margins and passes close to the most noticeable of the group of circular earthworks known as Knowlton Rings, the one with the ruined thirteenth-century church tower within it, and there are as well several large round barrows, conspicuous with their covering of trees in the midst of vast arable fields. But the ridge which runs parallel and about half a mile east of the main road is the watershed between the Allen and the Crane and Moors Rivers, and it seems more likely that this would be the way the Ridgeway went in early times, though today there is only a succession of lanes and footpaths, a way broken in at least two places.

Across the Allen a footpath and then a lane take it to Hinton Parva, and then there is a break for three-quarters of a mile until it comes to an old lane called Embley Lane, which continues the line to Hinton Martell. The line then disappears again until about half a mile north-west of Chalbury another lane which goes to Chalbury Farm continues it, and this crosses the minor road from Horton Inn to Horton to go past Horton North Farm to a crossing-place of tracks on the byway between Woodlands and the Wimborne–Cranborne road. From there it goes to Knowle Hill as a track and footpath, and then as a footpath over Rye Hill, where it comes to the main road just as the main road is about to curve around the estate of St. Giles's House. It can be seen quite plainly here how the main road has been diverted to keep outside the estate, suggesting that its original course, at this point, was in existence before the estate was enclosed, for the road seems as if it would run quite naturally between the gates instead of taking the sudden swerve through beech woods to avoid them.

The Ridgeway now follows the main road to Cranborne, first between magnificent beech woods and then as a wide hedged road with many yew trees at intervals in the hedges to give it a medieval processional air. Although the land on each side is now arable it is not difficult to imagine how it looked when it was downland pasture, with the shadowless darkness of the yews making a startling contrast to its pale tones. The spread of a ploughed-out tumulus can still be seen on the left as the woods of St. Giles's House are left behind.

It is impossible to say which route the Ridgeway took through Cranborne, but north of the little town a winding byway takes it north-north-east past the west side of Burwood Copse and by a tumulus to Martin Wood, leaving the hamlet of Boveridge a furlong or so to the east. The track, now metalled, goes through Martin Wood between low ferny banks and after crossing the county boundary comes out on to the downs just before the turning to Kite's Nest Farm. The long east flank of Pentridge Hill comes into view on the left, and on the right the ridge which falls to Damerham and holds the earthwork called Soldier's Ring on its west end. Passing over Tidpit Common Down the track falls gently to Tidpit, with its chalk quarry and a cluster of cottages tucked under the ridge. Here the track, which was also the old coach road, is metalled as far as the quarry and then becomes a wide green hedged lane as it begins its slow climb over Toyd Down.

From Toyd Down the coach road passed south-east of Toyd Farm, where it crossed the Wilton Way (see Map 4), and about a quarter-mile beyond the Wilton Way is today part of the minor road from Rockbourne to Salisbury. It seems likely that a track which forks east about half a mile south of Toyd Farm and cuts the angle between the coach road and the Wilton Way may be the more important line. Turning east-north-east it goes past Knap Barrow and Grans Barrow—two earthen long barrows about which little seems to be known—and after crossing the lane from Rockbourne to Toyd Farm goes on as a green track between large arable fields past Duck's Nest Barrow hidden in a circle of trees and undergrowth with one enormous yew tree on the summit of the mound. From Duck's Nest Barrow it goes on over Whitsbury Down to cross the county boundary and become one of the many trackways on Wick Down.

This plateau of downland is now nearly all cultivated, and the lines of some of the tracks have obviously been changed to suit the new farming methods of today, but the hard green rutted track which passes Duck's Nest Barrow looks very old, and on each side of it in places, despite the plough, can be seen vestiges of older trails going in the same direction. From Wick Down the track could join up with other ridgeways going to Salisbury Plain or the New Forest. A well-defined track continues the line north-east to Clearbury Ring.

Rather more than a mile north-west from Badbury Rings (see Map 1), at a coppice beside the Blandford–Wimborne road, a byway turns south-west along a low ridge above the Tarrant and comes to the riverside road from Shapwick to Blandford. It continues over this road to cross the Stour at Crawford Bridge at the south end of Spettisbury village close to Spettisbury Rings. Spettisbury Rings, or Crawford Castle as it is sometimes called, is an earthwork on a low hill south of the Stour with just enough room between it and the river for the main road and the railway. It lies a little over two miles west of Badbury, and from its banks Badbury can be plainly seen across the water-meadows. Crawford Bridge is mentioned in the Charter of the Abbey of Tarent in the year 1235. As many ancient bridges replaced fords or ferries of earlier times it seems likely that before the first bridge was built there was a river crossing here.

To return to the point where the byway crosses the riverside road from Shapwick to Blandford. Continuing towards Blandford the riverside road passes Keynston Dairy House at a deep bend in the river, and soon afterwards comes to the trackway which leads back north-east along the ridge to Buzbury Rings (see Chapter 28), so it seems possible that a link between the three earthworks once existed, though it is not suggested that the earthworks are of the same period.

From the north-west corner of Witchampton beside the river Allen and two and a half miles north-east of Badbury Rings, a minor road leads north-west to a ridge between the Long Crichel valley and the valley of the Tarrant. It must be close to the line of a former trackway leading through a gap in the woods between Tarrant Monkton and More Crichel. At Horse Down, where it leaves the woods, there is a meeting-place of ways where this minor road is continued north-west as a track along Crichel Down to the Salisbury–Blandford main road, passing by tumuli and through a dyke in doing so. Beyond the main road it continues over Tarrant Hinton Down, where there are many traces of British settlements, to Chettle Long Barrow less than a quarter-mile east of the site of the Roman road from Badbury to Ashmore. Beyond the long barrow it looks as if the track was superseded by the Roman road going past the camps in Bussey Stool Woods and on to a tumulus on Woodley Down east of Ashmore, where it becomes the minor road to Charlton Down close by Win Green. Here it joins the Great Ridgeway where the Ox Drove also joins it.

This track from Witchampton to the Great Ridgeway looks as if it might have been an alternative loop to the track which came to Witchampton from Badbury and continued north-west along the ridge separating the Gussage villages from Long Crichel. It may even have been the original route.

Ordnance Survey Maps

Wimborne and Ringwood. Sheet 131. 1 inch to 1 mile. Popular Edition, 1919
Dorchester. Sheet 178. 1 inch to 1 mile. 1946
Bournemouth. Sheet 179. 1 inch to 1 mile. 1945
Salisbury. Sheet 167. 1 inch to 1 mile. 1940

28

BUZBURY RINGS TRACKWAY

Approximately 15 miles

A TRACKWAY running south-west from Buzbury Rings, an earthwork just off the Blandford–Wimborne road (B 3082) about two miles east of Blandford (*see* Map 1), is named 'Trackway' on the 1-inch O.S. map, and it can be followed, though with difficulty in places, to a ford over the Stour at Charlton Marshall and then along a low ridge of downs to Lower Street, near Winterbourne Whitchurch.

The Blandford–Wimborne road (B 3082) actually goes through one part of Buzbury Rings, and on the north side of the road short lengths of its outer bank have been incorporated into a golf-course.

As it leaves Buzbury Rings the trackway is reduced to less than a footpath between the edge of a wood and an arable field, and most of the way to the ford at Charlton Marshall it is dank, deserted and overgrown, for it no longer serves any useful purpose. About fifty yards before it descends to the river it has been lost in a cultivated field and only the line of a hedge marks its course. Although the ford is not used nowadays and part of its entrance has been built up, a portion of its shelving bay still curves into the low river bank, and plants rising above the water mark the shallows.

On the other side of the ford the track ascends to the main road A 35 as a sunken, muddy, nettle-infested footpath, and across the main road it continues as a broad metalled lane shut in by the cob and tile-roofed boundary walls of private parkland. When the walls come to an end high banks covered with ferns and woodland plants and topped with tall chestnut trees take their place. Here, despite the generous width, the height of the banks and trees makes it a deep, cool, covered way. One barely notices the railway arch, for its bricks have become patterned with lichen and moss, at one with the speckled green shade. The metalling ends at the gates of a cemetery and the track narrows, continuing as the familiar dank, narrow tunnel between ramping hedges and clutching brambles, with mud and nettles underfoot.

As a hedged lane it goes along a low ridge that gradually rises to 330 feet after it has crossed Combs Ditch, a linear earthwork beginning on Whatcombe Down and continuing for nearly three miles in a south-easterly direction to Great Coll Wood. There are tumuli and minor earthworks in the vicinity of the track nearly all the way to Lower Street, whose name suggests Romanization here. Parts of the main Blandford–Dorchester road, which runs roughly parallel to the north on higher ground, look very much as if they are on the line of a ridgeway. If so the trackway from Buzbury Rings may have been a summer way of this ridgeway.

From Lower Street a winding byway brings it to Winterborne Whitchurch in less than half a mile. There seems no compelling reason why it should have come to an end at Lower Street or Winterborne Whitchurch. The upper reaches of the Winterborne stream would be no obstacle, for it is dry in summer. The line can be continued westward by an almost continuous series of tracks, footpaths, parish boundaries and metalled lanes, only touching one village, Cheselbourne, on its way to the meeting-place of tracks at Dole's Ash half a mile or so east of Piddletrenthide. Until this line comes to the east end of Streetway Lane, half a mile east of Cheselbourne, it is far from straight and passes through some of the quietest Dorset farmland, a region that seems more remote because of the windings of the byways between steep-sided slopes of small hills which often block the view and heighten the impression of being shut away from the rest of the countryside.

From Winterborne Whitchurch a minor road takes the line west past Chescombe Farm. The road then turns north-west, but half a mile on from the farm a short length of footpath and parish boundary leads west to a track which comes out on the Milborne–Milton Abbas road about a hundred yards north of Hewish Farm. From here a footpath and track bring it to Gallows Corner (see Map 16). One cannot escape the conclusion that Gallows Corner, three miles west of Winterborne Whitchurch and in the coaching era a crossroads for travellers going to Cheselbourne, Milton Abbas and north beyond Bulbarrow, must also have been a meeting-place of trackways. Today some of these ways have become blind or remain as dank overgrown lanes between fields.

Keeping its direction westward from Gallows Corner our line continues as a footpath and parish boundary to the east end of Streetway Lane. The half-mile of Streetway Lane to Cheselbourne and the further two and a half miles on to Dole's Ash is now a metalled road. At Dole's Ash it meets the track coming down from Nettlecombe Tout (see page 64) and joins it in its journey westward through Piddletrenthide and on to the Old Sherborne Road above Cerne Abbas (see Map 15).

Ordnance Survey Map

Dorchester. Sheet 178. 1 inch to 1 mile. 1946

29

THE DORSET COASTAL RIDGEWAY

<small>ABBOTSBURY CAMP TO POXWELL</small>

Approximately 12½ miles

THE Dorset chalk hills which carry the Great Ridgeway from Wiltshire across the county to Toller Down above Beaminster have a narrow coastal extension below Dorchester which goes roughly eastward to end in the cliffs above Swanage, and along this coastal ridge runs the trackway we have called the Dorset Coastal Ridgeway (*see* Map 1). This belt of chalk forms a high ridge which falls more steeply on the seaward side and is an impressive feature of the Dorset coastline. It is a fascinating feature also for the geologist, the botanist and the lover of Dorset landscape and seascape, for chalk is not the only substance making up the scarp. In many places it is overlaid by tertiary gravels and sands, so that in the woods and hedgerows oak and holly can be seen as often as beech and yew, and gorse and heather often take the place of downland turf on old pastures.

North of Bincombe and on the summits of Bronkham Hill and Black Down the sombre tones of the heath are particularly noticeable from a distance, but on a closer view Black Down and many another hillside in that region have their dark colour enlivened by silvery-grey dry walls of limestone outlining the fields. Beyond the hills the changing iridescence of the sea, the pale grey of Portland and the yellow-browns of the Chesil Beach are made more remote and seem to hold more light because of this contrast with the brooding darkness of the heathland. It is this geological make-up, with its varied deposits of gravels, limestone, chalk and Kimmeridge shale, and the fact that the sea is visible from almost every part of this coastal ridgeway, that give it its unique character.

The crest of the southern scarp is nowhere less than about 450 feet above sea level—at Black Down it reaches nearly 800 feet—and all along the ridge evidences of Dorset prehistory make it obvious, even if its geographical situation did not, that there must have been a way for travellers along it at least from the Bronze Age onward. Today there are gaps in the once continuous line, but it can be followed in the field, bridging the gaps and linking up farm roads, lengths of minor roads with open stretches across heath, arable fields and downland pasture.

While the Great Ridgeway in Dorset passes a dozen hill-forts the Coastal Ridgeway has only four along its route—Abbotsbury, Chalbury, Rings Hill and Maiden Castle. Maiden Castle, the largest and best known and the one which has been so thoroughly excavated that it seems as if little more can be discovered about it, lies about half way between the Ridgeway and Dorchester and about half a mile from the Weymouth main road. From the banks of the camp the Ridgeway can be clearly seen punctuated with round barrows following one another along the skyline in close and orderly procession, and showing that in the Bronze Age this southern part of Dorset must have supported a large population, unless the ridge was used exclusively for burials, which is hardly likely. Yet the barrows are so numerous one cannot escape the thought. Every ridgeway has its accompanying tumuli, but no other in Wessex has still so many strung out along the whole of its course. When one thinks of the numbers which must have disappeared during the last two thousand years and the multitude still remaining, the original number must have been great indeed. Not only do they line the trackway but they are also found in clusters in the fields just under the crest, following lesser ridges and spurs in short strings, and standing in pairs away from the main line as if dropped there as an afterthought. There are remains of long barrows as well, but most of these have suffered severely in early excavations, and have lost their shapeliness and in some cases are now barely visible.

The last hill-fort eastward is Rings Hill above Worbarrow Bay, but the tumuli continue along the Purbeck ridge so that one feels that the track led finally to the sea. The escarpment itself south of Dorchester is known as the Ridgeway, though whether it acquired its name because of its obvious ridgeway character or from the track which runs along it is uncertain.

Starting from the west the Coastal Ridgeway begins at Abbotsbury Castle Camp, which is a triangular-shaped earthwork at the west end of Wears Hill. Here the scarp has a capping of gravel, so that the earthwork has a rough uneven covering of bracken and heather, which does not give the same flowing contours to banks and ditches as when chalk lies just beneath ancient turf. On Wears Hill the ground on each side of the ridge falls away steeply, particularly on the south, and the prospects from it on a clear day are as magnificent as any in Dorset. To the south can be seen Portland and the sea, which gives a sense of illimitable space to the view, to the west the cliffs beyond Bridport, and beyond them the Devon coast. North-westward one can look across the Dorset vales to where the Great Ridgeway links together the distant hills of Lambert's Castle, Pilsdon Pen and Lewesdon Hill. Eggardon Hill and Camp are unmistakable about five miles to the north.

The track goes along Wears Hill and then along the edge of White Hill. The face of the scarp here has been moulded into wide terraces by landslips in the greensand, which are called Abbotsbury Plains. The track becomes a hedged lane for a short distance and runs inward from the actual edge so that the view is obscured, but beyond the lane the road opens out again and for over a mile becomes the minor road leading north-east to Winterborne St. Martin. Just beyond the Hardy Monument on the summit of Black Down the line leaves the Winterborne road and curves slightly south-east, here beginning the stretch of the scarp known as the Ridgeway, and which continues as a distinct ridge to a point beyond Poxwell.

Leaving the Hardy Monument on the right the track continues over Bronkham Hill where the tumuli lie thick. The Ridgeway is gated on Bronkham Hill and beyond it for a few miles. It comes to the chalk again beyond Great Hill, as one can tell by the many round barrows on each side which are no longer covered with shaggy heath but are green and shapely.

Just before it comes to a reservoir the track has been lost in one field, but on each side of the gateway a barrow stands as if to mark the way, leading beyond the reservoir to the road from Upwey to Winterborne St. Martin (B 3159). Across this road a clearly defined track, also a parish boundary, goes south-east with clusters of tumuli on each side to reach Ridgeway Gate on the main Dorchester–Weymouth road (A 354) in about a mile. The line continues across the Weymouth road above the railway tunnel, over the golf-course and on under the south edge of Came Wood as the road to Broadmayne.

As it comes to Came Wood the track passes a tumulus known as Culliford Tree. South of it Bincombe Clump, with its tuft of ragged and wind-tossed conifers, is a landmark for miles around. We have even picked it out on the skyline from Bulbarrow Hill.

Still following parish boundaries, the line of the Ridgeway for the four miles or so from Ridgeway Gate past Came Wood and along White Horse Hill is easily followed to a point above Poxwell. The track passes a long barrow, a cross-dyke and a gathering of tumuli on Bincombe Hill. Another line of barrows follows a track which branches south-west to Green Hill and Chalbury hill-fort. At a saddle on Green Hill there is a meeting-place of ways. One leads south-east as a metalled road to Sutton Pointz, another track goes to Bincombe to join a minor road leading north-west to the elbow bend in the Dorchester–Weymouth road on Ridgeway Hill, and other footpaths wind about Chalbury hill-fort and make their way variously to Preston, Jordon Hill and the coast.

This part of the Ridgeway, from Ridgeway Gate to the vicinity of Poxwell, must have been of great importance in the old days as it commands Portland and the harbourage of Weymouth Bay. Modern naval establishments make one realize that its great strategic importance is not lessened today. Chalbury hill-fort, set on an outlier of limestone above the bay, must have served a similar use in ancient times.

Poxwell to West Lulworth

Approximately 6½ miles

At Poxwell Corner the line branches, the main line following the crest of the downs to White Nothe. The more northerly branch goes along Moigns Down, passing Lord's Barrow and a group of tumuli called the Five Marys on its way to Winfrith and beyond (*see* Chapter 30).

The northern arm of the branch keeps above the small brook which comes from Holworth and goes through Upton, but the main branch of the Coastal Ridgeway has first to cross the narrow valley holding this brook between Poxwell and Upton before it can rise to the ridge and proceed with it along the coast. On the steep hillside north of the valley various tracks can be seen coming down to the stream, but which is the original track it is difficult to say. Whenever an ancient road crosses a valley there are usually a number of ways to the next ridge of high ground. On the south side it was impossible to explore any other possibility but the deeply sunken narrow road to Upton because of an R.A.F. establishment on the lower slopes of the shoulder of the ridge. This road, however, once the stream is crossed, soon begins to rise steeply, its almost vertical hedged and wooded high banks suggesting weather scouring as well as centuries of use. One can easily imagine it a rushing torrent in heavy rain-storms. A gap in the hedge on the right reveals a track going off along the hillside as well as a fascinating glimpse of the sea, and suggests an easier gradient to reach the crest of the ridge, but it is marked 'Private', and today leads only to a farm.

At the top of the hill the metalled road becomes a wide farm track, with the ground falling very sharply in places to the little valley separating the coastal ridge from Moigns Down. On the seaward side the track is open to a view of the sea beyond Weymouth Bay and Portland. Two round barrows, one on each side of the track, seem to indicate the way, but this stretch is so unmistakably a ridgeway that no indication of the route is necessary. Gates lead the track into the National Trust property of Ringstead Bay.

The track, still gated, continues to White Nothe and beyond it follows the crest of the cliffs to near Dagger's Gate, where there is a meeting-place of tracks and parish boundaries. One track, now metalled, goes north and connects the Coastal Ridgeway with the subsidiary track from Poxwell to Winfrith. The continuation of this metalled track south brings it to Newlands Farm in about a furlong and then goes on east to West Lulworth. Here it meets the B 3070 road coming south from Wool and, in its last mile, the War Department country of Lulworth Camp. Immediately north of Lulworth Camp a minor road goes east along the edge of the grounds and woods of Lulworth Castle to East Lulworth and up into Purbeck. Ronald Good says that the evidence of early itinerists shows that this line from Ridgeway Gate into Purbeck is probably one of the earliest highways in Dorset.

Dagger's Gate to Ballard Point

Approximately 14 miles

But to return to Dagger's Gate and the Coastal Ridgeway, which from Abbotsbury to this point has flowed along without much serious interruption. After Dagger's Gate there are two possible ways the old track may have taken. At first glance the direct line seems along the Burngate ridge, for the tumuli on its slopes show that a track must have existed here from prehistoric times, going inland by way of East Lulworth to the summit of the Purbeck ridge. But the main branch of the Ridgeway would surely have continued to Rings Hill Camp and beyond, where the spine of Purbeck runs almost unbroken, except for passes at Corfe and Ulwell, for about twelve miles to Ballard Point. This may seem a blind ending today, but coast erosion and landslips have altered the coastline through the ages, and in any case Swanage Bay is not very far away.

This ridge to Ballard Point above Swanage Bay, that runs like a backbone along the Isle of Purbeck, must have been the route of the main southern track. Its position alone makes one come to this decision, though no continuous trackway leads along it today. It would not necessarily come to an end at Rings Hill, its most easterly hill-fort, for beyond the hill-fort there are minor earthworks and tumuli all the way, and the precipitous cliffs make natural fortresses that give protection seaward from Worbarrow Bay to Swanage Bay. Northward this ridge overlooks the lower part of the Frome and the Piddle, thus providing an important look-out on the landward side also.

To return again to Newlands Farm just south of the meeting-place of tracks at Dagger's Gate. From this point the metalled track to West Lulworth seems the obvious line, and then a footpath keeping just north of a dyke which runs for a mile and a half along the narrow crest of Bindon Hill where the ground falls away steeply on either side. At the east end of Bindon Hill the footpath goes down into the Arish Mell gap, the pass separating Bindon Hill and Rings Hill, and then follows a farm track leading back to Sea Vale Farm. A footpath branches from this track and climbs the west end of Rings Hill past a tumulus to the hill-fort at its summit. Keeping to the crest of the very narrow summit the footpath passes the earthwork and a tumulus called Flower's Barrow and goes along the ridge of Whiteway Hill, where it joins a metalled road and keeps with it along Povington Hill and West Creech Hill to about half way under Great Wood. Here the metalled road turns north to go over Creech Heath to Stoborough about a mile south of Wareham, and about this area tumuli lie thick on the heath-land. The Coastal Ridgeway, however, continues east along Ridgeway Hill and Stonehill Down to the Corfe gap. Parts of the coast and the downs about the Lulworth area are War Department country, inaccessible to the ordinary traveller.

The ridge is split in two by the Corfe gap, in which the ruin of Corfe Castle set on high looks today as if it had been placed there to provide a romantic focal point. The way the original track dropped down to cross the gap must have been lost long ago when the castle and its outer fortifications were constructed, while the way up the other side has been eradicated by cultivation.

On the east side of the Corfe gap the downs rise to a narrow ridge which widens out before narrowing again as it comes to Ballard Point overlooking Swanage Bay some six miles on.

Ordnance Survey Maps

Dorchester. Sheet 178. 1 inch to 1 mile. 1946
Bournemouth. Sheet 179. 1 inch to 1 mile. 1945

30

FROM POXWELL TO WINFRITH

Approximately 5 miles

THIS track, which leaves the Dorset Coastal Ridgeway at Poxwell Corner (*see* Map 1), has a prominent if less elevated ridge to take it to Winfrith than the ridge which holds the main branch, and from its position there can be no doubt that it is a true ridgeway. On the north the ridge drops down to the valley of the Frome and on the south the green Chaldon valley lies between it and the cliffs of the escarpment overlooking the sea. But perhaps the most remarkable thing about this ridge is the expanse of Dorset countryside to be seen from its summit, and the feeling it gives as one travels along it of being very high above the valley world. Yet its greatest height is only 411 feet above sea level where it crosses the minor road to Holworth about a mile and a half east of Poxwell. Even Badbury Rings beyond the Stour valley can be seen on a clear day.

From prehistoric times there must always have been some kind of a high-way along it, though except at each end it touches no villages, and it seems likely that the highway persisted as a continuous road until the beginning of the nineteenth century. Taylor's map of Dorset, published in 1765, shows a continuous highway between the Cairn Circle near Poxwell and Winfrith; and Ronald Good, in his *Old Roads of Dorset*, says: 'There can be little doubt that this road formed, at the time, the main route towards Weymouth.' It seems to have continued as a favoured route, perhaps because of its open situation and because of the fine prospects, even when there was an alternative lower route by Warmwell Corner. Greenwood's map of 1829, however, shows that this ridge road had become a minor and incomplete route by the early nineteenth century. It is difficult to tell why it fell into decline. Only tracks and footpaths make up its line today, and it is a quiet, unfrequented way, traffic using instead the lower modern roads in the valley north of it.

It rises from the tree-shaded Poxwell Corner to the open downs as a track, passing in its first hundred yards what the latest O.S. map calls a Cairn Circle, that is, a ring of stones which once encircled a tumulus. This miniature stone circle has a diameter of about fourteen feet and is made up of fifteen stones, three of which are larger than the others, but none of them of a size difficult to handle. These Dorset 'stone circles'—for there are several to be found on or near trackways—are not of the same type as the larger ones found in Wiltshire and elsewhere in Wessex. Archaeologists have a theory that they are the result of the influence of Neolithic culture on the Beaker Folk who settled in Dorset and who, some two thousand years ago, buried their dead beneath round barrows and then sometimes surrounded the mounds with a close circle of stones or placed a ring of stones inside the mounds before covering them with earth. Early excavators, as well as time and weather, having denuded the mounds of their covering of brash and earth, only the 'stone circle' remains to mark the spot.

The track rises to Moigns Down, crosses the by-road going south to Holworth and in half a mile or so comes to the road leading down to East Chaldon, where the crossing is marked by Lord's Barrow. Eastward a parish boundary and a footpath take up the line to pass a row of tumuli known as the Five Marys and drop gently down the shoulder of the ridge to meet a lane which takes it to the south-west corner of Winfrith Newburgh.

One of the reasons why the four miles or so of ridgeway from Poxwell to Winfrith may have been important in prehistoric times is that it could have provided a link between the southern Coastal Ridgeway and the trackways leading north over the heathland to the chalk downs of north-east Dorset and so on to Salisbury Plain. There is also the line taken by the B 3071 road going north from West Lulworth past Burngate Farm and crossroads and coming to Wool Bridge over Quarr Hill to provide another link with the coast and the heath ridgeways north of the Frome.

From Winfrith the track could have continued over the heath to the crossing of the Frome at Wool, where it would meet the track coming from West Lulworth, and then have continued beyond the river to Woodbury Hill just east of Bere Regis, going on from there to link up with the Buzbury Rings trackway near Winterborne Whitchurch. If there was any communication between the northern and southern Dorset trackways this line seems the most obvious as well as the most direct route. The probability that such a link existed is made more likely by the tumuli and earthworks it passes on its way, and the fact that such a linking up would have been of great value to travellers to and from the southern coast from Cranborne Chase and the Wiltshire Downs. There has been a bridge at Wool since medieval times and the earliest bridges were generally built at river crossings already in use as fords or ferries.

The track from Winfrith could have reached Wool by going north-east on the line of a minor road which joins the main Dorchester–Wareham road near East Knighton and then on to Wool by the line of the main road (A 352). Over the river the main road turns east to Wareham after going north for a furlong or so, but the track would have continued north, rising to the shoulder of Tout Hill and following the ridge to Gallows Hill on Bere Heath where, between the Frome and the Piddle, it would have met the ridgeway that comes from Dorchester to Wareham. North of Gallows Hill it would have to face a crossing of the Piddle near Chamberlayne's Farm, and there are a number of fords in the vicinity to make this possible. It would pass End Barrow and then Hundred Barrow on Rye Hill before coming to a crossing of a tributary of the Piddle at Bere Regis, where there is another ancient bridge.

East of Bere Regis stands Woodbury Hill with an earthwork on its summit whose double ramparts and fosse enclose ten acres. Woodbury Fair, held on the hill, was once of considerable importance, beginning on 18th September and lasting for five days. On one of these days it held a great sheep fair to which shepherds travelling the ridgeways and green droves brought their flocks from all over the south and south-west.

The track from Tout Hill to Bere Regis is now metalled, but north of Bere where the heath is left behind and it comes to the chalk again the line becomes a track following the ridge of Bere Down, crossing the Badbury–Dorchester Roman road and then going on as a footpath past Elderton Clump and tumuli on West Down. From West Down it again becomes a track but changes to a footpath as it joins the by-road going into Winterborne Whitchurch. At Lower Street, before it comes to Winterborne Whitchurch, it joins up with the trackway coming from Charlton Marshall as a continuation of the Buzbury Rings trackway.

Ordnance Survey Map

Dorchester. Sheet 178. 1 inch to 1 mile. 1946

31

RIDGEWAYS ON THE GREAT HEATH

Approximately 7 miles

TWO trackways linking up with the Ridgeway coming from Poxwell to Wool run roughly east and west across the Dorset heath along the low water-shed between the Piddle and the Frome (*see* Map 1). They serve the area which lies between Wareham and Dorchester, reaching to Wool in the south and Bere Regis and Puddletown in the north. The more northerly of the two leads from Bere Regis to Puddletown, where it joins the Ridgeway along the Waterston ridge north of Dorchester.

It leaves Southbrook just below Bere Regis as a lane which branches south-west from the trackway along Rye Hill, and goes to Black Hill. It passes over this hill first as a footpath and then as a track, going through a cluster of tumuli which lie thickly about it, and after bending round the north end of a copse descends as a lane to the east end of Turners Puddle.

At Turners Puddle it fords the Piddle to reach Throop on the other side of the river, and following a parish boundary and a metalled track rises to Throop Clump and the tumulus on the ridge which is the watershed between the Piddle and the Frome. As an open metalled track it goes west along the ridge, and soon after passing the by-road coming south from Briants Puddle comes to an enormous pit on the heath known as Culpepper's Dish. The mouth of this pit makes a perfect circle on the ground, its smooth sides being covered with heath and narrowing down in a conical shape like that of a funnel.

After crossing the road from Warmwell to Affpuddle on Affpuddle Heath the track swerves a little south of west under Sares Wood, and then curves north-west as a parish boundary and tracks along the north edge of the woods of Southover Heath to reach South Admiston. Just west of this village it joins the by-road to Puddletown and leaves the heath to rise to good farming land and join the Puddletown Ridgeway west of the village.

DORCHESTER TO WAREHAM

Approximately 14 miles

Even today the minor road from Dorchester to Wareham which follows the crest of the ridge separating the Piddle and the Frome is the most direct route between the two towns, and much of this road must be on the line of a ridgeway. With chalk underfoot only the plough can obliterate all traces of a trackway, but the nature of gravel and sand, which does not pack hard, makes a terrain such as heath a place where any unmetalled road not in constant use must soon become lost. With the actual traces of an old road difficult or impossible to follow, there remains the evidence of the position of the ridge which gives direct access from the chalk downs above and beyond Dorchester to the shores of Poole Harbour, an access necessary to the traveller of early times. There is also the fact that along the ridge can still be seen minor earthworks and tumuli of prehistoric date. It also shares another ridgeway characteristic of keeping above later settlements. From Tincleton, four miles east of Dorchester, to Wareham, ten miles to the east, it passes no villages.

It is likely that Wareham was a riverside centre in pre-Roman days for the people whose burial mounds are strung out along the heath ridgeway. We know that the Romans realized that it was the only land approach from the west and strengthened and fortified it accordingly, while it was an important town in Saxon Wessex, so that one cannot escape the conclusion that this ridgeway was of considerable importance.

West of Wareham and along the same watershed the modern Wareham–Dorchester road (A 352) keeps just above the river as far as Wool, but a furlong beyond Worgret, about a mile west of Wareham, the Ridgeway branches north-west over Worgret Heath as a metalled road. For the next mile or more a linear earthwork called Battery Banks runs parallel to it, while parish boundaries follow it for several miles. At Gallows Hill on Bere Heath it crosses the ridgeway that goes north to Winterborne Whitchurch, and reaches its highest point of 250 feet. It now takes a more westerly course to come to Clouds Hill, where it runs through a scattering of tumuli. From Clouds Hill for the next mile or so through the southern edge of Oakers Wood to Waddock Farm on the crossroads with the Warmwell-Affpuddle road, the line is so straight that one suspects either Roman or modern road-makers have been at work on it. The road keeps closer to the river for its next two miles to Tincleton, where a link may have led north-east to join the previous heath ridgeway leading to the Puddletown Ridgeway. Or the link may have branched two miles farther west above Norris Mill at a tumulus where a track leads north through the woods of Puddletown Heath across Castle Hill to White Hill south of Puddletown village.

Whether the Ridgeway continued west beyond this point or beyond Tincleton is open to doubt. A continuation which looks probable today might have taken it to Stinsford and from there to keep north of the Frome for a mile or so before crossing it at Burton, where there is an ancient ford. By doing this it could have joined up with ridgeways south of Dorchester. It may have crossed the Frome at the ford on the east side of Dorchester which was replaced by Grey's Bridge in the eighteenth century, but this would only be possible in a dry season, if at all. Daniel Defoe, in his *Tour through Great Britain*, gives a picture of the roads east of Dorchester and this particular Frome crossing which makes one doubt if in early times this would be a possible way. Of the approach to Dorchester from the east he states that the road '… lies over part of the common or moor, through a considerable length of waters, subject to floods in times of heavy rains, and through a ford on the River Frome which is a very dangerous passage '.

It does seem more likely that the earliest travellers left the heath at or near Tincleton and made their way along the Waterston ridge.

Ordnance Survey Map

Dorchester. Sheet 178. 1 inch to 1 mile. 1946

32

THE PUDDLETOWN RIDGEWAY

Puddletown to Dorchester

Approximately 5 miles

THE Puddletown Ridgeway which goes west from Puddletown village along the Waterston ridge and provides a link with the ridgeways on the Great Heath between Dorchester and Wareham and the ridgeways north of Dorchester (*see* Map 1) is yet another of the early trackways used as a coach road in the eighteenth and nineteenth centuries, and which survive today as lanes, usually running under the crest of the downs and enclosed by tall, free-growing hedges. These lanes look narrow at first sight. It is only when one measures the distance between the hedges that one realizes how the neglected hedgerows have encroached inward and reduced what was originally a wide rutted way to the width of a footpath. In some of them parallel sunken ways like a broken ditch can still be detected beneath the thick undergrowth. When these lengths of old road have not been kept in use the hedges grow closer and closer together, saplings and briars spring up in the centre and in some places form barriers of thorny growth impossible to pass through.

Such a rough tangled lane leads off from Puddletown, fifty yards or so from the inn on the Dorchester–Bournemouth road (A 35). This lane is marked Ridge Way on the 1-inch O.S. map and follows the watershed between the Cerne and the Piddle. The Ridgeway continues as a lane for nearly three miles, until it comes to the B 3143 road from Dorchester. It is margined with rough herbage and still shows signs of metalling, perhaps put down when it was last used as a coach road. Tall old elms, ivy-clad, venerable rugged thorns and massed thickets of shrubs on each side make it a hidden way burrowing across the hills. In places the road is deeply sunken between high wooded banks, so that the view is shut out and, in summer, one walks in a green shade. Only at field gates and gaps in the hedges does one become aware of the open country beyond and the wide upland skies, but whenever one gets a glimpse of the world outside there on the north-east skyline stands Bulbarrow Hill.

After about a mile or so from Puddletown the lane loses its hedge on the right and comes to a triangular crossroads that is of no importance nowadays except to the farmer. Here a footpath leading off north-east across an arable field seemed to be heading straight for Bulbarrow and we were tempted to leave the Puddletown Ridgeway and follow it; but having learned from experience it is wiser to keep to one ridgeway at a time we resisted the impulse, with the reservation to follow it another day.

We discovered later that this footpath is marked as a lane on the earlier O.S. maps, and having now become a footpath over a cultivated field may soon be lost. Several tracks and footpaths in this area, particularly west of the B 3143 road, have been lost or diverted since the pasture on the south side of the Waterston ridge has been ploughed in recent years. This footpath leads to the modern road along the Piddle valley. On the other side of the road the line to Bulbarrow is taken up by a metalled road winding roughly north past Druce Farm and Chebbard Farm to Cheselbourne, where it continues by the side of Cheselbourne Water to come to a junction with the old coach road from Cheselbourne to Piddletrenthide which has Streetway Lane as its eastern arm (see Map 15). Still rising, the road goes between Highdon and Henning Hill and past a tumulus called Giant's Grave to Hartfoot Lane, where it descends to cross the Devil's Brook and then rises quickly to Ansty Cross, to continue to Bulbarrow as the high road along the west side of Moots Copse (see Map 16).

It looks as if this road from Druce Farm, as well as the old lane which branches from the Piddle valley road a mile or so west at Higher Waterston to go by Dole's Hill Plantation and join the Cheselbourne road at an awkward turning a quarter-mile south of the Giant's Crave, may be variants of much older tracks lost or diverted in medieval or later times. The Cheselbourne charters, of which there are several, suggest considerable Roman remains in this area, so it may be that the continuity of the track was lost as early as Roman-British times. A glance at the 1-inch O.S. map will show that, in a shield-shaped area of roughly eight or nine square miles, with Dole's Hill Plantation in the centre, and enclosed by the Cheselbourne–Piddletrenthide road on the north, the valley road from Piddletrenthide to Puddletown on the west, and the minor road from Druce Farm to just beyond Cheselbourne on the east, there is no continuous track which looks as if it belongs to the period of the field system and the many tumuli to be found on its downs.

To return to the Puddletown Ridgeway. West of the crossroads near Puddletown the lane continues open on the north, a green way rising gently all the time. The map shows a footpath leading to Robin's Barrow a quarter of a mile or so on, but the footpath is now lost in a cornfield. Robin's Barrow has also disappeared, and only broken ground and a square iron water-tower mark the spot where it once stood. Beyond Robin's Barrow, near an overgrown pit, the track becomes a lane which has degenerated into a jungle of thorny growth. After half a mile or so the hedged tangle comes to an end near a field gate opening on to the B 3143 road to Dorchester.

Across the road the track goes on, still rising gently. After a mile or so, passing a couple of round barrows, one each side of the path, the track goes through a gate and becomes a wide green road, running between great fields falling a little on the left, and on the right rising to a belt of woodland. Soon, however, it comes out into a great bowl of cultivated downland around Wolfeton Clump.

Here the track has been lost in the plough. It was impossible to tell which way it continued, though several ways were faintly discernible through the corn. One way went westward, another led south-south-west in the direction of the Dorchester crossing of the Frome. The line has been lost here, or perhaps split up into several branches and diverted round the arable fields to suit the needs of the farm and farm buildings. One path, however, across the open fields, comes after a mile or so to an old lane, narrow and deeply rutted, enclosed by high banks with old thorns and trees above the banks, which tumbles down the hillside in steep descent and is a true gipsy lane, for it is still used by them. This lane leads finally to water-meadows and a ford over the Frome, its continuation taking it as a raised path between marshy fields to the north side of Dorchester. The Ridgeway, however, may have turned south-west at Wolfeton Clump to go to Wolfeton Eweleaze and then on to the Old Sherborne Road passing above Charminster. It may also have crossed the Cerne at Charminster to join the Long Ash Lane Ridgeway (*see* page 69).

Ordnance Survey Map

Dorchester. Sheet 178. 1 inch to 1 mile. 1946

LIST OF BOOKS AND PUBLICATIONS

BELLOC, HILAIRE, 1923, *The Road*. British Reinforced Concrete Engineering Co. Ltd.
CODRINGTON, G. T., 1904, *Roman Roads in Britain*. S.P.C.K.
COX, R. HIPPISLEY, 1914, *The Green Roads of England*. Methuen.
CRAWFORD, O. G. S., 1922, *Man and His Past*. Oxford University Press.
— 1922, *The Andover District*. Clarendon Press.
DARTON, F. J. HARVEY, 1936, *Alibi Pilgrimage*. London.
— 1936, *The Marches of Wessex*. London.
FAGERSTEN, ANTON, 1933, *The Place Names of Dorset*. Uppsala.
FOX, CYRIL, 1932, *The Personality of Britain*. National Museum of Wales, Cardiff.
GOOD, RONALD, 1940, *The Old Roads of Dorset*. Longmans of Dorchester.
— 1940, *Weyland*. Longmans of Dorchester.
MARGARY, I. D., 1954, *Roman Roads of Britain*, Vol. I. Phoenix House.
PLACE, ROBIN, 1954, *Down to Earth*. Rockcliffe.
THOMAS, EDWARD, 1913, *The Icknield Way*. Constable.
WILLIAMS-FREEMAN, J. P., 1915, *Field Archaeology (Hampshire)*.

Antiquity
  'Cerdic and the Cloven Way', O.G.S. Crawford, June 1931.
  'Butser Hill', Stuart Piggott, June 1930.

Archaeological Journal
  'Ancient Highways and Trackways', G.B. Grundy, 1918, 1934, 1935.

Out of Doors Magazine, Brian Vesey-Fitzgerald, Nov. 1953–Nov. 1954.

Proceedings of Dorset Natural History and Archaeological Society
  'Saxon Charters of Dorset', G.B. Grundy, Vols. 55-61, 1934-9.

Proceedings of the Hampshire Field Club
  'Old Track from Walbury Camp', Christopher Burne, Vol. VIII, 1924.
  'Old Roads in Central Hants', C.F.C. Hawkes, Vol. IX, 1925.
  'The Belgae through Hampshire', J.P. Williams-Freeman, Vol. XII, 1928.
Wiltshire Archaeological Magazine

'Saxon Boundaries of Downton', Rev. A. Du Boulay, 1909.

'Durrington Walls', P. Farrer, 1918.

'Anglo-Saxon Boundaries of Bedwyn and Burbage', O.G.S. Crawford, 1921.

'A Middle Bronze Age Urnfield. Easton Down', J.F.S.Stone, F.S.A., 1933.

'Hoard of Bangles from Ebbesbourne Wake', H. de S. Shortt, F.S.A., 1949.

'Sorviodunum', J.F.S.Stone, F.S.A., and D.J. Algar, 1955.

Wiltsire Notes and Queries, Vol. I.

INDEX

MAPS

KEY

■■■■■■■■■■■■■■	*Great Ridgeway*
▲▲▲▲▲▲▲▲	*Dorset Coastal Ridgeway*
▫▫▫▫▫▫▫▫	*South Hampshire Ridgeway*
┼┼┼┼┼┼┼┼┼┼┼	*Lymington Ridgeway*
○○○○○○○	*Icknield Way*
●●●●●●●●●	*Harrow Way*
✕——✕——✕	*Lunway*
•••••••••••••••	*Inkpen*
·············	*Other Trackways, etc.*
——— ═══	*Modern Roads*

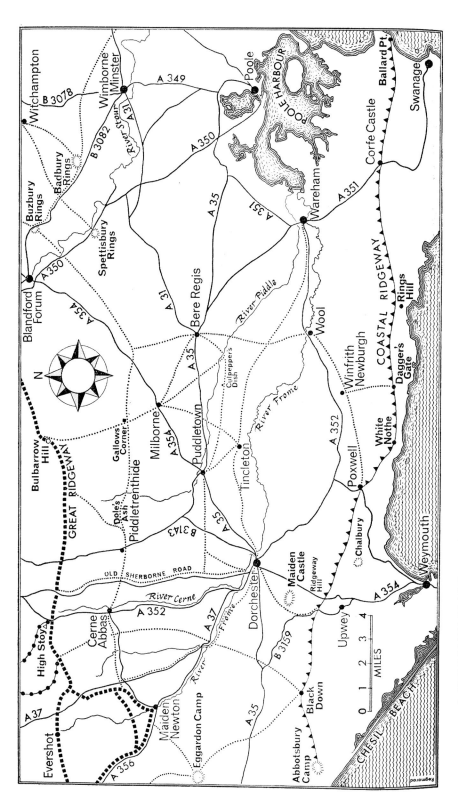

I. THE DORSET COASTAL RIDGEWAY; THE BUZBURY RINGS RIDGEWAY; TRACKWAYS ON THE GREAT HEATH

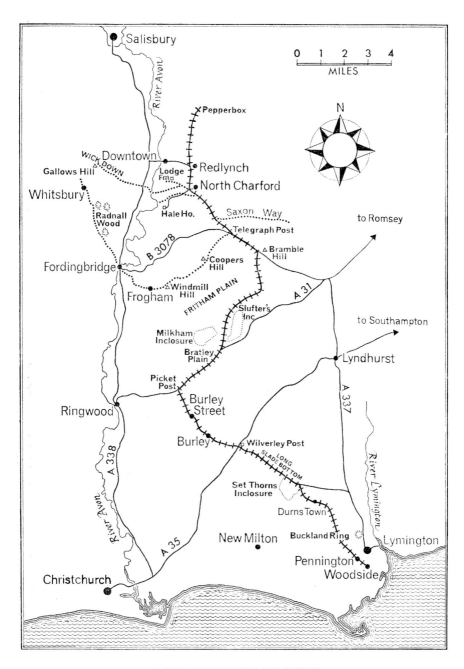

2. THR LYMINGTON RIDGEWAY

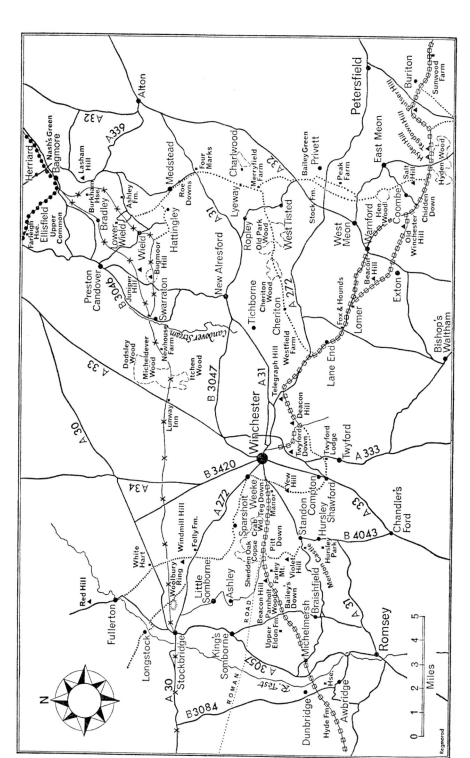

3. THE LUNWAY AND THE SOUTH HANTS RIDGEWAY, AND CONNECTING TRACKWAYS

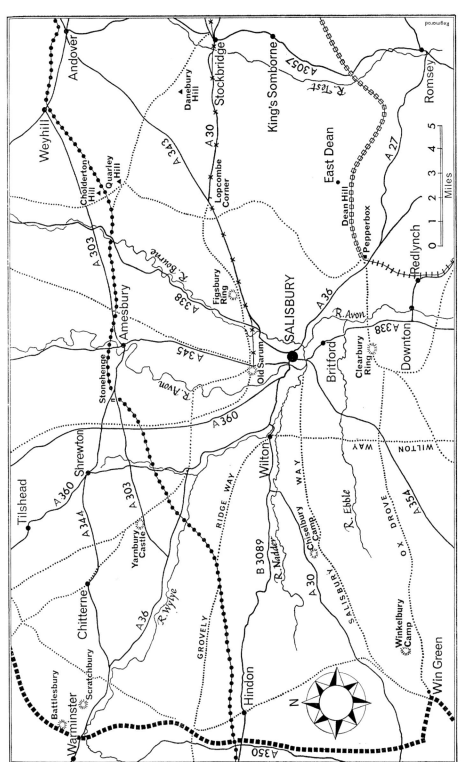

4. THE DORSET COASTAL RIDGEWAY; THE BUZBURY RINGS RIDGEWAY; TRACKWAYS ON THE GREAT HEATH

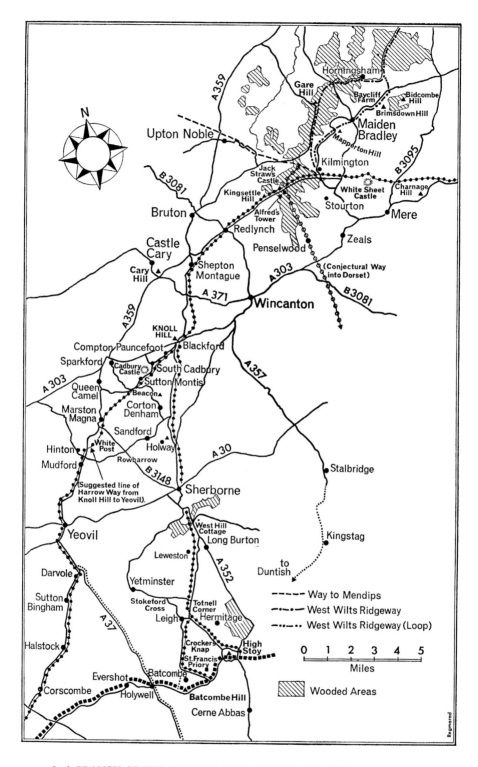

5. A BRANCH OF THE HARROW WAY JOINING THE GREAT RIDGEWAY

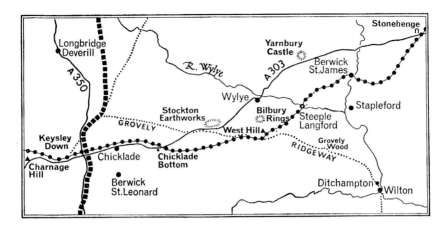

6. THE HARROW WAY FROM STONEHENGE TO CHARNAGE DOWN

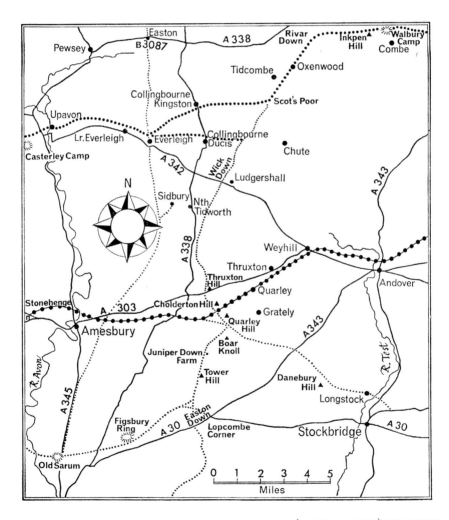

7. THE HARROW WAY IN RELATION TO THE INKPEN (NORTH HANTS) RIDGEWAY

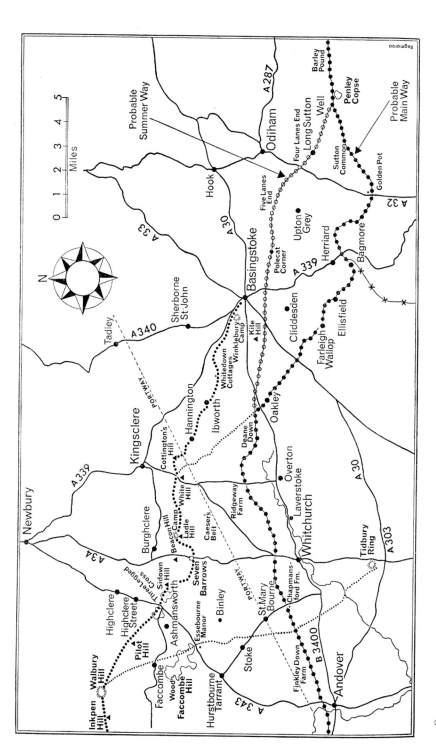

8. THE HARROW WAY PASSING SOUTH OF BASINGSTOKE AND IN RELATION TO THE INKPEN (NORTH HANTS.) RIDGEWAY

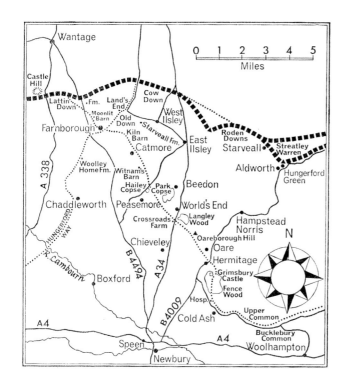

9. LINKS WITH THE
GREAT RIDGEWAY ON
LATTIN DOWN

10. WILTSHIRE BRANCHES
OF THE GREAT
RIDGEWAY

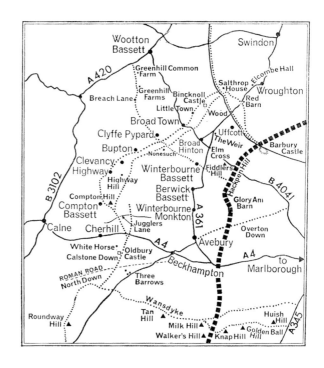

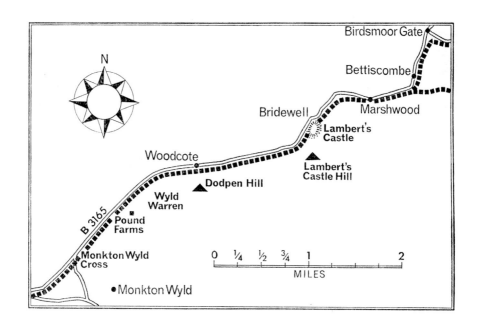

11. and 12. THE GREAT RIDGEWAY FROM BIRDSMOOR GATE TO THE SEA

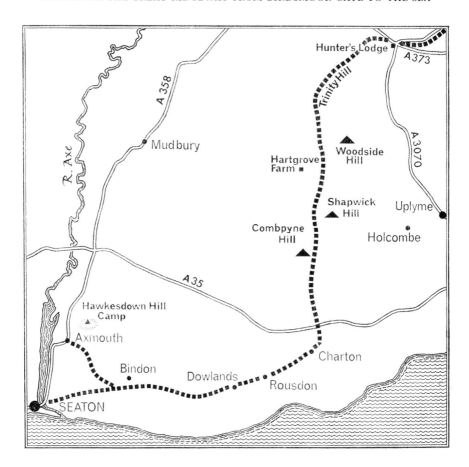

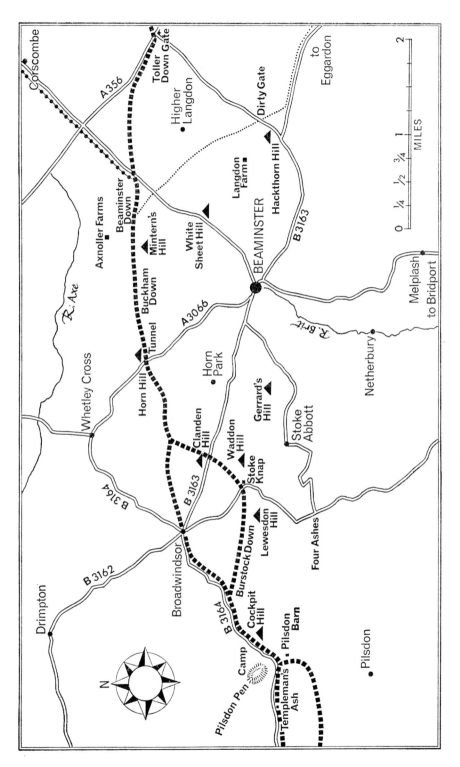

13. THE GREAT RIDGEWAY FROM TOLLER DOWN TO PILSDON PEN

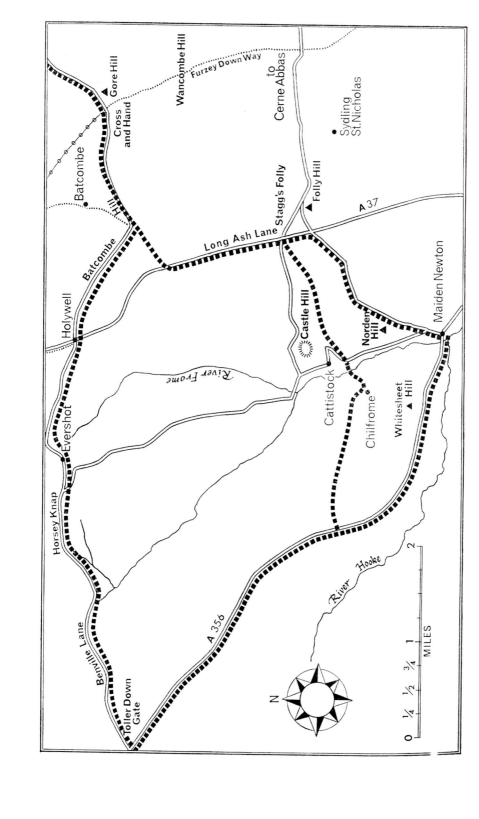

14. POSSIBLE COURSE OF THE GREAT RIDGEWAY AT THE FROME GAP

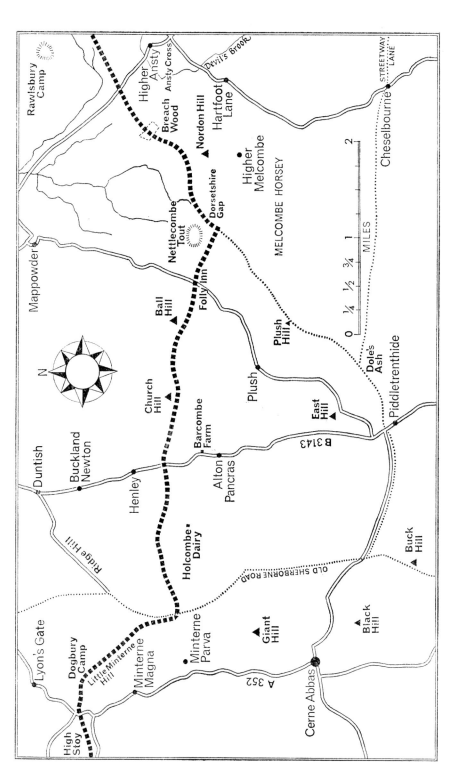

15. THE GREAT RIDGEWAY FROM BULBARROW TO HIGH STOY

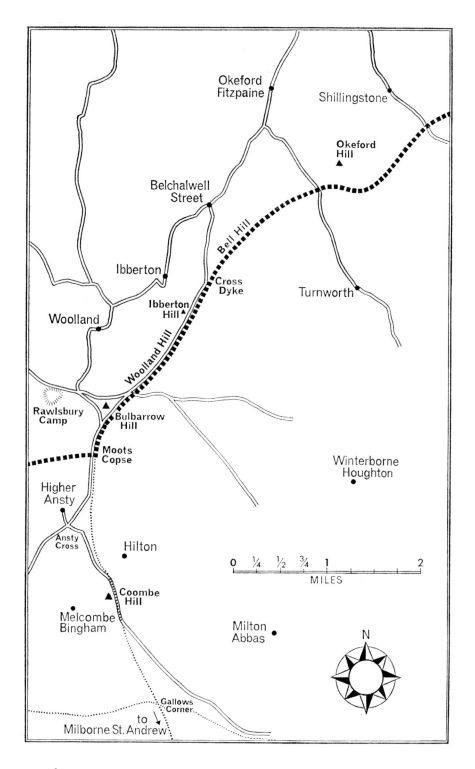

16. THE GREAT RIDGEWAY FROM SHILLINGSTONE HILL TO BULBARROW

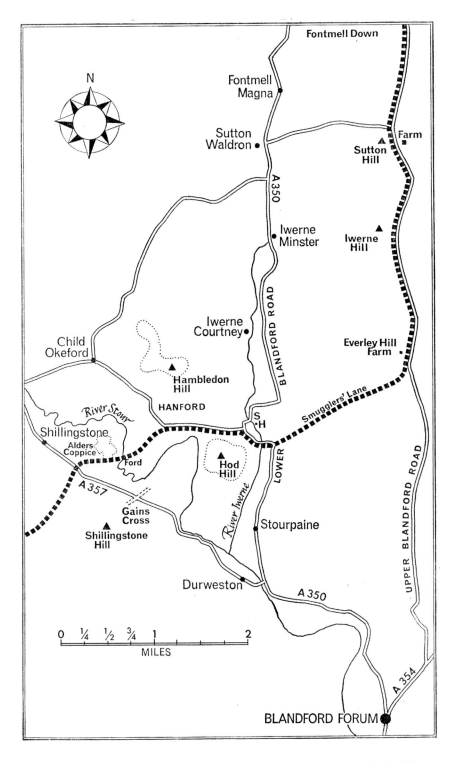

17. POSSIBLE LINE OF THE GREAT RIDGEWAY ACROSS THE STOUR GAP

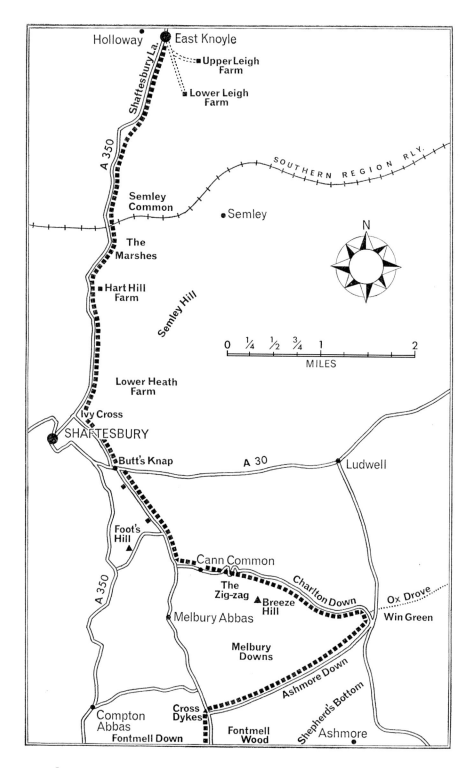

18. THE GREAT RIDGEWAY FROM EAST KNOYLE TO FONTMELL DOWN

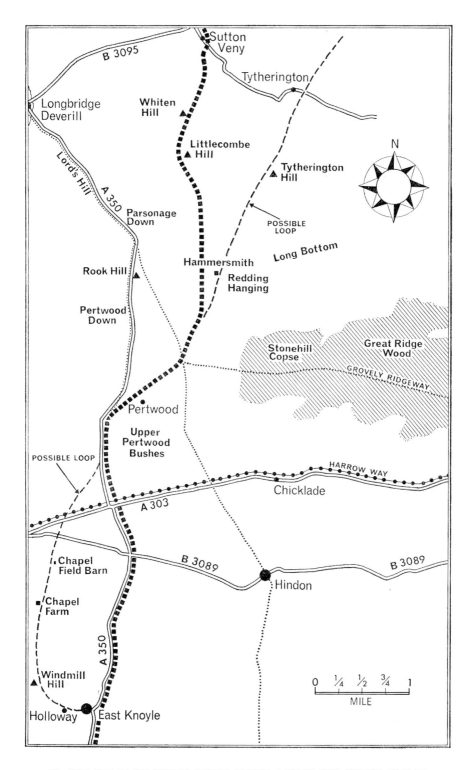

19. THE GREAT RIDGEWAY GOING SOUTH ACROSS THE WYLYE VALLEY

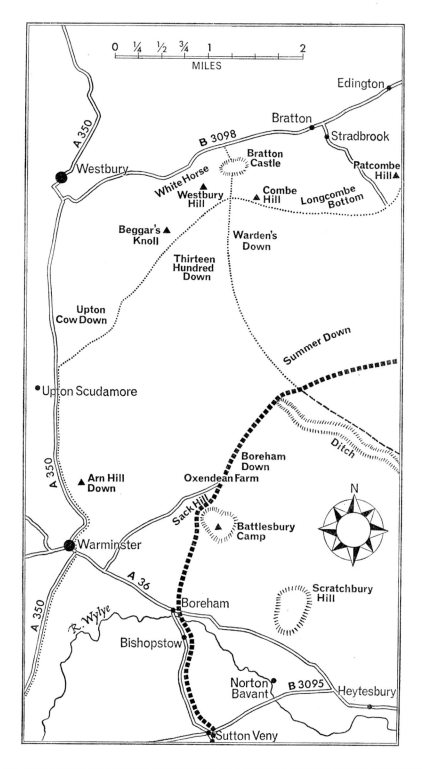

20. THE GREAT RIDGEWAY AND OTHER TRACKWAYS IN THE IMBER DISTRICT

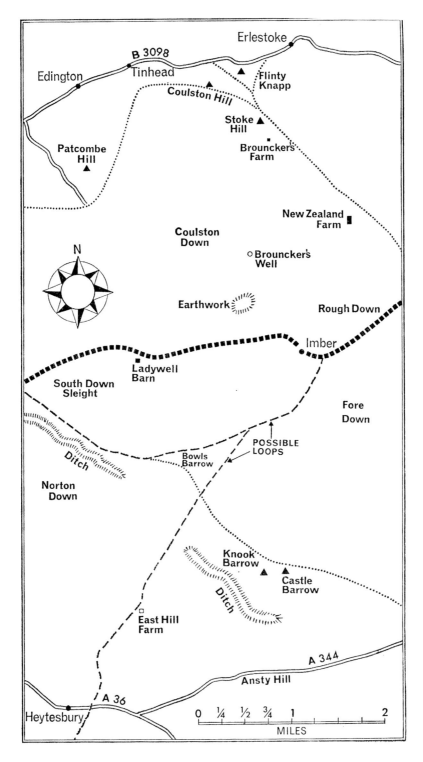

21. THE GREAT RIDGEWAY AND OTHER TRACKWAYS IN THE IMBER DISTRICT

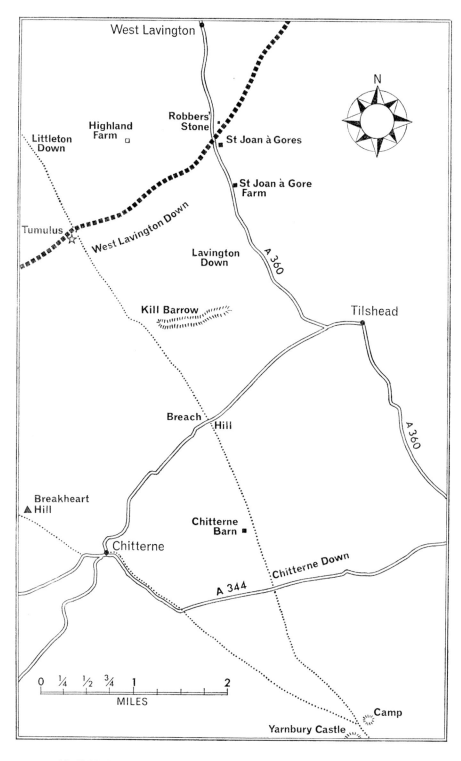

22. THE GREAT RIDGEWAY CROSSING WEST LAVINGTON DOWN;
TRACKWAY TO YARNBURY CASTLE

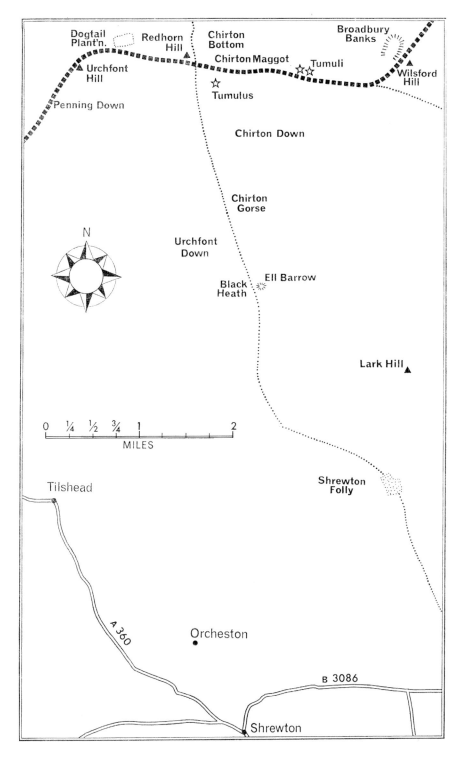

23. THE GREAT RIDGEWAY FROM WILSFORD HILL TO WEST LAVINGTON;
TRACKWAY TO SHREWTON FOLLY

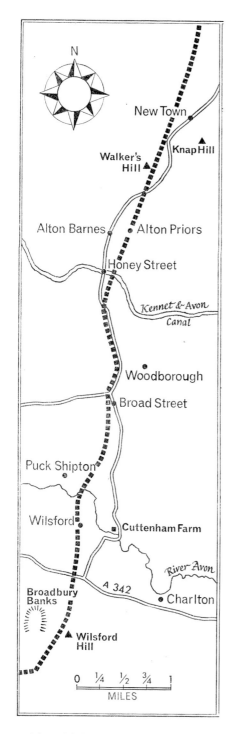
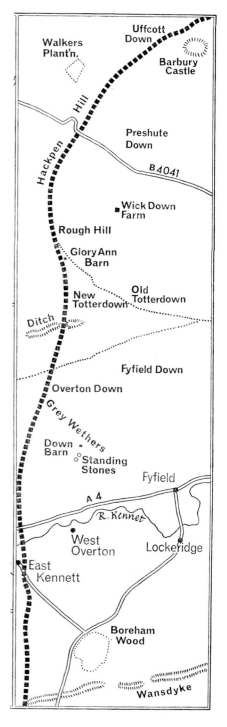

24. & 25. THE GREAT RIDGEWAY FROM BARBURY CASTLE TO WILSFORD HILL

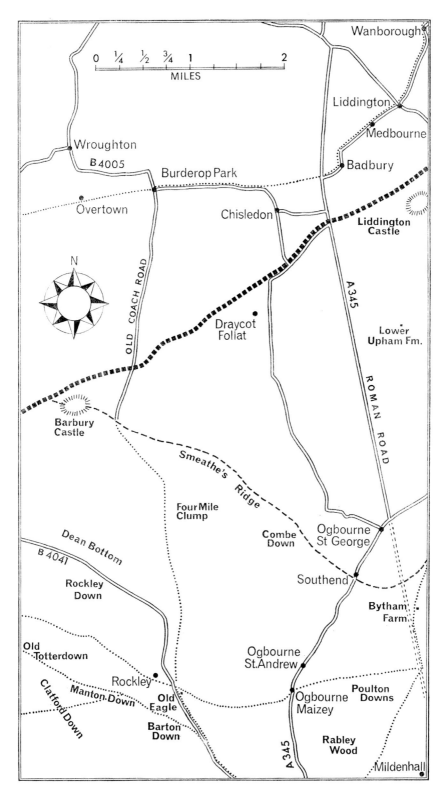

26. THE GREAT RIDGEWAY FROM LIDDINGTON CASTLE TO BARBURY CASTLE,
AND PROBABLE LOOP

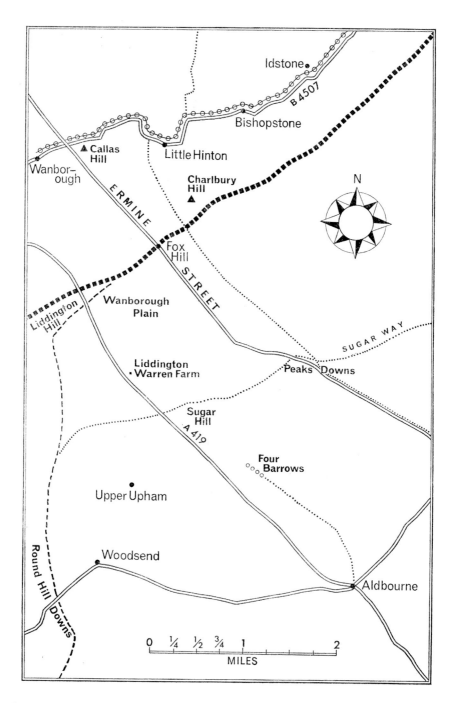

27. THE GREAT RIDGEWAY PASSING FOX HILL; LINK WITH THE ICKNIELD WAY
AND SUGAR WAY

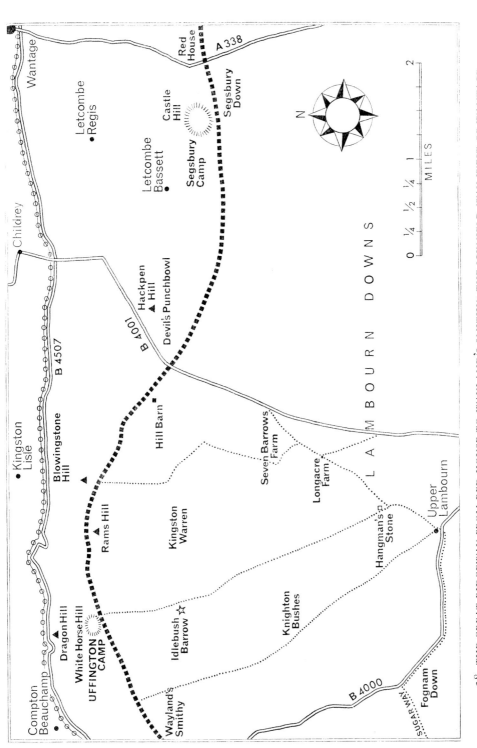

28. THE GREAT RIDGEWAY FROM RED HOUSE TO WAYLAND'S SMITHY; THE ICKNIELD WAY WEST OF WANTAGE

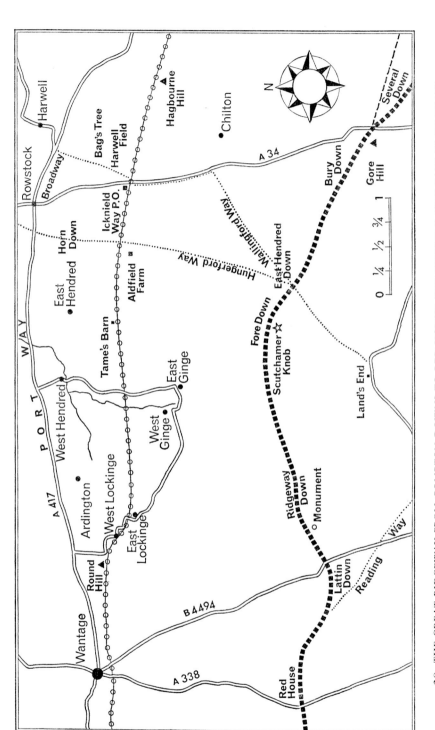

29. THE GREAT RIDGEWAY FROM COMPTON DOWNS TO RED HOUSE; THE ICKNIELD WAY EAST OF WANTAGE

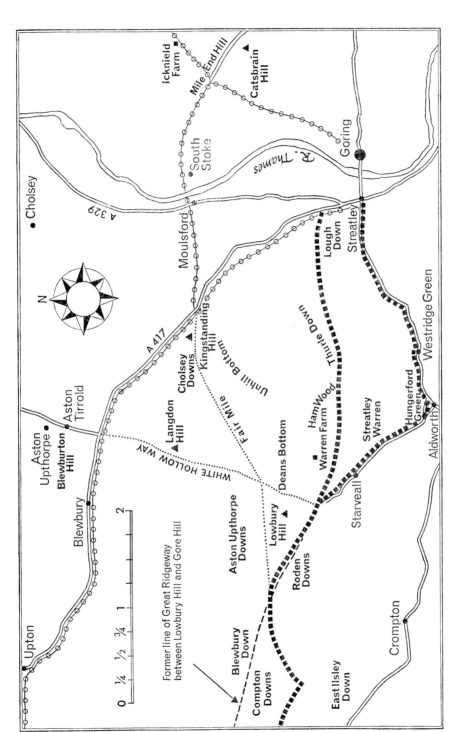

30. THE GREAT RIDGEWAY AND THE ICKNIELD WAY GOING WEST FROM STREATLEY